C000090341

THE GOVERNANCE OF WALES

The Welsh Office and the Policy Process 1964-1999

Russell Deacon

Welsh Academic Press
Cardiff

Published by Welsh Academic Press, an imprint of

Ashley Drake Publishing Ltd
PO Box 733
Cardiff
CF14 2YX

First Impression - September 2002

ISBN
1 86057 0399

© Russell Deacon 2002

The right of Russell Deacon to be identified as the author
of this work has been asserted in accordance with the
Copyright Design and Patents Act of 1988.

All rights reserved. No part of this publication may be reproduced,
stored in a retrieval system, or transmitted, in any form or by any means
without the prior permission of the publishers.

British Library Cataloguing-in-Publication Data.
A CIP catalogue for this book is available from the British Library.

Cover design by: www.darkangeldesign.com

CONTENTS

Acknowledgements   v
Foreword   vii

Chapter I
Evidence of Distinctiveness in Policy Making   1

Chapter II
The Historical Context of the Welsh Office and Policy Making   14

Chapter III
Internal Influences on the Welsh Office Policy Process:
The Welsh Secretary   41

Chapter IV
Internal Influences on the Welsh Office Policy Process:
The Office Juniors   68

Chapter V
Internal Influences on the Welsh Office Policy Process:
The Civil Service   88

Chapter VI
External Influences on the Welsh Office Policy Process: Parliament   116

Chapter VII
The Remaining Major External Influences on the Welsh
Office Policy Process   135

Chapter VIII
Completing the Policy Jigsaw: The Territorial Policy Community   159

Chapter IX
The Welsh Office and the Policy Process in Action: The Establishment
and Development of a National Curriculum for Wales   177

Chapter X
Welsh Office to the National Assembly: The Policy Process   216
Appendix 1   230
Appendix 2   232
Bibliography   241
Index   265

This book is dedicated to
Alexandra Elizabeth Deacon

ACKNOWLEDGEMENTS

The National Assembly for Wales is now at the centre of politics in Wales. Before it arrived, however, the Welsh Office had been the crucible of Welsh policy making. From its inception in 1964 until its demise in 1999 it became the administrative machine by which government policy was shaped to Welsh circumstances. Importantly for Wales, it was the Welsh Office which evolved into a body capable of delivering and servicing the National Assembly. For thirty-five years it fought the Welsh corner in government but also acted as a mechanism by which the government in Westminster and Whitehall could force their own policies on Wales. Those figures within, it especially the Welsh Secretaries, were always hard working, often controversial and politically ambitious. The civil servants beneath them worked equally hard in what was the civil service's smallest department.

This book sets out to record the development and extent of the Welsh Office and the policy process. Although the book is not a history of the Welsh Office' by its very nature it does cover the departments inception, development and expansion in all aspects that relate to policy determination. The book begins by reviewing the nature of the policy making process at the Welsh Office. The empirical evidence that identifies the distinctiveness of Welsh policy is explored. The study then explores each of the groupings that influenced the Welsh Office and the policy process. These groupings ranged from the Prime Minister and his Cabinet to the Welsh media and European Union, and examines how each of these groups directly or indirectly created or altered Welsh Office policy output. The book concludes by seeing how all of the policy actors interacted in order to produce a unique Welsh policy, the National Curriculum for Wales.

My interest in the Welsh Office first occurred whilst working for it's European Affairs Division between 1989-1991. I was impressed by the number of very bright and academically able people working there. My employment also coincided with the periods of Peter Walker and David Hunt. Walker was constantly bringing Wales into the news due to his battles with avoiding the impacts of Thatcherism in Wales. This was something which highlighted to me the extent to which Wales could benefit from its own government department. It was only later, however, when working as an academic, that I became aware that there was very little material on the Welsh Office from which to examine its impact on government policy within Wales. With increasing academic and public interest on Welsh politics it became ever more important that a thorough study of the Welsh Office was available in print. With this in mind, I started a research project in order to rectify this. In the meanwhile the Welsh Office developed and in turn became the National Assembly for Wales. At the same time, the thirst of scholars and those interested in knowing about the Welsh Office's role in the political process increased and a book upon the Welsh Office seemed ever more important. During this period I interviewed nearly one hundred people. Much of the material supplied for the book came from personal interviews of former Welsh Secretaries, ministers, politicians, civil servants and those surrounding the Welsh Office. They have helped to provide the overall detail in the book.

Lastly, I must pay my thanks and acknowledgements to those who have made this book possible. My biggest thanks must go to my wife and confident Tracey Deacon. I would also like to thank Ashley Drake for publishing this book. Over the last eight years I have had the support of a number of people I would like to thank: my Ph.D supervisor Professor Michael Connelly, my parents Garry and Mandy Deacon, my family Wally Barnes and Vivienne James, the late Derek James, University colleagues, Steve Belzak, Trefor Lewis, Dr Russell Holden, Dr Alys Thomas, Mark Wilson, and friends Suzanne Mainwaring, Heleen De Wulf, Gareth Thomas and Katrin Schmitt.

FOREWORD

By Rt Hon Alun Michael MP

This study of the Welsh Office and its impact on the policy process could not have come at a better time for the student of politics and for practitioners too. The book fills a gap that has existed for many years, and as the Welsh Office ended its life in 1999, this book is able to look at the whole history.

It is timely, but it may also help to mould future events. It is still far too early in the life of the National Assembly for Wales to judge its work or to predict its success or failure and it makes sense to look objectively at the work of its predecessor. Indeed, when our top civil servant Sir Richard Wilson (himself a Welshman) was asked how soon it would be fair to judge the performance of the Assembly, he suggested "at least five, ten - perhaps 15 years".

Our age constantly demands instant results, but we would be wise to take a longer view and - as I suggested in the Assembly's early days - nurture our "fragile young dragon". While doing so we should study our own history, for those who ignore their own history are often condemned to repeat its mistakes. And fascinating though we all find the period of Owain Glyndwr, the peaceful warriors of a more recent Government Department also have a fascinating story to tell.

In some ways it is interesting to see the same battle lines of political conflict causing problems for the Assembly as dogged the Welsh Office throughout its existence. Those who believe in devolution, then and now, have to contend with those who want all power to stay at the centre, while fighting off who want to use devolution as a Trojan Horse for separation. And within the Labour Movement, those who reject or fear the destructive force of nationalism have often also rejected devolution rather than recognising it as a democratic and constructive credo.

The early days of the Welsh Office saw it placed in the hands of a true and heroic champion of devolution. Few were more passionate advocates than Jim Griffiths, who became Secretary of State for Wales with experience of high office and the authority within the Labour Movement of having been Deputy Leader of the Labour Party. As a passionate enemy of nationalism, he was able to define what the new Government

Department **was** and what it was **not**. Indeed, it can be argued that he knew, understood and was able to deal with the threat of nationalism more effectively than someone like George Thomas who saw matters in a far more simplistic way.

Over the years, those who have championed the administrative independence of the Welsh Office have sometimes surprised us and perhaps themselves too. My own favourite was the occasion when the Secretary of State for Education, Sir Keith Joseph announced that he was setting up an inquiry into the Youth Service in England and Wales. Hardly was the ink dry on his press release before a second was issued from an incandescent Nicholas Edwards who had not been asked for his agreement to this initiative. "The Welsh Office would be doing things in its own way in Wales", he announced. It sent civil servants and youth leaders into a tailspin to invent a different route almost overnight - but is was a strong blow for the decision-making rights of the Welsh Office.

Inevitably, the top layer of officials at the Welsh Office were stretched very thin. Arriving from the Home Office, I was shocked how much major policy work could depend on one or two officials, and the extent to which the retirement or illness of one or two people could put a narrow area of policy-making at risk. The arrival of the Assembly has increased the pressure and made inevitable a strengthening of the team. While it is an easy headline to criticise the cost, the processes of accountability and debate both require more resource and will improve the quality of decision-making as the Assembly starts to come of age.

Perception can be a frustrating challenge now as it was then. Still, on occasions, we hear that naïve question from an interviewer: "If the Assembly can't take a decision without consulting Westminster or Whitehall, doesn't it mean that devolution has failed?" Of course it doesn't - what we have is the positive and creative tension of devolution rather than the narrow parochialism of separation or the stultifying process of central dictat. Yet it was often assumed that the Welsh Office was wrong to adopt statutory instruments written first in Whitehall. Surely the test should be whether the answer is right for Wales, not who wrote it - and the scrutiny of the new Assembly processes provide the opportunity for public scrutiny which was lacking in the Welsh Office days. As long as Assembly Members (AMs) ask the right questions, there's a chance we will gain a great deal.

At times the crosscutting nature of the Welsh Office was a great strength. The first steps towards a mental handicap strategy were taken shortly before the 1979 general election and sought a "joined up" approach.

On the ground, housing fell to the District Council, social services to the County and other support to the Health Authority. At the all-Wales level, howerer, all came under the aegis of the Welsh Office, and the combination of exhortation and a little extra money was enough to persuade all the partners to come on board. Crosscutting work between Government Departments can be difficult and time-consuming, though in fairness there can be "silos" even with a department like the Welsh Office.

One of the great achievements of the Welsh Office was to prepare the way for the arrival of the Assembly and for its own demise. I was particularly struck by the extent to which over-stretched officials rose to the challenge time and time again, with enthusiasm and good humour, during the lead up to the Assembly's birth.

There were drawbacks of course - one journalist commented that he had failed to realise how new it would be for former Welsh Office officials to have to deal with reporting to public committees, being questioned by Members, and having the Press and the public sitting in on highly technical and sensitive discussions: "These are things which the staff of the smallest district council have to do every day - yet it was a totally new set of tasks and relationships for which nothing had prepared them," he said.

The good news is the way officials have sought to adapt to these new conditions without losing the high standards of objectivity, public service and loyalty, which characterise the civil service at its best, a point is worth stressing. The loyalty is fine-tuned - loyalty to the office held by a Minister, loyalty to the Department, loyalty to the civil service and its ethic, and loyalty to Wales. Make no mistake about the last: those who suggest that officials should leave the Home Civil Service to become a separate "Welsh Civil Service" would, in truth, destroy a great strength in the Welsh official team. It might drag the team down to the level of a small old-style district council but it could not add one iota to the loyalty with which officials now seek to serve the people of Wales through the new Assembly institutions, as they did before through the Welsh Office and its Secretary of State.

Finally, the great strength of this book is that it looks at the role of the Welsh Office and the work of policy creation right through the existence of "our" Department of State. It looks behind the public face of the Welsh Office. Much contemporary comment in the Press and media focuses on the conflicts and the disagreements - inevitably, it's the rows that make the news. People like Jim Griffiths didn't shrink from conflict, but they sought first to be builders, and they had scope to be different at times and to shape the wider political agenda at others. More recently, the same can be said of people like Cledwyn Hughes and John Morris - both of whom were always more concerned to get things done and to carry others with them than to seize personal advantage or a quick headline.

It is a fact of life that newspapers generally describe events that are in the news, rather than tracing how events were actually shaped - both by visible players like Ministers and by the officials at the Department and through their relationship with Whitehall colleagues. If students, political commentators and politicians in Wales are to understand the relationship between the Welsh Assembly and Parliament, they need first to step back in time and understand how this worked in the days of the Welsh Office. This book will be valued by many for filling a gap and providing fresh and useful insights into the process of decision-making. By understanding the past, it will help us understand what the future offers and how to help shape a "Better Wales" for the future.

Alun Michael

Chapter I

Evidence of Welsh Office Distinctiveness in Policy Making

Introduction

For nearly four decades the Welsh Office was present in Wales. To the outside world it remained mysterious. Dominated by powerful and frequently ambitious politicians. Sometimes the Welsh Office appeared to be all powerful yet at other times it gave the impression of being more of a Welsh lamb than a Welsh dragon. For those who lived in Wales, however, it had an important influence over their lives of which they were often unaware. So what exactly was the Welsh Office? What made it tick? Did it achieve anything and if so how? Until now these questions have never been fully answered. This book seeks to remedy this.

The first chapter starts by examining the evidence for the Welsh Office determining its own Welsh Policy agenda. Because little scholastic work has been undertaken in recent years on the Welsh Office, this has led many in academic circles to view the former department as being merely a rubber stamping mechanism of Whitehall in Wales (see Goldsmith, 1986, Kellas, 1989, Griffith, D., 1996). Evidence presented in this chapter indicates that it was much more than this. James Kellas noted of policy making at the former Scottish Office that:

> 'The British civil service was a close-knit organisation which checked out initiatives before they were adopted, and Scottish/English differences were often considered bad practice administratively. Despite these restraints, however, it must be emphasised that many differences did emerge from the policy process' (Kellas, 1989, p. 217).

Kellas's remarks about Scotland could also be said to have applied to Wales, if to a lesser degree. The first chapter is devoted to looking at the extent of the policy differences in Wales compared to those in England. It starts by analysing how much of this policy was either created or modelled directly by the Welsh Office, before its implementation in Wales. It goes on to define the various areas of Welsh Office policy that were distinct from, or an enhancement upon, those in the rest of the United Kingdom.

Section 1.1. What is policy?

Lynton Robins (1987, p. 1) noted that 'very little in our physical and social environment results from either 'natural' or 'inevitable' processes. Almost all developments are politically determined'. This process of political determination is known as government policy. The exact nature of policy, however, is not always easy to identify. One of the pioneers in the work on policy was David Easton. Easton saw policy as an allocation of values within society. Values are used in a broad sense 'to encompass the whole range of rewards and sanctions that those in positions of authority are able to distribute' (Ham, 1992, p. 94). These values are then allocated by means of policies. Ham notes that policy may involve a web of decisions rather than one decision and that those who make decisions are rarely responsible for their implementation (Ham, 1992, p. 94).

Although many academics, as well as Easton, have tried to define policy, few have agreed on the exact meaning of the word. Friend said that policy 'is essentially a stance which, once articulated, contributes to the context within which a succession of future decisions will be made' (cited in Ham and Hill, 1993, p. 11). Cunningham argued that 'policy is rather like the elephant – you recognise it when you see it' (cited in Ham, 1992, p. 94). And Wildavsky stated that 'Policy is a process as well as a product. It is used to refer to a process of decision making and also to the product of that process' (Wildavsky, 1979, p. 387).

This study, however, uses the definition of policy defined by James (1997). He defines it as: 'a course of action which the government has taken a deliberate decision to adopt' (p. 3). He distinguishes this from a government's philosophy; 'policies', James indicates, 'are the practical plans with which the government's philosophy is put into practice'.

Section 1.2. The Welsh Office and the Welsh Policy Making Process

James (1997) stated that 'At any particular time there exists a policy agenda: those issues on which the government either wants to act or feels compelled to act' (p. 4). James went on to state that in Whitehall policy making is very much based on individual departments so it 'is probably truer to say that each department maintains it own policy agenda' (p. 5).

It is the contention of this section that during its existence the Welsh Office maintained its own policy agenda and therefore it sets out to provide the empirical evidence to back up this contention.

Burch distinguished between two broad kinds of policy output:

1. rules, regulations and public pronouncements (e.g. Acts of Parliament, Orders in Council, White Papers, ministerial and departmental circulars).
2. public expenditure and its distribution (cited in Jones, 1997, p. 449).

Hogwood (1992) identifies five directions of 'ideal-type' form of policy. These are (pp. 18–26):

1. *Policy innovation* involving the entry of the government into an activity in which it has not previously been involved.
2. *Policy succession* involving the purposive replacement of existing policies by others in the same area of activity.
3. *Policy innovation and maintenance* characterises the 'continuous replacement' (updating) and addition to an existing range of policies.
4. *Policy termination*, which is the mirror image of policy innovation. It involves the complete winding down of the policy in question.
5. *Policy reversal* involves not only policy termination but also the introduction of a new policy which has an objective in the opposite direction.

The Welsh Office was involved directly in both Burch's and Hogwood's policy output and details of these are provided within this chapter.

Section 1.3. Evidence of a distinctive Welsh Office policy agenda

In 1973 Geraint Talfan Davies, later Controller of BBC Wales, stated of policy making at the Welsh Office that:

> 'Those who fought for so many years for the establishment of a Secretary of State for Wales had constantly emphasised Wales' distinctive problems and the possibility of finding peculiarly Welsh solutions to them. Now, however, the lament is often heard that, far from finding these solutions, the Welsh Office has become a mere echo of Whitehall' (Talfan Davies, 1973, p. 100).

In the 1980s, Goldsmith looked at all three territorial ministries in the UK and noted that:

> '....the Welsh Office appears largely unwilling and perhaps unable to transmit the Welsh dimension upward into Imperial policy debates. Hence there is a marked tendency for the Welsh Office to accept core policy initiatives and to adopt them with little variation' (Goldsmith, 1986, p. 154).

In 1996 Dylan Griffith, in a major work on the Welsh Office, concluded that there was little evidence of 'any distinct Welsh Office policy agenda outside of unique Welsh circumstances' (Griffith, D, 1996, p. 163). Thus, over three decades, various commentators and academics have examined the Welsh Office, and have come to the same conclusion that, in essence, it is a branch of Whitehall in Wales. Such a designation, they believed, did not enable the Welsh Office to do much more than implement White-hall designed policies in Wales.

This section challenges the perception of those academics and com-mentators that state that there was a total lack of any distinct Welsh policy. It notes the comments of Bulpitt who stated in his study on territorial politics 'that administrative departments are treated as a homogeneous unit, where in fact substantial differences can exist between them and their attitude to policy making' (Bulpitt, 1983, p. 28). This section high-lights five distinct areas which provide a clear indication that there were Welsh policy differences, and the processes by which these were devel-oped in order to generate a distinct Welsh policy agenda. Sufficient evi-dence is presented to indicate that there was a significant amount of gov-ernment policy in Wales which was distinct from that applied to Eng-land. The difference will become clear on the following pages.

The public acknowledgement of policy differences

The pre devolution structure of the UK government meant that the Welsh Office remained a department of the Home civil service. It had the same internal management structures and was run according to the same pro-cedures as the 22 or so other ministries based in Whitehall (Norman et al, 1996, p. 300). But this did not mean it could not mould its own policy agenda on certain issues just as these other departments frequently did. Farrell and Law (1995, 1997) in their studies of education in Wales made it clear that there were distinctions between the systems of education in England and Wales and that it was the Welsh Office which was the key actor in creating these differences (Farrell and Law, 1997, p. 176). They highlighted a number of instances in which the Welsh Office or Welsh Secretaries rejected City Technology Colleges and limited the expansion of Grant Maintained Schools. Similarly, they developed distinct Higher and Further Education Funding Councils and Curriculum Authorities to those in England, which have in turn pursued Welsh policy. Other examples also abide, in 1994 for instance, Redwood, was able to avoid John Patten's proposed 'initiative for a Mum's Army of volunteers in schools' by enjoying considerably his administrative autonomy and simply 'observing the English experiment' (Williams, 1998, p. 52).

It should also be remembered that the Welsh Office was one of the smallest government departments. This meant that it lacked the resources and political clout to sustain its own policy agenda on the whole of its extensive functional remit. As a result circulars which emerged from Whitehall 'emerged simultaneously from Cathays Park, differently numbered and signed by a different hand, usually with a common interest' (Jones, 1988, p. 91). On the majority of general UK policy which it covered therefore, the bulk of the policy was fashioned by a far larger Whitehall department. On matters of health for instance, it would be the Department of Health that did the greater part of the policy creation work. It was these 'lead departments' whom the Welsh Office 'was continually relying on for advice' (Wardell to author). Although these 'lead departments' fashioned much of the policy output, there was still substantial scope for the Welsh Office to fashion its own policy alternatives. It was the role and status of these lead departments, however, that convinced many that the Welsh Office was nothing but a rubber stamping machine for Whitehall.

Welsh Secretaries often had policies modelled specifically around their own personal concept of a Welsh agenda. The 1992 Conservative Party Manifesto for Wales made this clear when it stated that:

'Wales has its own Department of State – the Welsh Office – with a wide range of responsibilities and headed by the Secretary of State with a seat in the Cabinet....Recognising the special needs and difficulties of Wales. ...If government spending in Wales is to continue to meet Welsh needs, it is clearly necessary that Wales should have a strong voice at the Cabinet table' (Conservative Party, 1992, p. 8).

Under the Conservatives both the Welsh Office and the Welsh Secretary were often keen to publicise these distinctions, in either Conservative Party or Welsh Office literature. In 1992 the Conservative Party produced a booklet entitled: *The Dragon Awakes: A Decade of Development* which highlighted the previous ten years of distinctive Conservative economic policy in Wales (Conservative Party, 1992). It emphasised the fact that, whilst Conservatives in England had been publicly against state intervention in the economy, in Wales the opposite practice had occurred. The reasoning behind this publication and others, may be perhaps that they viewed that there were votes to won by being seen to fight the Welsh corner and/or getting a better deal for Wales. There were clear examples of the promotion of a distinct Welsh policy agenda by three Welsh Secretaries. Perhaps the most interesting and vivid were:

1. *A pro-active economic policy.* Peter Walker pursued an openly interventionist approach to stimulating the Welsh economy, whilst Thatcherite policy in England advocated a policy of non government interference. Walker's policy was seen as both increasing Wales' indigenous industries and attracting inward investors. It became such a successful policy that Margaret Thatcher in one instance had to directly intervene to curtail its success. She prevented a Toyota car plant from going to Wales, and redirected it to Derbyshire, because of pressure from English Conservatives (Walker, 1991, p. 217).

2. *A smooth transition to local government reform.* David Hunt restructured Welsh local government without the use of a Public Commission, as happened in England. The role of the English Commission and its reorganisation proposals ended very much in farce. The government ignored many of the Commission's recommendations and constantly changed the guidelines; its Chairman eventually resigned in protest. The Welsh local government reorganisation was clearly undemocratic, in that the introduction of unitary authorities was the only option offered. Its lack of complexity, however, was envied in England, a factor that has been highlighted by Welsh Tories (Stewart, 1995, p. 12).

3. *Protecting the old hospitals.* At the same time as Virginia Bottomley, then Health Secretary, announced the closure of St Bartholomew's Hospital in London, John Redwood was preventing older hospitals from being closed in Wales. He stated that "it is a myth that it is cheaper to close the older hospital and do everything better in a new larger one" (Western Mail 26/5/95, p. 2). It was something that Redwood ensured made the headlines in the national press as well (Williams, 1998, p. 55). His policy delighted not only the local Welsh

populations who were fighting to keep these hospitals open, but also Welsh opposition politicians. Even English Conservative MPs, angry at London hospital closures, highlighted Redwood's approach compared to Bottomley's.

For Welsh Office officials, these policy differences provided a justification for their separate departmental existence. It was also an indication that they were capable of managing or creating policy in Wales, based on local needs without the need for too much Whitehall interference.

Bending UK policies to suit Welsh needs

When UK wide or English/Welsh legislation or policy was drawn up, the Welsh Office had to consult with those in Wales who would be affected by new legislation. The large volume of legislation meant that it was constantly consulting the Welsh policy community on new government policy, often via adapted Green or White Papers, ranging from local government reform to changes to the health service. Once any Welsh policy concerns were identified by the Welsh Office it sought to have them taken into account in the proposed legislation (Welsh Office officials to author). There were a number of examples of beneficial amendments for Wales in English/Welsh primary legislation. Some of these were (Welsh Office to author):

1. Section 4 of the *Tourism Act 1969* provided grants for the improvement of tourism facilities in Wales but not England.
2. The *Children Act 1989* was amended to ensure that more detailed Children's service plans were produced in Wales than were for English Social Service authorities.
3. More generous payments could be made to voluntary organisations than in England, under Sections 28 (1) (a) and 28 (2) of the *NHS Act 1977*, as amended by the *Health and Social Services and Social Security Adjudication's Act 1983*.

There were also occasions in which environmental needs which took precedence in England were lessened in Wales so as not to deter economic considerations there. Unlike in England, Welsh planning regulations stated that Green Belts need not necessarily extend in a continuous band around urban areas. The Welsh guidelines in 1995 'differ slightly from those in England, particularly in not mentioning sprawl but in advocating

protecting the setting of all urban areas not just those of historic towns'
(Elson and MacDonald, 1997, p. 176).

Creating Welsh legislation and policies that are unique to Wales

Sometimes to implement government policy in Wales, specific legislation
was created. Although only eight Acts of Parliament pertaining to Wales
were passed between the Welsh Office's creation and the *Referendum Scotland and Wales Act 1997*, which led to its abolition. They defined important differences in both the economy, language and government of Wales
(Griffith, P, 1996, pp. 63–64). In the 1960s and 1970s, these Acts concerned legislation for the Welsh language, proposals for a Welsh Assembly (1978) and the creation of the Welsh Development Agency (WDA)
and the Development Board for Rural Wales (DBRW). In the later years of
the Welsh Office, new legislation concerned the introduction of unitary
authorities, further Welsh language policy and the construction of the Cardiff Bay Barrage. Outside of 'Wales Only' Acts there were also a large
number of England and Wales Acts with delegated legislation for Wales.

It was the area of secondary legislation that created the greatest number
of differences between Wales and the rest of the UK. Here are three examples provided by the former Welsh Office to the author which illus-
trate how it fashioned secondary legislation to the advantage of Wales:

1. *Housing* – Welsh Office Circular 30–86 Housing for Senior Managers stated that senior managers, as part of an inward investment into
   Wales which involved building a new factory, they could get special
   planning permission in order to build themselves a new house.
2. *Community care* – Wales had more beneficial regulations concerning
   the funding of community care. Local government funding in England
   for community care was given in the form of a Special Transitional
   Grant. This stated how the money was to be spent and on what. In
   Wales, money was rarely given with strings attached. Similarly, English local authorities had to produce annual community care plans prepared solely by their Social Services departments. In Wales these were
   produced annually in three year rolling plans. These were constructed
   not only by the Social Services and Housing departments of local authorities but also together with Welsh district health authorities.
3. *Renovation grants* – regulations for the renovation of privately owned
   housing have also been tailored to meet Welsh circumstances. In 1995,

for instance, there was a £24,000 limit for mandatory renovation grants in Wales (£20,000 in England); concerning a minimum of 100 homes in a Welsh renewal area (300 in England).

Perhaps the greatest example of the Welsh Office determining its own policy through altering primary and secondary legislation, as mentioned earlier, was in the field of education. By the end of the 1990s the major differences between Wales and elsewhere were as follows (Welsh Office to author):

- there was a separate Curriculum and Assessment Authority (ACAC) for Wales;
- there were Higher and Further Education Funding Councils under a joint Chief Executive; this did not occur anywhere else in the UK during the Welsh Office's existence;
- the statutory requirements at Key Stage 4 (age 14 to 16) were different in Wales in that technology and a modern foreign language were not included. This provided more room for choice, including vocational options;
- there were different arrangements for the local management of schools and the drive to raise the standard of research in higher education, which were financed partly by earmarked funds provided by the Secretary of State;
- opted-out schools were funded directly from the Welsh Office, rather than by a quango, as happened in England;
- Welsh was a statutory subject within the National Curriculum in Wales;
- the subjects of History, Geography, Art and Music reflected Welsh culture and its past.

It should be noted therefore that although 'Wales Only Bills' were relatively rare, English/Welsh legislation still allowed significant differences to occur between England and Wales, via secondary legislation.

Creating Welsh Office policy that later became UK-wide

Wales did not receive a one way flow of policy ideas from England. From time to time it produced its own policy initiatives, which were then adapted for the wider UK. Within Wales, both the Welsh Secretary and his junior ministers were able to create their own policy initiatives. Sir Wyn Roberts described the role of ministers within this process as 'the dynamos within the Welsh Office, developing Welsh policy issues and implementation' (Roberts to author). Marsh et al (1998) saw this ministerial policy role as agenda setting on a UK-wide basis. If these policy initiatives proved to be successful in Wales they later became UK wide. Perhaps the three most notable examples of this concerned: Social Services, Housing and Education:

1. In 1983 Sir Wyn Roberts launched the Welsh Mental Handicap Strategy. This provided a working model from which the 1993 UK-wide community care reforms were created.
2. Peter Walker launched the concept of 'Flexi-ownership' for public sector housing tenants in 1989. This gave secure tenants the right to buy their homes at a weekly outlay broadly the same as their existing rent. Flexi-ownership became a pioneer of the Rents to Mortgages scheme later contained in the *Leasehold Reform, Housing and Urban Development Act 1993* (Western Mail 9/6/95, p. 2).
3. John Redwood developed plans to improve educational standards, through targets for schools and the Popular Schools' Initiative (Welsh Office to author). This policy was then developed for English schools.

Why evidence of distinct Welsh Office polices did not reach the light of day

The Ancient Greeks had a legend which concerned two whirlpools: Scylla and Charybdis. Those who got distracted into seeking to avoid drowning in Scylla would often plunge into Charybdis and vice versa. The Welsh Office had a similar dilemma. For both politicians and administrators in the Welsh Office the highlighting of beneficial policy could have caused both inter-departmental and political jealousies within the ruling party. But the failure to point out policy differences also undermined the justification for having a separate department in the first place.

The personal values of the Welsh Secretary played a key role in the willingness of the Welsh Office to develop independent policy initiatives. For a Conservative Welsh Secretary at the Welsh Office, however, the Scylla and Charybdis syndrome could be particularly acute, especially if they represented an English seat. Between 1992–97 Wales only had six Conservative seats, just 2% of the Conservatives' total number of UK seats. When compared with Berkshire, the English County in which the former Welsh Secretary, John Redwood, held his seat, a different picture emerged. This county was a fraction of the land size of Wales and had a quarter of the population, yet it had seven Conservative MPs, one more than the whole of Wales. To whom then should a Conservative government pay more attention? The people of Berkshire who normally backed them overwhelmingly, or those in Wales in which they were a minority? If the Welsh Secretary was seen to be unduly favourable to Wales, or if Wales was getting a better deal than the 'loyal' home counties, then the Cabinet would come under considerable pressure from their own MPs to redress this. But the fact that the Conservative Party only had a handful of seats to lose meant that they were more willing to let Welsh Office ministers experiment on new policy initiatives. They had fewer constituents either to please, pander or protect.

The Welsh Office administrators suffered a similar problem if the Whitehall departments became aware of the differences. They therefore devised a simple rule regarding policy differences with England: 'protest if England was getting a better deal than Wales but if Wales was the better off, say nothing' (Welsh Office officials to author). This rule became increasingly difficult to apply, however, when a Welsh Secretary wished to highlight his policy successes and this was picked up either by the media, English politicians or Whitehall departments.

John Redwood and the showing of the 'Union' card

The Conservatives have always campaigned heavily against Welsh nationalism. Yet this did not mean that Conservatives in Wales did not view themselves as being Welsh, quite the contrary. During the 1970s and 1980s they sought an identity as 'a party of Wales' rather than 'a party in Wales' (Butler, 1985). To aid them in this role they had a strong leader in the form of Nicholas Edwards (1974–87). He was a Welsh born MP, with a Welsh seat. The last Welsh based Conservative Cabinet member prior to Edwards was Peter Thorneycroft, in the early 1960s. Even when Edwards had left the Welsh Office, his successors (Walker and Hunt) were keen to carry on emphasising the distinctiveness of Welsh Office policies via such economic policies as the 'Valleys Initiatives'. Matters changed, however, when John Redwood arrived at the Welsh Office in 1993.

John Redwood was perhaps the strongest unionist to have governed Wales directly. In an article in the *Sunday Telegraph* in June 1994 (The Sunday Telegraph, 19/6/94, p. 22), Redwood made it clear that it was 'general UK policies' rather than any distinct Welsh Office policy that was responsible for the transformation of the Welsh economy. In that year's European elections he campaigned not for a strong Wales in

Europe but for a 'strong Britain in Europe' (Redwood, 1994, p. 19). The Welsh Dragon was replaced by the Union Jack on the Welsh Development Agency's Wales European Centre. John Major, at the Conservative's 1995 Llangollen Conference, in turn declared that 'Wales benefits enormously as part of the United Kingdom' (Western Mail, 9/6/95, p. 2).

Redwood's Union rhetoric was also apparent in the Welsh Office's Departmental Reports during his period as Welsh Secretary, Table 1.1. In both 1993 and 1994 these reports detailed ten publicly stated medium term objectives. Six of these mentioned Wales or Welsh in their title. In 1995, John Redwood's only full year at the Welsh Office, the number of objectives had dropped to seven and direct references to Wales were curtailed to just two. After Redwood departed and Hague took over, the number of objectives rose up to eleven and references to Wales went up to six.

Table 1.1
Indications of distinct Welsh Policy in Welsh Office
Annual Reports 1993 to 1997

Year	Number of medium terms objectives/aims	Direct references to Wales	Welsh Secretary
1993	10	6	Hunt
1994	10	6	Hunt/Redwood
1995	7	2	Redwood
1996	11	6	Hague
1997	11	5	Hague

Source: Welsh Office Departmental Reports 1993 to 1997.

For the remaining year of its life the Welsh Office returned to the status quo in terms of stressing the Welshness of departmental aims and objectives.

Conclusion

In the pre devolution period, Wales, like Scotland and Northern Ireland, could not be considered a different political system because ultimate political and economic control of the policy making process lay outside of them in London (Moore and Booth, 1989, p. 18). For the London based media and for many of the politicians at Westminster it was most often a case of 'for Wales, see England'. It was difficult for them to perceive than any differences existed at all between England and Wales.

In the following chapter we will see how Wales had a low profile in the Whitehall hierarchy. In Wales, however, there was a set of national institutions which have been constructed in order to implement government policy, which were not merely sub-units of the ministries in White-hall. The same was true of Scotland and Northern Ireland, but not in England where regional offices contained only a handful of Whitehall department functions, covering Environment, Trade and Industry, Transport and Employment (Constitution Unit, 1996C, p. 40). Therefore it was not unrealistic to expect that when a region was given administrative devolution, it would also develop a degree of policy devolution. There was substantial evidence to indicate that this was the case to a significant degree within the Welsh Office. The degree of autonomy differed across policy areas, with the more Welsh the policy, for example, the Welsh language, the greater the degree of policy autonomy.

Any government department that was in existence for more than thirty years was perhaps bound to make its policy creation process distinct from other ministries. The Welsh Office's opportunity to do this was enhanced by its geographical separation from the culture of Whitehall. A physical distance that had also been aided by the linguistic, cultural, historical, and political differences which make Wales distinct from England. Different Conservative Welsh Secretaries, for political reasons, were keen in the past to highlight the differences in policy between England and Wales. Yet in the Conservative government's later years there was a tendency to dismiss them and instead praise the benefits of a closely integrated UK. If one looked behind the public rhetoric though, there were numerous examples of government policy being implemented differently from that in England. Almost without exception these proved to be of advantage to Wales.

Jones (1997) details five groupings which influence government policy in order of their closeness to the centre. These were (p. 452):

1. At the core: The Prime Minister, Cabinet, Cabinet Office, Policy Unit and policy advisers.
2. Next in importance were ministers, civil servants, inquiries, key economic groupings and think tanks.
3. Followed by Parliament, party sources, select committees and the opposition.
4. Getting closer to the periphery were extra-parliamentary parties and party groupings.
5. On the near edge of the periphery were the cause groups, the media and academics.

In the remainder of this book each of these influences on the policy process will be examined in the context of the Welsh Office.

Chapter II

The Historical Context of the Welsh Office and Policy Making

Introduction

The Welsh Office was in existence for almost 35 years. In its time it was the hub of the public sector in Wales and the source of many of the Welsh media's political news stories. Even after its passing its origins and subsequent development are still not fully documented. Welsh historians tend to concentrate on the Welsh Office's first ten years, whilst the Welsh media now only concern themselves with the issue of the National Assembly for Wales. It is the objective of this second chapter, therefore, to provide a brief coverage of the Welsh Office's development mainly up to the May 1997 general election, which saw the fate of the Welsh Office sealed forever. The evolution of the Welsh Office dramatically increased the scope of government policy deviation within Wales. This chapter identifies the extent to which this has occurred under various Welsh Secretaries. It does not detail the part played by the Welsh Secretary in the policy process, this is dealt with in Chapter III.

The chapter has been divided into two parts. Section 2.1. provides an outline of the establishment of a Welsh Office/Secretary. Section 2.2. assesses administrative and political developments from 1964–1997. Within this section particular reference is made to the transfer of powers and the type of policy areas favoured by consecutive Welsh Secretaries. For a more detailed account of important events and dates affecting the development of the Welsh Office, see Appendix 2.

Section 2.1. The establishment of a Welsh Office/Secretary

Henry VIII united the public administration systems of Wales and England under the Acts of Union (1536–1542) (Graham Jones, 1992, p. 17). From the mid sixteenth century onwards the administration of Wales was gradually integrated fully into that of England. It then evolved as an element of the English administrative system. In the centuries that followed, the links between England and Wales were strengthened by 'physical proximity, population movement and common legal and educational systems' (Madgwick and Woodhouse, 1995, p. 219). It was not until the last half of the nineteenth century that a Welsh national consciousness developed to such an extent through the Liberals and the Cymru Fydd (Young Wales) movement, that the status quo was challenged (Daniel, 1969, p. 102). As the pressure for greater political, administrative and cultural development gathered pace, the Liberal governments provided greater administrative devolution to Wales (Daniel, 1969, p. 102).

Despite the numerous attempts to bring about substantive administrative devolution to Wales, it took 72 years from the first attempt to create a Welsh Secretary in Parliament in 1892, until the Labour government eventually did so in 1964 (Graham Jones, 1992). The question therefore is why did it take so long? This section seeks to answer this question by examining the role of each of Wales' political parties in the establishment of the Welsh Office.

In general the Liberal Party, and more lately the Liberal Democrats, have consistently favoured political and administrative devolution for Wales. Within Wales, in the late nineteenth and early twentieth century, its policy was generally pro-devolution for Wales (Roberts, 1985, p. 76). The main obstacle in the decentralisation of administrative authority from London to Cardiff was that, unlike Ireland and Scotland, Wales lacked any tradition of being treated as a separate administrative unit (Randall, 1972, p. 353). Both the Conservatives and the Home civil service 're-sented a division of authority on an area or national basis' and always stressed the advantages of unified administrative control (Randall, 1972, p. 353). The Liberal Party gave Wales a more sympathetic hearing when they returned to power in 1906. Over the next twelve years they established separate Welsh departments within existing ministries for education, agriculture, insurance and health (Randall, 1975, p. 471). The Liberal Party's last days as part of the government (1919–21) were concerned more with the internal problems that eventually split the party, rather than with any notion of comprehensive Welsh devolution. In later years the Party committed itself to implementing large-scale administrative and political devolution for Wales, but by then it was no longer in a position, electorally, to act on its policies.

The Conservatives were always opposed to any devolutionary measures that could be seen to decrease the power of the Union between England and Wales. Most Conservative politicians regarded the whole issue of devolution as a total irrelevance (Osmond, 1985, p. 229). Yet it was the Conservatives, via Anthony Eden, in October 1951 that accepted that Wales 'Has her own special needs and the conditions which, must be fully recognised and met' (Randall, 1972, p. 357).

As soon as the Conservatives came to power in 1951 they created a minister for Welsh Affairs. It was the new Scottish Home Secretary, David Maxwell Fyfe, who was given the additional responsibility of Welsh Affairs. It seems that a Scotsman, a Celt, was appointed because the government lacked a Welshman at a senior enough level (Jones, Barry, 1994, p. 267). Maxwell Fyfe grew to some prominence in Wales and became affectionately known as 'Dai Bananas' as a result of the predominance of Fyffes bananas in Wales (Hennessy, 1989, p. 468). From 1951–1957 this post was held by the Home Secretary, and from 1957–1964 by the minister of Housing and Local Government. To help Maxwell Fyfe, David Llewellyn, then MP for Cardiff North, became the additional minister at the Home Office charged with assisting in Welsh affairs. Later this position was to be filled by Lord Brecon, formally, Vivian Lewis.

Lewis had been a Conservative Councillor who was made a Peer solely to enable him to do this job. Before his appointment few MPs had heard of Lewis; this therefore caused a furore throughout Wales. Lady Megan Lloyd George stated that the government had 'had to scour the country for a Welsh Conservative' (Stead, 1985, p. 108). George Thomas was even less complimentary when he described Lewis's promotion as being 'catapulted like a Russian sputnik from the recesses of Breconshire past the aldermanic bench to the outer space of another place' (Stead, 1985, p. 108). Despite these misgivings, both Lord Brecon and his Parliamentary chief, Henry Brooke, built up a number of contacts with local authorities and voluntary bodies throughout Wales, thus ensuring that the Welsh voice was heard frequently in Cabinet (Griffiths, 1968, p. 163). Sir Keith Joseph, later to become one of the stalwarts of Thatcherism, was the final Conservative minister to hold the post.

The Conservatives' position on Wales in the 1950s also stood in sharp contrast to that of the official Labour Party position. Within the Labour Party pro-unionist Welsh Labour MPs, led by Aneurin Bevan, were concerned more with the battle to introduce Socialism than aid nationalism. They therefore continued to veto any effective devolution of power to Wales. Although the introduction of a Minister for Wales marked an important evolutionary step on the way towards a Welsh Secretary, it did not encourage the Conservatives to go any further along the road of administrative devolution.

The Labour Party, which had politically dominated Wales for most of the twentieth century, had within its power the ability to create a Welsh Office/Secretary between 1945 and 1951: they did not. The party's only pro-Welsh measure was the establishment of an unelected Advisory Council for Wales and Monmouthshire in 1949 (known commonly as the Welsh Council). It was made up of members from local authorities, industry and other Welsh interests. The majority of Labour MPs in Wales had little interest in devolution in the immediate post war period. They were more concerned in preserving those wartime employment improvements which had stemmed from the establishment of massive ordinance factories in North and South Wales (Morgan, 1995, p. 449).

This indifference was combined with the powerful figure of Anuerin Bevan who was totally opposed to any Welsh devolution. The views of Bevan, often tipped as a future Labour leader, held immense sway within the Labour Party. In the first 'Welsh Day' debate in the Commons in 1944 he sardonically asked: 'How are Welsh sheep different from English sheep?' and claimed the whole idea of even a Welsh debate was a waste of time (Morgan, 1995, p. 449). Such views did not help promote the idea of a Welsh Secretary/Office within the party in the immediate post-war period.

The Wales Labour Party remained split between those who wanted to see more devolution of power to Wales and those that preferred the status quo. Throughout the 1950s an even smaller nationalist group who wished to see an elected Welsh Parliament also supported the campaign for a Welsh Secretary of State. In March 1955 S.O. Davies, Labour MP for Merthyr Tydfil put forward a Private Members Bill for a Welsh Parliament (Osmond, 1978, p. 101). Only six of Wales' thirty-six MPs supported the Bill. Five were Labour MPs, who were consequently reported to the Party's National Executive Committee for opposing the party line, which was still firmly against any political devolution. S.O. Davies was constantly called before the Welsh Regional Council of Labour to account for going against Labour's national policy (Osmond, 1995, p. 160). The Conservatives' change of heart in establishing a Minister for Welsh Affairs had passed relatively painlessly within the Conservative Party. Although this act was nowhere near the formation of a Welsh Secretary/ Office, as most nationalists wanted, it was still much more than the Labour Party of that time was prepared to do.

Osmond suggests that Wales Labour Party was never fully converted to the idea of the need for Welsh devolution (Osmond, 1995, p. 160). The divisions within the party over the need for a Welsh Secretary/Office were to stay fixed. The splits were clearly seen on the issue of a Welsh Parliament. During the 1950s, three future Welsh Secretaries were prominently involved in campaigning either for or against this Welsh Parliament. Cledwyn Hughes showed strong support for the concept of a Welsh Parliament. James Griffiths was more guarded in his reactions. He did not wish to see the Welsh people signing what he regarded as a 'blank cheque'. Griffiths required much more clarification of what a Welsh Parliament was to be before he could agree to it. George Thomas condemned the idea of a Parliament and the idea of a Secretary of State for Wales as 'unnecessarily detracting from the union within the UK' (Osmond, 1978, p. 101).

When moves towards a Welsh Parliament failed, efforts were redirected towards a Welsh Secretary/Welsh Office. Dr Huw T. Edwards, Chairman of the Welsh Council, was one of those Labour politicians who was converted from the idea of a Welsh Parliament to that of a Welsh Secretary. In 1957 the Welsh Council under his guidance provided a detailed and reasoned case for the co-ordination of government activity in Wales into a Welsh Office. A large number of the arguments put forward by the Council for a Welsh Secretary were centred around making government policy more relevant for Wales (Randall, 1972, Rowlands, 1972). Harold Macmillan, then Prime Minister, replied directly to the Council but only after a lengthy delay. A Welsh Office would be 'too small for (purposes of) efficiency' he argued (Osmond, 1978, p. 102). The Council protested that its well documented arguments had been overlooked and sent a unanimous memorandum contesting the Prime Minister's own arguments. The government did not give way and the Council resigned *en bloc* (Osmond, 1978, p. 102). The government in turn tried to discredit the Council's Chairman by accusing him of being either 'power-crazy or a hopeless erratic romantic' (Stead, 1985, p. 106). Another leading Welsh Labour MP, James Callaghan, was also converted to the idea of a Welsh Secretary. He had been converted upon hearing about 'how a Scottish Secretary, sitting in the Cabinet could gain priority for the Forth Bridge instead of (plans for) one crossing the Severn' (Morgan, 1980, p. 388). Where would Wales be in the future without such power? Although both Edwards' and Callaghan's support did much to promote the cause of a Welsh Office/Secretary within the Labour Party it was not decisive.

Osmond (1995, p. 160) cites Aneurin Bevan, James Griffiths (Labour's deputy leader), and the party's leader, Hugh Gaitskell, as being behind the eventual decision to establish a Welsh Office. In July 1959 the Labour Tripartite Committee containing Bevan, Gaitskell and Griffiths met to discuss devolution. As seen earlier, Bevan was against any policy which he felt would 'divorce Welsh political activity from the mainstream of British politics'. Griffiths was still passionately for a Welsh Secretary/ Office and Gaitskell remained neutral (Osmond, 1995, p. 160). Gaitskell provided three possible options for Welsh devolution:

1. A Royal Commission on Devolution
2. A Welsh Grand Committee
3. A Minister for Welsh Affairs with a seat in the Cabinet.

Bevan dismissed the first two options as a mere 'exercise in shadow boxing' (Osmond, 1995, p. 161). He supported option three, but only if the Welsh Secretary was granted effective executive power. Osmond suggests that it was the emotional commitment of James Griffiths to the concept of a Welsh Secretary which eventually persuaded Bevan (Osmond, 1995, p. 161). Whatever the reason Bevan's conversion seems to have been the vital step forward in ensuring a Welsh Secretary. In the autumn of 1959 the Wales Labour Party published *Labour's Policy for Wales*, which gave a firm commitment 'to the appointment of a Secretary of State for Wales with a seat in the Cabinet and with departmental responsibilities, to be exercised through a Welsh Office' (Griffiths, 1976, p. 112). Griffiths's plan for a Welsh Office was now endorsed by the Labour Party Executive and the party's conference, and was consequently included in the 1959 Manifesto (*Forward with Labour: Labour's Plan for Wales*). Although Labour lost the 1959 general election Griffiths ensured that this pledge was also repeated in the 1964 Labour Party general election manifesto (*Signposts for a New Wales*). This time Labour won. Even after the victory was won, however, a number of Welsh Labour MPs continued to try to limit the power and role of the Welsh Secretary. Ness Edwards, the MP for Caerphilly, led a group of Welsh MPs in urging Harold Wilson to confine the Welsh Secretary's powers to those of oversight rather than direct administrative functions. The Wales Labour Party over the coming decades never united over the concept of increased devolution to Wales.

Plaid Genedlaethol Cymru (the National Party of Wales) was established in 1925. It was dominated at first by policies relating only to Welsh language and cultural issues (Davies, 1985, p. 127). The party made little impact politically in the interwar years (Jones, 1994, p. 267). By the early 1950s, however, it had moved on to campaign actively on constitutional issues such as the Parliament for Wales Campaign. It had an increasing political presence in the general elections of the 1950s, especially in Labour dominated south-east of Wales. This was felt by some Welsh historians such as John Davies, to be 'a major factor in causing the Labour Party to include a Secretary of State for Wales among its objectives' (Davies, 1985, p. 136). The evidence, however, points to the fact that it was nationalists within the Labour Party rather than those outside of it that led to the creation of a Welsh Secretary. Plaid Cymru showed no signs of an electoral breakthrough in the 1950s when the Labour Party was forming its policy on a Welsh Secretary/Welsh Office. They came last in virtually every parliamentary by-election held between 1950 and 1959, and lost the majority of their deposits in those seats they contested in the general elections during that period. It wasn't until they won their first seat in the 1966 Carmarthen by-election that Labour began to consider Plaid Cymru's nationalist aspirations as being a serious threat (Jones, 1994, p. 268). The first Plaid Cymru success to seriously worry Labour came seven years after Labour had concluded their plans for a Welsh Secretary and Welsh Office in their 1959 manifesto and therefore too late to influence Labour's devolution plans. The republican noises made by Plaid Cymru only damaged the cause of those nationalists within the Labour Party. To this effect a number of Wales Labour MPs, such as Ness Edwards and George Thomas, were extremely hostile to any proposals on devolution they felt would encourage or were linked to Plaid Cymru (Osmond, 1995, p. 162).

The period leading up to the establishment of the Welsh Office can therefore be divided into two distinct phases:

1. *The battle between pro- and anti-administrative devolutionists, 1886–1959.* The desire to have both political and administrative power devolved from the centre of power in the UK, Westminster and Whitehall, to the Welsh nation began to gather pace in the mid nineteenth century. The battle began in earnest in 1886 when the political grouping known as the *Cymru Fydd* movement started to promote Welsh political and administrative devolution. Six years later the National Institutions (Wales) Bill 1892 was introduced to the House of Commons. It proposed the creation of a Secretary of State for Wales, but was soundly defeated within the House. Over the next 67 years battles between pro- and anti-devolutionists raged in Conservative, Labour and Liberal Parties until one party, Labour, had both enough pro-devolutionists and the opportunity to make the establishment of a Welsh Office a potential reality.

2. *The winning of the argument and the implementation of the policy.*
After accepting that a Welsh Office/Secretary should be created, the
Labour Party from 1959–1964 drew up plans for its establishment
and then championed the cause by eventual implementation.

Even when the Welsh Office was established, however, the fight to
maintain its role as an effective and influential government department
continued.

Section 2.2. Administrative political and policy development at the Welsh Office 1964–96

There was one issue behind the establishment of a Welsh Secretary that
united all of the pro-devolutionists and that was the importance of the
Welsh Secretary as an instrument of Welsh policy creation. For some
seventy years pro-devolutionists in Wales argued for the need to adapt
UK policy to suit Welsh circumstances. The role of the Welsh Secretary
was seen as being fundamental in allowing Wales to have its own policy.
There were constant calls for a Welsh input in the policy process, via a
Welsh Secretary, over 60 years. The Welsh Liberal, MP Alfred Thomas,
stated in 1890 that a Welsh Secretary 'would bring about legislation
adapted for the wants of the Principality'. In 1914 a Welsh Conservative
MP, William Ormsby-Gore, made it clear that he was against the uni-
form treatment of problems in Wales and England. He thought that only
the appointment of a Welsh Secretary would enable these problems to be
solved 'in their own way' (Randall, 1972, p. 361). Clement Davies, the
Welsh Liberal MP, promoted the Welsh Secretary in 1937 as a man 'in
the Cabinet when policies are being settled, great issues decided, new
legislation proposed, representing the Welsh views' (Randall, 1972, p.
364). In 1958 the Chairman of the Welsh Council, Huw. T. Edwards,
cited the need for a Welsh Secretary/Office because 'Whitehallism has
not the slightest prospect of ever understanding Welsh aspirations'
(Osmond, 1995, p. 163). It was putting a Welsh angle of government
policy that was the *raison d'etre* for having a Welsh Secretary.

Ted Rowlands, a former Welsh Office minister, saw the establishment of the Welsh Office as raising 'great expectations for nothing less
than a new deal for Welsh affairs in Whitehall and the Principality'
(Rowlands, 1972, p. 339). In the area of policy creation or adaptation
Rowlands believed that the Welsh Secretary had created a 'Voice for

Wales' in the Cabinet, and access to the vital inter-departmental policy committees in which to put forward Wales case. Harold Wilson announced on the day of the appointment that the 'Secretary of State for Wales will be able to express the voice of Wales, and put pressure on other government departments to see that Wales gets a fair crack of the whip' (Western Mail, 1/12/64). The Welsh Secretary was also able to influence 'Whitehall policy-making to take note of special factors relating to the region within the broad framework of national policy' (Rowlands, 1972, p. 339). Whilst Rowlands was extolling the policy making virtues of the Welsh Secretary, others poured scorn on the opportunity to break away from the English policy agenda concerning the amount of policy variation possible. The Western Mail stated in its editorial that 'the man would make the office' (Western Mail, 1/12/64). Randall (1972, p. 362) noted:

> "The view, however, rests on a rather naive assumption about the degree of independence and variation possible under a Secretary of State for Wales...In practice, however, there are great pressures tending towards a uniformity of administration. A Welsh Secretary of State still remains a member of the ruling party and so from the outset there is the obvious limitation presented by party loyalty or outlook. More important, however, is the pressure towards uniformity provided by the Welsh Secretary's membership of the Cabinet and his day-to-day contact with departmental colleagues. A Secretary of State does not operate in a vacuum but forms an integral unit of the political process subject to its pressures and restraints".

Thus, almost from its outset, the Welsh Office was seen on the one hand as being an instrument of Welsh distinctiveness and on the other as merely a branch of Whitehall in Wales. Although the extent of Welsh policy creation is explored in greater depth in the rest of this study, it is important to note that a Welsh Secretary's success in office was identified with the extent to which he successfully adapted government policy to suit Welsh needs (former Welsh Secretaries to author). This section seeks to review some aspects of policy adaptation or creation in the context of the growth of the Welsh Office.

The growth of the Welsh Office's policy remit

The growth of the Welsh Office policy remit from 1964 was sometimes the result of a process of rational planning by the government, and at other times merely due to *ad hoc* opportunism by whoever was the Welsh Secretary in power at the time. There were four distinct phases of policy development between 1964–1999:

1. *Creation and development of the Welsh Office.* The years between 1964 and 1974 saw the establishment of the Welsh Office, and a gradual rise in the amount of policy areas for which it was responsible. It was also a period in which the interests of the Welsh Office had to be defended from other, predatory, government departments.
2. *The devolution years.* Between 1974 and 1979 functions and powers were transferred from other Whitehall departments to the Welsh Office, on a planned basis. This was in anticipation of an elected Welsh Assembly taking over the running of Welsh Office policy making.
3. *The evolution of the Welsh Office under Thatcherism, 1979–1997.* In the period following the failure of Labour's political devolution proposals the Welsh Office's political leadership was occupied solely by the Conservatives. They increased its powers incrementally. The period saw an increase in the Welsh Secretary's personal powers, both in respect of the use of the Welsh Office's fiscal resources, and in relation to government policy implementation.
4. *Devolution and the end of the Welsh Office, 1997–1999.* The general election of 1997 saw the end of the Conservatives reign at the Welsh Office. Instead there was the introduction of a devolutionist Welsh Secretary, Ron Davies, who was determined to see the Welsh Office policy remit transferred to a democratically elected Welsh Assembly. This phase is referred to in the final part of this book.

Section 2.2.1 The establishment and development of the Welsh Office (1964–74)

The first Welsh Secretary was James Griffiths, the former Deputy Leader of the Labour Party, at the age of 74. Griffiths had been awarded the new post in recognition of his tireless campaigning on behalf of the creation of a Welsh Office (Tonypandy to author). Griffiths, and his new Permanent Secretary Goronwy Daniel, experienced some initial problems over recruiting enough Welsh staff for the new ministry (Hennessy, 1989, p. 468), and in ensuring that their responsibilities extended beyond merely overseeing the implementation of Whitehall directives (Griffiths, 1968).

To this end, they often engaged in acrimonious wrangles with other Whitehall departments and members of Griffiths' own Party over the transfer of powers and functions to the new Welsh Office. (Daniel to author). The behind-the-scenes wrangling meant that it was well over a month after the election victory before the Prime Minister defined the Welsh Secretary policy remit as being:

"responsible for housing, new towns, town and country and planning and the organisation of local government... (in addition) responsibility for roads, including trunk roads in Wales. Oversight within Wales of the execution of national policy by the Ministry of Agriculture, Fisheries and Food, the Department of Education and Science, the Ministry of Health, the Ministry of Transport, the Board of Trade and the Ministry of Labour" (Griffiths, 1968, p. 167).

Although the scope of this policy remit appeared to put Wales on an equal footing with Scotland in respect of its territorial administrators, this was not so. The majority of the Welsh Office's remit was merely in respect of 'oversight' of policy and not the 'responsibility for' it as was then the case with the Scottish Office. The Welsh Office therefore had 'only a fraction of those responsibilities envisaged by the Council for Wales and the Labour Party manifesto' at the time of its establishment (Madgwick and James, 1979, p. 1).

Sir Goronwy Daniel, the first Permanent Under Secretary at the Welsh Office, was well aware that other government departments were far from unhappy about the few powers of the new Welsh Office. The Mandarins of Whitehall were keen to prove that the Welsh Office would be ineffective. A major policy mistake by the Welsh Office could well have proved its undoing. Sir Goronwy, therefore, took great pains to ensure that there were no 'slip-ups'. Every new function the Welsh Office took over was carefully planned for and executed. No grounds for a rethink of the Welsh Office's existence would be offered and therefore none were found (Daniel to author). A full description of the key powers allocated to the Welsh Office and key policies created during the period 1964 to 1996 is contained in Appendix A.4.

In the mid to late 1960s, Welsh Secretaries such as Cledwyn Hughes (1966–68) and then George Thomas (1968–70), a former Welsh Office junior minister, carried on the acquisition of functions (Robertson, 1993). As soon as the Welsh Office overcame its fears concerning the practicality of administrative devolution the department grew from strength to strength (Talfan Davies, 1973, p. 97). This increase in policy functions meant that within five years of the Welsh Office's establishment, the internal administrative structure had taken on an appearance similar to that of most other Whitehall departments. The Welsh Office was organised into a series of divisions based around policy functions (local government, housing etc.) and internal departmental administration. Each of these divisions was provided with its own budget. This set-up is still the basis of the administrative structure today. It was also during this period that the Welsh Office created its first non-departmental public body (NDPB or quango, as they are now better known), this was the Welsh Arts Council, established in 1967.

During the late 1960s Welsh nationalism was on the rise. Plaid Cymru's political strength was being increasingly felt. Extreme nationalism also developed. Shortly after 3.30 am on Saturday 25th May 1968 a bomb blasted the Welsh Office building in Cathays Park. Although no one was hurt, extreme nationalism in Wales had reached such a height that the following year a bomb attempt during the Investiture of the Prince of Wales. Cledwyn Hughes and George Thomas responded to the rise in nationalism in differing ways. Cledwyn Hughes sought an expansion of the Welsh Office and even greater political devolution to Wales. George Thomas, however, who was initially against a Welsh Office being established, preferred socialism to nationalism. He rejected many of the demands of Welsh nationalists and sought closer socialist ties within the United Kingdom, rejecting totally any notion of political devolution. For his views he earned the scorn of many nationalists both inside and outside of his own party (Thomas, 1970, p. 5). The objective of Welsh Office policy was often to head off the nationalist dragon which in the late 1960s was breathing new separatist fire. The Investiture of the Prince of Wales in Caernarfon helped. This was aided by both Hughes and Thomas policies to aid the Welsh Language, Welsh local government reform, the depopulation of rural Wales, and the lack of industrial diversification in the declining South Wales coal mining areas (Rowlands, 1972, p. 346). At last there was a Welsh Office that seemed to be steering policy to help the lives of ordinary Welsh people. Not everything went to plan, however. Plans to bring Health to the Welsh Office were rejected by the Cabinet, by among others, James Callaghan who feared this would just further promote the nationalists. This increased the divide between Thomas and Callaghan that was to come to the forefront some years later when Thomas became Speaker and Callaghan Prime Minister (Morgan, K.O., 1997, p. 361).

By the end of the 1960s the Welsh Office had evolved into the ninth largest government employer in Wales with some 750 staff in eight administrative divisions. This was still someway behind the Post Office's 16,151 and the Inland Revenues 4,490 employees (Western Mail 10/9/69). The year 1969 also saw the establishment of the Crowther (later the Kilibrandon) Commission into devolution in the UK. This would look at the future of the Welsh Office amongst other territorial ministries across the UK. On its first meeting in Cardiff, Welsh Office Permanent Under Secretary Sir Goronwy Daniel stated that there was a danger of Welsh policy being determined solely 'a Civil Service elite' with only limited accountability to Westminster (Western Mail 16/9/69). Sir Goronwy went on to suggest that an elected body could make the Welsh Office accountable for its policy creation. This same argument was to resurface again and again over the next three decades. This was not a view which held much sway with George Thomas. One of his last acts as Welsh Secretary, together with Eirene White was to ensure that Wales Labour Party's policy view on an elected Council in Wales was that it should have as few powers as possible (Western Mail, 5/11/69).

When Edward Heath achieved his surprise election victory in 1970 he was determined to have the smallest ministerial government possible. He consequently cut 17 Ministers in his Government from Wilson's 101. One of these posts was a junior position from the Welsh Office. The two remaining posts were filled by MPs with English constituencies. David Gibson-Watt, (great, great grandson of James Watt the discover of steam power) MP for Hereford, took over the junior post. Peter Thomas, the MP for Hendon South, London, became the first Conservative Welsh Secretary as well as Chairman of the Conservative Party. Thomas was a fluent Welsh speaker and he had previously been the MP for Conwy, North Wales. Although Thomas's Welsh credentials were not questioned, his lack of commitment to the Welsh Secretary's post was.

As Thomas also held the post of Conservative Party Chairman from 1970–72, at the same time as being Welsh Secretary. This gave the appearance of the Conservatives regarding the post of Welsh Secretary as more of a part time job. Thomas maintained that he fulfilled his duties to both Party, Welsh Office and constituents by working seven days a week (Thomas to author). In the end Peter Thomas's reputation as an absentee landlord was partly disproved by the fact that he was able to gain control for the Welsh Office of two of the largest public sector spenders in Wales. These were education (primary and secondary), and some major elements of the health service (Thomas, 1987, p. 146).

Despite his Welsh credentials Thomas's appointment started the debate, on whether or not an MP for an English constituency should have headed the Welsh Office and determined the government's Welsh policy (Western Mail, 18/12/86; Western Mail, 28/5/93; The Times, 28/5/93). The Conservatives pointed out that the United Kingdom has a unitary and not a federal constitution (Turpin, 1990, p. 212). Under the British constitution a Welsh Secretary did not need to come from, nor hold a constituency in Wales (Yardley, 1995, p. 54). This meant that any ministerial appointments were in the 'best man for the job' category, regardless of constituency location. The Conservatives also pointed out that Welsh MPs had themselves represented departments other than the Welsh Office, including Prime Minister, James Callaghan, who had a Cardiff constituency. Therefore it followed that non-Welsh MPs should have been able to represent Wales.

The other three main political parties in Wales in their arguments highlighted the contradiction in the Conservatives' arguments when applied to Scotland. There a Scotsman, for the last fifty years of its existence, had headed the Scottish Office. If a Scotsman always ran the Scottish Office why couldn't a Welshman always run the Welsh Office. Another issue arose concerning the lack of accountability of a non-Welsh MP. It was argued that a Secretary of State without a Welsh seat was less accountable to, and out of touch with, the Welsh electorate. He was immune from the consequences of the actions he took, because he had nothing to lose electorally. The Welsh population or a portion of the population dissatisfied with his performance could not vote him out of office. Finally they argued that it took a Welsh-based MP to fully understand and deal with the complexities of Welsh political and administrative life. Not somebody who was merely passing through as a stage in their political career, as was judged to be the case with David Hunt, John Redwood and William Hague.

The Conservatives in the general election of October 1974, under Thomas, promised an increased role and powers for the Welsh Secretary as an antidote to increasing demands for political devolution from the other political parties in Wales. The Conservatives lost that election, however, and shortly afterwards Thomas was to lose his post as Shadow Welsh Secretary when Margaret Thatcher became leader of the Conservatives. A move that shocked his former boss Edward Heath (Heath, 1998, p. 537).

Section 2.2.2 The devolution years (1974–1979)

Jim Bulpitt noted that by the second half of the 1960s a credibility gap had appeared in the politics of both Whitehall/Westminster and the periphery. In these circumstances it was not surprising that there was some sort of political revolt, notably in Wales and Scotland where the collaborative system (Union) was weakest and where the nationalist parties had made the greatest impact. This revolt was marked not only by the rise of these nationalist parties, but by the growth of a situation in which most of the 'established *corporations* of Scottish and Welsh politics, (churches, business, trade unions and professions) began to take a more critical attitude towards the existing nature of the Union' (Bulpitt, 1983, p. 174).

Prior to 1997, the political devolution debate in Wales reached its height in the five-year period between 1974 and 1979. Much of this debate was related directly or indirectly to the Welsh Office and its role in the policy process. It was the desire of a number of politicians to bring the Welsh Office's policy process much closer to the people of Wales via political devolution (Osmond, 1978, p. 21). When the Kilibrandon Commission on the Constitution reported back in April 1974 there was strong support for an elected Welsh Assembly within its recommendations.

It was up to the new Welsh Secretary John Morris (1974–1979) to see how to best deal with The Kilibrandon Report in the Constitution and Labour's 1974 election pledges. Morris was close to the Prime Minister. He had supported Callaghan in the 1976 leadership contest and became one of his closest supporters in Cabinet (Callaghan, 1987, p. 443). He was therefore able to pursue his policy ambition of political devolution, although not always with as much government support as was required. He proposed that an elected Welsh Assembly should take control of those policy areas enjoyed by the Welsh Secretary and his ministers, and called for a referendum in which he hoped that the Welsh people would support his call for change. To this end, the transferring of new policy areas to the Welsh Office from other government departments was quickened. New policy areas transferred included total control of Agriculture and for the first time control over Manpower Planning, Industry and Export Promotion, and Higher and Further Education. These transfers ensured that the new Assembly would be able to control the administration of government policies over a wide spread of areas. The remit of the new Assembly would therefore encompass powers over areas such as: agriculture, local government, education, housing, health, economic development, Welsh language and culture, and the establishment and monitoring of Welsh quangos (Osmond, 1978). It was also during this period that one of Wales' most powerful and controversial quangos was created, the Welsh Development Agency, in 1975. This was seen by some as further acknowledgement of the failure of central control, in this instance in economic policy (Harvie, 1982, p. 12).

John Morris fought a bitter battle to ensure that devolution succeeded. Six of his fellow Welsh Labour MPs, however, including the future Labour Leader Neil Kinnock, joined ranks with the Conservatives in 1978–79 in order to defeat the concept. Ironically, they used the same arguments that had been made in order to suppress the establishment of a Welsh Office/Secretary, a concept that by now all political parties accepted as being beneficial to Wales. These arguments against an Assembly revolved around the following points: it was not needed because Wales already had sufficient representation at Westminster; it might also lead directly to an independent Wales dividing the United Kingdom and ruining the economic and social base upon which Wales prospered (Osmond, 1985, p. 57). They were arguments that found many supporters and far fewer dissenters. The referendum was held on St David's Day 1979. The result was a resounding four out of five Welsh electors voting against the setting up of a Welsh Assembly (May, 1994, p. 23). John Morris had lost; as he considered resignation (Morris to author), the Labour government crumbled and collapsed on a Vote of No Confidence, which did not, however, directly concern the issue of devolution.

During the late 1970s a new funding arrangement was also worked out for the Welsh Office which would allow future Welsh Secretaries the chance for greater policy deviation from England. Prior to this arrangement funding for the Welsh Office had often been on a case by case basis for each functional area, with the Welsh Office often losing out to both the other two territorial departments and the Whitehall departments (Thain and Wright, 1995, p. 309). This was meant to change in 1978 with the establishment of the *Barnett Formula*. This formula allocation was established by Joel Barnett, Labour Chief Secretary to the Treasury, and thereafter took his name (Heald, 1994, p. 149). It was based loosely on the population size of Scotland, Wales and England, expressed as a ratio (10:5:85). The Barnett Formula provided the Welsh Office with a long period of virtual fiscal autonomy, in which a Welsh Secretary could switch some funding from one area to another at his own discretion (Thain and Wright, 1995, p. 309). It proved to be more fiscally generous to Wales than to England but still less generous than that going to Scotland or Northern Ireland (Rhodes, 1992, p. 102). A more generous funding arrangement did mean, however, that Welsh Secretaries for the next decade avoided much of the Treasury versus department battles undertaken by their Cabinet colleagues (former Welsh Secretaries to author).

As the devolutionary dust was beginning to settle, and with political devolution "on the back-burner" it was clear that the coming decade would hold a more stable future for the Welsh Office. The Welsh Office had gained substantial powers and devolved autonomy from Whitehall, though it still remained very much part of the Whitehall set-up. It now drew closer to the power enjoyed by the Scottish Office; at least in the number of departmental functions it was responsible for administering (see Table 2.1).

Section 2.2.3 The evolution of the Welsh Office under Thatcherism

In 1979 the Welsh Labour Party was laid low by the double poll defeats of the devolution referendum and its general election failure. It was therefore the Conservative Shadow Welsh Secretary who took over the running of the Welsh Office in May 1979. Nicholas Edwards (1979–87) became the first, and only, Conservative Welsh Secretary to have his Parliamentary seat in Wales. Edwards letter recalled his years at the Welsh Office in his autobiography *Westminster, Wales and Water* (Crickhowell, 1999). Those seeking to read Edwards' own account of his years as the longest serving Welsh Secretary should therefore refer to this book.

Edwards avoided the constitutional and policy minefield of devolution which had dogged his Labour predecessor; instead he concentrated on economic policy issues. He used the Welsh Office principally as an administrative tool for the implementation of his Party's economic policies. Over the next eight years Edwards concentrated on tailoring Thatcherism to meet the particular circumstances of Wales and did this in a series of calculated steps. He sought to ensure that the Welsh Office would in future have far greater control over directing local economic regeneration within Wales. A major step was gaining control over the allocation of Rate Support Grant to local authorities. This enabled the Welsh Office to direct local authority spending more closely towards the government's own policy needs (Crickhowell to author).

Despite the incoming Conservative government's plans to reverse many areas of the Labour government's policies, not all areas of Welsh Office policy were altered. In a dramatic reversal of the Conservative Party's 1979 policy aim of 'quango-bashing', the Welsh industrial quangos were spared. Nicholas Edwards, although a Thatcher loyalist, started his term in office by stating that there was no "virtue to be gained simply by destroying what one's predecessors have created" (Osmond, 1985, p. 15).

The institutions that had been set up by the Labour Party were now adapted for Conservative use (Butler, 1985, p. 158). The prime example of this was the use both Nicholas Edwards', and later Peter Walker (1987–90), made of the Labour-created Welsh Development Agency. This became the spearhead of their drive for increased inward investment and economic development in Wales (Crickhowell and Walker to author). Edwards also created the Cardiff Bay Development Corporation which started the economic regeneration of southern Cardiff and, ironically for the key anti-devolutionist, later housed the National Assembly in a building named after him – Crickhowell House. The period from 1979 onwards also saw something of renaissance for the funding and promotion of the Welsh language (Butler, 1985, p. 165), a policy that continued apace even under the English based, and non Welsh-speaking Welsh Secretaries that followed Nicholas Edwards.

Nicholas Edwards was not alone in putting the Welsh economy at the top of his list of policy priorities for Wales. The first three Conservative Welsh Secretaries' policy agendas were dominated by the desire for nothing short of a full economic renaissance for Wales (Crickhowell, Walker and McManus to author). Edwards, Walker and David Hunt (1990–93) toured the world in search of companies willing to invest in Wales. They tuned the whole Welsh public administrative system to maximise investment opportunities. Peter Walker later recalled how one inward investor described the Welsh public investment machinery: he "had developed plants throughout Europe, but never before dealt with such an efficient organisation . . . The WDA, the Welsh Office and local authorities all working as one team" (Walker, 1990, p. 222).

Politically the Welsh Secretaries of the Thatcher era in the shape of Edwards, Walker and Hunt stood more towards the centre of the Conservative Party than to its Thatcherite right wing (Crickhowell and Walker to author). Nicholas Edwards was also the Thatcher government's longest serving Cabinet Secretary. His longevity as Welsh Secretary, and his subsequent senior position in the Cabinet, did much to help strengthen the position of the Welsh Office in Whitehall (former Welsh Secretaries to author).

His successor, Peter Walker, was an equally powerful figure in the Thatcher government. He was an acknowledged Cabinet 'wet', meaning he was on the left of the Cabinet. He was a follower of what he himself described as the 'middle way' of British politics, in essence a consensus politician in the one-nation Conservative tradition (Walker, 1991, p. 47). His chosen successor David Hunt, whom Walker helped pick (Walker,

1991, p. 67), was also from a similar political mould. Their left of Conservative centre credentials went down well in Wales; a country that itself is generally politically left of centre. All remained very strongly Conservatives but they were realists, in that they knew that Wales was a Labour Party fiefdom. To succeed therefore, co-operation and consultation with the local authorities was needed in order to implement policies more rapidly and effectively (Griffiths, P. 1996, p. 65). In turn the local authorities themselves tended to appreciate that these 'Middle-Way' politicians mellowed the harsher realities of Thatcherism. Thatcherite policy was synonymous with non- state intervention, and leaving industry and commerce to the full rigours of the economic market. Yet these Welsh Secretaries were very much interventionists, pointing to the positive results of their policies on the Welsh economy. The period between 1979 and 1995 saw the final transition of the Welsh economy   based mainly on mining and steel to that of one based on light manufacturing and the service sector (Prentice, 1993, p. 43). This closer involvement of the Welsh Office in the Welsh economy ensured that the Welsh Office was constantly being devolved new powers and responsibilities.

In 1990 Welsh Office ministers provided further evidence of their interventionist policy credentials. In the Conservative leadership election of that year the three Welsh Office ministers (Hunt, Roberts and Grist) voted first of all against Thatcher, and in the next round against the Thatcherite candidate, John Major. Hunt was in fact the only Cabinet Minister to vote against Thatcher (Major, 1999) They instead supported a fellow Welshman, Michael Heseltine, who was deemed to be on the Cabinet's left. It was therefore somewhat ironic that three years after those at the Welsh Office rejected Thatcher and her preferred candidate, John Redwood, one of the architects behind Thatcherism, a former head of Mrs Thatcher's No 10 Policy Unit, (Thatcher, 1993, p. 438) was appointed Welsh Secretary.

Redwood did not easily fit into the mould of any of his Welsh Office predecessors. Edwards saw his style of policy as a departure from all of the other Conservative Welsh Secretaries (Crickhowell, 1999). Morgan saw that his appointment signalled the end of the Disrealian 'one-nation' Conservatives at the Welsh Office (Morgan and Mungham, 2000, p. 64). Redwood was a strong advocate of the economic 'market place', albeit acknowledging the need for some 'restraint [by government] for the public good' (Redwood, 1994, p. 22). He wanted to show Wales 'how global capitalism could penetrate the valleys and the hills' (Williams, 1998, p. 52). Ideologically he was opposed to too much state interference. He had a reluctance to impose 'higher-tier guidance on the activities of lower-state functions, and a belief that the guidance that was being released was unnecessarily detailed and cumbersome' (Tewder-Jones, 1997, p. 65). This meant that in some areas such as planning, Wales was left in a 'timewarp as policies and decisions in England kept apace with the new planning framework, leaving the development industry and local planners in Wales without a comprehensive national planning framework' (Tewder-Jones, 1997, p. 65).

Redwood pursued a mainly pro-unionist stance with the occasional devolutionist contradiction. On his pro-union side he linked Welsh Office policy administration more closely to that of an overall UK wide agenda. He refused, for instance, to allow a separate Rural Green Paper for Wales or for the WDA to fly the Welsh flag in Brussels, insisting on the Union Jack instead. The only two major Welsh Acts which were passed during his period in office, the Welsh Language Act 1993 and the Local Government (Wales) Act 1994, had been left to him by his predecessor, David Hunt, both of which were Acts he would not personally have brought in (Williams, 1998). Redwood did not readily acknowledge that Welsh economic regeneration was the primary result of the efforts of the Welsh investment machinery. Instead he has stated that any Welsh economic success was primarily due to 'general UK policies' (Redwood, 1994, p. 22). In 1995 he returned nearly £100 million pounds of unspent Welsh Office moneys to the Treasury instead of spending it in Wales (Western Mail 26/3/96), the first and only time a Welsh Secretary has ever done this.

Redwood also had, however, a devolutionist policy side and pursued policies independently of those occurring in England. On matters such as NHS, quango and local government reform he introduced policies to Wales that were quite distinct and more beneficial in nature to those being carried out in England (see Chapter I.). Redwood's Local Government (Wales) Act 1994, for example, provided the opportunity for Area Committees to be constructed, at the behest of just 10 councillors, within the new unitary authorities. Although partly developed in order to stave off opposition within his own party to the changes (Griffiths, P, 1996, p. 65), these Area Committees have significant devolutionary powers. They are able to (Welsh Office, 1995C):

- use the name of any designated area they desire, such as Montgomeryshire, Rhondda or Radnorshire; all of which disappeared as districts in their own right in May 1996.
- have substantial powers delegated to them by the unitary council within

whose control they fall; though this does not include money-raising powers.

The 1994 Act went much further than any other legislation applying to Scotland or England (Welsh Office to author). Once established, Area Committees are very difficult to abolish. Area Committees, therefore, can allow for a large amount of decentralisation of local government power. In theory this created the potential for dozens of self governing sub districts within the Welsh counties, in reality only a few were ever established. It did provide, however, a clear example of Redwood's devolutionary side.

Redwood's desire to reform the Welsh public sector may have had other motives apart from merely tailoring government policies to suit the needs of Wales. Economic regeneration in Wales from the mid 1970s onwards led to the establishment of a number of powerful economic quangos, such as the Welsh Development Agency and the Land Authority for Wales. These in turn were joined by a host of other Welsh quangos relating to everything from the NHS Trusts to the post Welsh local government reform Staff Commission. Previous Welsh Secretaries often took the praise for these quangos' successes, especially the industrial quangos records on inward investment. Mr Redwood was there, however, not to take the credit for their successes but instead, to take some of the blame for their failings. Over his two years in office these failings were numerous and often public. The majority of criticism was reserved for two quangos: the Welsh Development Agency (WDA) and Development Board for Rural Wales (DBRW). Various Parliamentary and Audit Commission Reports on both quangos proved to be damning and saw 'heads roll' in both organisations. They brought a number of problems to the public's attention. These included:

- Many millions of pounds spent on unauthorised redundancy payments (Local Government Chronicle, 22/10/93, p. 6)
- Irregular payments to members via a car leasing scheme (Western Mail 13/5/94, p. 5)
- The employment of a convicted fraudster as Marketing Director of the WDA (Morgan and Ellis, 1993, p. 28)
- Several irregular retirement packages amounting to around £½ million to quango members (Morgan and Ellis, 1993, p. 28).

Unsurprisingly, this public concern about Welsh quangos, linked with Redwood's own ideological fervour to reduce the role of the state, set the scene for much of his public agenda. To this effect Welsh quangos had their accountability to the Welsh Office tightened and their budgets and staffing cut (Welsh Office to author). In the NHS a high profile campaign to reduce the amount of NHS form filling was introduced. The NHS's District Health Authorities were reorganised with a ban put on the recruiting of new administrators. The idea was to reduce 'the men in grey suits' [administrators] (Redwood, 1994, p. 63) and increase the men in 'White Suits', the doctors. Even the Welsh Office's budget and staffing levels were reduced. Until Redwood was appointed, the Welsh Office's powers grew every year. He appeared to be the first Welsh Secretary to actively and publicly seek to reduce the role of both the Welsh Office and its subsidiary bodies in policy making. Redwood, in essence, favoured the expansion of local government as opposed to regional government and quangos. His overall policy of reducing the role of the state was to become a major campaign theme when he stood for the Conservative Party leadership in 1995.

Redwood, however, promoted perhaps more personal dislike than any Welsh Secretary before or after, from the Welsh nation. As we have seen his ideological position was foreign to much of Welsh political life. His misguided attempt at miming the Welsh national anthem, recorded on TV, was shown again and again by the BBC, especially during his leadership bid. This did much to undermine his image within Wales and beyond. Together with his refusal to sign letters in Welsh this seemed to show a contempt for the Welsh people. According to John Major he did not 'take to the Welsh people, or they to him . . . He rarely intervened in Cabinet [on their behalf]' (Major, 1999, p. 621). Others saw this poor public reaction to Redwood as being beneficial to the future campaign for a Welsh Assembly. Morgan and Mungham (2000, p. 66) note that:

'. . . what ultimately gave the Tory-led Welsh Office the appearance of being in but not of Wales was the occasion when John Redwood, in an effort to champion public expenditure cuts, returned an estimated £112 million from Wales to the Treasury, resources which might have been invested in economic or social renewal. From a Welsh standpoint it seemed that here was a Secretary of State using the Welsh Office not to promote Wales, but to champion a creed which was largely alien to the country. Inadvertently, John Redwood proved himself to be a powerful recruiting officer for the cause of democratic devolution in Wales.'

Major believed that Redwood ran for leadership of the Conservatives because he was about to be sacked from the Cabinet for being an ineffective member of the Cabinet (Major, 2000, p. 621). Redwood indicated that he went because he had lost faith in the Prime Minister. Whatever the true reason Redwood's leadership challenge brought the media spotlight onto a former Welsh Secretary like never before. When John Redwood's Conservative Party Leadership challenge failed, however, a new Welsh Secretary was appointed. The six remaining Conservative MPs in Wales were overlooked. Once again an English-based MP was appointed, this time from Yorkshire – William Hague. The Welsh political Opposition once more voiced its anger when yet another English based MP come to govern Wales, and responded by boycotting his first appearance at Welsh Question Time.

Major recalls in his biography that when he told Hague he was appointed he remarked 'Grand, I'll learn the Welsh national anthem straight away' (Major, 1999, p. 646). This had an impact on Hague he could never have imagined at the time. Ffion Jenkins, the civil servant chosen to coach him in his Welsh, ended up becoming his wife. Thus the Welsh Office was to leave a far greater legacy on William Hague than he did on the Welsh Office.

When he arrived at the Welsh Office Hague was a man somewhat haunted by the ghost of a tough Law and Order speech made at the Conservative Party Conference in 1977, when he was just 16 years of age. After this speech he was hailed as the 'Churchillian boy wonder' (Waller and Criddle, 1996, p. 687). It was something which the media and those introducing him at public events liked to remind him of. The twenty years between making this speech and his appointment to the Welsh Office appear to have mellowed his public views. Although he continued with some of Redwood's policies such as playing up the virtues of local government in order to undermine moves towards a Welsh Assembly (Morgan and Mungham, 2000, p. 66). In other areas, however, he reversed a number of Redwood's policy initiatives. One of his first steps upon taking office was to introduce a rural Green Paper on agriculture and the environment specifically for Wales, something Redwood had refused to do. Hague also undertook a U-turn on John Redwood's plans to reduce the Countryside Council for Wales' budget, transferred a number of its functions to Welsh local government and increased the WDA budget. With the policy reversals and the toning down of his previous Thatcherite credentials Hague appeared to be a more consensual politician than Redwood. Redwood's adviser Hywel Williams saw him as clearly 'dismantling of

Redwoodian Wales', something which Redwood ignored because he had himself no desire to revisit the past (Williams, 1998, p. 188). Edwards saw him as following in the tradition of himself, Walker and Hunt (Crickhowell, 1999). When Hague went onto become the leader of the Conservative Party, however, his closeness to Margaret Thatcher once more rose to the surface. He bought his predecessor John Redwood into his Shadow Cabinet, sacked him and then brought him back again. Both became more united in their policy ideals than they were at the Welsh Office. Hague's Welsh Office legacy was not to be economic policy, or any specific policy issue. Instead it was an issue relating to children's homes. Hague, himself, acknowledged his greatest legacy as being the commissioning of the North Wales Child Abuse Inquiry which went on to shape both Labour and Conservative Party policy on children (Western Mail 15/8/00).

Ron Davies', and Alun Michael's periods as Welsh Secretary are referred to in the final section of this book.

The Welsh Office and the expanding policy agenda

Table 2.1. illustrates the extent of the Welsh Office's development over the three and a half decades of its existence. With each period of expansion its power to alter and create distinct government policy for Wales grew.

Table 2.1
The expansion in the Welsh Office's policy remit 1964–1999

1964	Housing, Local Government, Town and Country Planning, New Towns, Water & Sewerage, Forestry, National Parks, Ancient Monuments & Historic Buildings and the Welsh Language, Regional Economic Planning, National Parks, National Museum and National Library and Highways transferred to new Welsh Office
1967	Welsh Arts Council established, Welsh Office's first quango
1968	Tourism and Health transferred to Welsh Office
1969	Welsh Office gained joint control over Welsh agriculture with MAFF.
1969	Welsh Tourist Board established
1970	Primary and Secondary Education transferred to Welsh Office
1971	Child Care relinquished by the Home Office to Welsh Office, Sport Council for Wales established
1971	Welsh Office created Welsh Water Authority in response to recommendation in the Welsh Councils Report : The Water Problem

Table 2.1 *contd.*

1974	Reorganisation of Health Care in Wales; Welsh Office now acted as a Regional Health Authority for Wales
1975	Industry and Export Promotion arrive, transferred from the Trade and Industry.
1975	Civil Service Commission review established a Welsh Office Permanent Secretary's Division.
1976	Welsh Development Agency and Development Board for Rural Wales established.
1978	Full responsibility for Agriculture (most functions) transferred from MAFF.
1978	Higher & Further Education (excl. Universities) Teachers and Manpower Planning.
1979–89	The 1980s marks the 'decade of the quango.' The Welsh Office expanded its powers through a network of quangos, these included: a Schools Curriculum Council for Wales; the Welsh Language Education Development Committee; Tai Cymru/Housing for Wales; a Welsh Language Board; a Welsh Health Promotion Authority; the Technical Education Councils, CADW, a body established inside the Welsh Office to administer and promote sites of historic interest; and the Cardiff Bay Development Corporation.
1980	Nicholas Edwards was given almost total discretion over how the 'Welsh Block' (Treasury allocated money to Wales) was spent.
1981	Transfer of power over the Welsh Rate Support Grant to the Welsh Office, increasing fiscal autonomy.
1991	Cadw became the Welsh Office's first Executive Agency.
1992	Employment training transferred to Welsh Office. Welsh TECs come under Welsh Office control.
1992	Welsh Office assumed direct funding for the University of Wales.
1993	Welsh Funding Councils established for further and higher education in Wales.
1994	The Welsh Office was given the power to model Welsh Local government in its desired image.
1997	A Labour government came into power with the commitment to abolish the Welsh Office and replace it with an elected Assembly.

Thus by the mid 1990s the Welsh Office had established an extensive formal policy remit.

This chapter has determined the major policy objectives of those Welsh Secretaries who served between 1964–97. Much of their achievements have been mentioned in this section. Each Welsh Secretary had an over-riding personal policy objective and through interviews and the various Welsh Secretaries' own writings it is possible to detail them, Table 2.2.

The following chapters will examine all those who determined Welsh Office policy.

Table 2.2
Welsh Secretaries' personal policy objectives (1964–1999)

Welsh Secretary	Term	Main Personal Policy Objective	Secondary Personal Policy Objective
James Griffiths	1964–1966	Devolution – administrative	Administrative reform
Cledwyn Hughes	1966–1968	Devolution – political	Economic
George Thomas	1968–1970	Economic	Social e.g. leasehold reform
Peter Thomas	1970–1974	Economic	Devolution – administrative
John Morris	1974–1979	Devolution – administrative and political	Economic
Nicholas Edwards	1979–1987	Economic	Devolution – administrative/fiscal
Peter Walker	1987–1990	Economic	Resisting certain aspects of Thatcherism
David Hunt	1990–1993	Economic	Local government reform
John Redwood	1993–1995	Economic	Reform social and administrative
William Hague	1995–1997	Economic	Restoration of consensus
Ron Davies	1997–1998	Devolution – Political	Economic
Alun Michael	1998–1999	Devolution – Political	Youth, NHS and Economic Policy

Source: Welsh Secretaries to author, Walker, 1992, Redwood, 1995.

Conclusions

The battle concerning the Welsh Office's creation was a slow and painful process. Almost half a century of hard campaigning preceded its creation. For decades the Labour party, which created the Welsh Office, was torn between pro and anti-Welsh nationalist factions; it was only when the latter dominated that the Welsh Office came into existence. In its first fifteen years it had to cope with predatory Whitehall departments, anxious not to lose any of their own powers. Over its final 20 years it developed into a multi-functional ministry carrying out the majority of non benefit-related, revenue raising and social security government functions in Wales. The last Welsh Secretary proper, Alun Michael filled a post far more powerful than that created by the Welsh Office's founding father, James Griffiths. Griffiths's department had few powers and staff of just over 200. Michael had over ten times as many staff as Griffiths, and personal powers that were almost Viceregal in nature. The Welsh Office had indeed moved far in thirty-five years.

One of the overriding reasons many gave for the establishment of the Welsh Secretary was as a way of ensuring that government policy could be made far more responsive to the needs of Wales. Each Welsh Secretary brought specific policy ideas to Wales. For most of them their aim was to see Wales become an economic success. Others had different goals, such as increased political devolution. All Welsh Secretaries between 1964–1997 were expansionists, bringing fresh powers and functions to the Welsh Office. This increase in both powers and expenditure was not matched by a subsequent rise in the number of Welsh Office civil servants, however. Instead the administration of these functions was often devolved out to a myriad of new Welsh quangos, which in itself has created problems for Welsh Secretaries.

The thirty-five years of the Welsh Office saw periods of rapid growth in power followed by periods of consolidation. It was likely that James Griffiths would have been proud of the development and expansion of the Welsh Office at its end. It achieved and surpassed his dreams for a Welsh Office. As a man who supported political as well as administrative devolution, however, he would have been perhaps more delighted still to see the Welsh Office consumed by the Welsh Assembly.

Chapter III

Internal Influences on the Welsh Office Policy Process:– The Welsh Secretary

Introduction

The name of Welsh Secretary finally officially disappeared under Paul Murphy's reign when the post's name was changed to Wales Secretary although it was still widely known as Welsh Secretary. This was undertaken in order to reflect changes occurring in devolution across the UK. Prior to this event, however, there was a long history of Welsh Secretaries setting the policy agenda in Wales. In Chapter I we saw that the Prime Minister, Cabinet, Cabinet Office, Policy Unit and policy advisers were at the core of policy initiatives. In this respect the Secretary of State for Wales was the key policy figure at the Welsh Office. It was the succession of Welsh Secretaries, however, more than any other group of people, that shaped the distinct Welsh Office policy agenda. Cabinet Secretaries tended to see 'policy initiation as their most important role' (Headey, 1974, p. 172). This chapter seeks to define how the various Welsh Secretaries enabled distinctly Welsh policy to be framed. It examines their role in the policy making process.

First, it examines how the Welsh Secretary was appointed. Richard Rose stated that 'ministries work best when the skills and ambitions of the ministers run parallel with the requirements of the ministries that they head' (Rose, 1987, p. 74). It was therefore of vital importance to the development and maintenance of a distinct Welsh Office policy profile that the 'right' person was chosen to head it. There is no literature detailing how the process of choosing a Welsh Secretary was carried out. Not one of the former Prime Ministers autobiography's from Wilson to Major contains a single reference to it. This first section therefore relies on academic studies, on the process of choosing Cabinet ministers in general and primary research in the form of interviews with former Welsh Secretaries. The Welsh Office, Conservative and Labour Parties and former Welsh Secretaries had given assurances that the process was no different from choosing any other Cabinet Minister. This meant that there was little or no consideration given to the fact that this Cabinet minister was responsible for coordinating policy for major elements of the government in Wales, as well as a covering the remit of almost a dozen Whitehall departments.

The second part of the chapter assesses what the relationship between the Prime Minister and the Welsh Secretary was like. The Prime Minister had the power to 'select and dismiss ministers and to assign portfolios to them; to create Cabinet committees and choose their chairmen and members' (James, 1992, p. 99). As part of this process, the Prime Minister could also help determine Welsh Office policy output. It was clear that a good working relationship with the Prime Minister was beneficial both to the policy aspirations of the Welsh Office and the Welsh Secretary (Walker, 1991, p. 232). It is difficult to gauge the strength of these relationships between the Welsh Secretary and Prime Minister. Biographies or autobiographies of recent Prime Ministers make only occasional reference to it. There are only two direct references to the relationship between a Prime Minister and their Welsh Secretary. John Morris and James Callaghan were close (Callaghan, 1989) whereas John Redwood and John Major were not (Major, 1999). The other Prime Ministers make no mention of previous Welsh Secretaries, let alone their relationship with them. This section therefore relies on interviews with, or the biographies of, previous Welsh Secretaries to indicate the strength of the relationship.

Being a member of the Cabinet had important implications for the Welsh Secretary. He, for there was never a female Welsh Secretary, was able to take part in a number of important Cabinet Committees and numerous Subcommittees. This enabled him to contribute actively to the policy-making process. This also meant that he was bound by the doctrine of 'Collective Ministerial Accountability'. The third section assesses how both the Cabinet Committee system and Collective Responsibility could be used to the Welsh Secretary's advantage, and to his detriment. A number of academics ranked the Welsh Secretary as generally one of the least influential ministers in the Cabinet (Rose, 1987; King 1994). The consequences of such a lowly position are assessed in this section.

There was no job description defining the exact role and function of the Welsh Secretary in respect of policy. Although nationalists always pushed the Welsh Secretary to be a proactive politician who strongly fought his policy corner for Wales. The final section examines the Welsh Secretary's proactive policy role within Wales.

Section 3.1. Choosing the chief Welsh Office policy creator – A Welsh Secretary

The post of Welsh Secretary, like that of any other Cabinet position, could not be given to just anyone. By convention the Prime Minister could only choose a Welsh Secretary from members of either the House of Lords or House of Commons (Birch, 1993, p. 132). In theory this provided over 1600 potential post holders. In reality, however, they were left with only between 300 and 400 Lords and MPs to chose from. The reason the pool of potential ministers was so small was because not every Lord or MP was suitable to be a minister. The Prime Minister had to, firstly, exclude those Lords or MPs from the Opposition parties. Secondly, he rejected Parliamentarians from his own party who were deemed too incapable, unambitous, rebellious, past their sell-by date, or just too politically embarrassing to obtain office (Rose, 1987, p. 77). By convention, Cabinet posts in the three territorial ministries were never offered to members of the House of Lords (Butler and Butler, 1994). It was probable that the reason behind this was that most Welsh Office parliamentary business was conducted through the House of Commons. Parliamentary procedures such as Welsh Question Time, and the committee and report stages of Bills often needed the presence of a Cabinet Secretary to ensure that things ran smoothly. A Cabinet Minister who could go into the House of Commons proved vital to the running of the Welsh Office.

The Prime Minister had to take into account party political factors when he chose his Welsh Secretary. There was a need for him to balance different party factions within the Cabinet (James, 1992, p. 101). The appointments of Peter Walker and David Hunt were clearly made in order to put 'wet' (leftward leaning) Conservatives in office (Walker, 1991, p. 202, James, 1992, p. 100). John Redwood's appointment was aimed at doing exactly the opposite, and putting a right wing member in the Cabinet. It was the Welsh Office which acted as a recipient for these political balancing acts.

The Welsh Office had also been used to introduce younger members into the Cabinet, partly in order to 'cultivate younger talent' (James, 1992, p. 101). Six of the ten Welsh Secretaries were in their forties when commencing the post. Of recent Secretaries, David Hunt was 48, John Redwood 42, and William Hague a mere 34. Incidentally, Hague became the youngest Cabinet member since Harold Wilson in 1945 (Wales Yearbook, 1996; Butler and Butler, 1994, p. 67).

There were two final *caveats* which applied to choosing a Labour Welsh Secretary. The first concerned the fact that a new Labour Prime Minister, upon winning the general election, was obliged to ensure that his new Welsh Secretary came from the Shadow Cabinet. Members of the Parliamentary Labour Party elected all members of the Shadow Cabinet. When Labour came into office Tony Blair was obliged to transfer Shadow Cabinet posts into the Cabinet proper. He did not give all new Cabinet members the same portfolio they held in the Shadow Cabinet. For instance Shadow Scottish Secretary, George Robertson was given Defence. The Conservative Party did not have the same obligations. In 1979 Margaret Thatcher only kept those Shadow ministers she believed had maintained 'an effective performance in Opposition and the election campaign', one of whom was Nicholas Edwards (Thatcher, 1993, p. 27). The second *caveat* was that any Labour Welsh Secretary also had to hold a constituency in Wales (Bold to author), something which has also never applied to Conservative governments. After the 1997 General Election there was only one Welsh MP in the Shadow Cabinet, Ron Davies, thus both *caveats* together ensured that Shadow Welsh Secretary Ron Davies became Welsh Secretary.

Over the life of the Welsh Office Cabinet posts were nearly always offered to MPs who had served several terms in Parliament (Hennessy, 1989, p. 488). Over the course of the twentieth century Cabinet ministers had on average served for fifteen years in the House of Commons before their first appointment (Jones and Kavanagh, 1994, p. 102). This was not the case at the Welsh Office. Only one Welsh Secretary from 1970 onwards, John Morris, had served this period. Over the last two decades Parliamentary service prior to appointment, with the exception of David Hunt, had gradually been reduced (see Table 3.1). John Redwood and William Hague, for example, spent only six years in Parliament before appointment to the Welsh Office, just half of the time of their Scottish counterparts. Thus Welsh Secretaries had considerably less Parliamentary and policy experience than their territorial counterparts, (see Table 3.1).

Although over its last twenty-five years Welsh Secretaries' duration in office, on average, passed that of the Northern Ireland Office, even this figure is slightly misleading (see Table 3.2). The average duration in office for the last four Welsh Secretaries was just 22 months[1], compared to 37 months for those in Scotland and 42 for those in Northern Ireland. This meant that Welsh Secretaries had a shorter time in which to create policies and see them develop. Rose has suggested:

'. . . it takes a year to prepare (policy) proposals, a year to carry them through Parliament and a year to ensure that they are being administered in accordance with intentions' (cited in Headey, 1974, p. 173)

Table 3.1

Number of years after entering Parliament before territorial Cabinet Secretaries
obtained their first Cabinet Post (1970–1999)[2]

Welsh Secretary	Years in Parl't	Scottish Secretary	Years in Parl't	Northern Ireland Secretary	Years Parl't
Peter Thomas	14	Gordon Campbell	18	William Whitelaw	17
John Morris	15	William Ross	18	Francis Pym	12
Nicholas Edwards	9	Bruce Millan	19	Merlyn Rees	11
Peter Walker	9	George Younger	15	Roy Mason	15
David Hunt	14	Malcolm Rifkind	12	Humphrey Atkins	18
John Redwood	6	Ian Lang	11	James Prior	20
William Hague	6	Michael Forsyth	12	Douglas Hurd	10
Ron Davies	14	Donald Dewar	13	Tom King	13
Alun Michael	11			Peter Brooke	10
				Sir Patrick Mayhew	9
				Mo Mowlan	10
Averages	11		15		13

Source: Butler and Butler, 2000, Who's Who, 1996.

Table 3.2

Number of month's territorial Cabinet Secretaries
served in their territorial office (June 1970 – May 1999)

Welsh Secretary	Term in office (Months)	Scottish Secretary	Term in office (Months)	Northern Ireland Secretary	Term in office
Peter Thomas	45	Gordon Campbell	45	William Whitelaw	21
John Morris	62	William Ross	25	Francis Pym	4
Nicholas Edwards	97	Bruce Millan	37	Merlyn Rees	30
Peter Walker	35	George Younger	85	Roy Mason	32
David Hunt	36	Malcolm Rifkind	48	Humphrey Atkins	28
John Redwood	24	Ian Lang	55	James Prior	36
William Hague	22	Michael Forsyth	22	Douglas Hurd	12
Ron Davies	16	Donald Dewar	22	Tom King	46
Alun Michael	6			Peter Brooke	33
				Sir Patrick Mayhew	60
				Mo Mowlan	22
Averages	38		43		29

Source: Butler and Butler, 2000

Even if recent Welsh Secretaries had started their own policy initiatives from day one of their arrival at the Welsh Office they would not see them completed. They were caught in a cycle of developing their predecessor's policies whilst having little time to develop their own. Marsh et al (1998) also noted that the shorter a minister's stay in a department the more likely it was that he would have to follow the predecessor's policy programme and be forced to take on a minimalist role themselves in the policy creation process. This factor could help explain why there was so little primary legislation at the Welsh Office over the last decade of its existence, just three Acts (on devaluation, the Welsh language and local government reform).

The longest serving Welsh Secretary, Nicholas Edwards, believed that a Welsh Secretary's policies could only continue in the long term if he was lucky enough to have a predecessor who was sympathetic to his own policy values. Edwards cited an example from his own policy agenda whereby the Cardiff Bay Barrage was continued. This was because:

'Fortunately, Peter Walker proved to be as enthusiastic about the scheme as I was; and in due course David Hunt played the same card that I had and took the new Prime Minister down to the waterside, where he made firm commitments . . .' (Crickhowell, 1999, p. 97).

Thus the Cardiff Bay Barrage, which was to remain in political controversy for the following decade, only occurred because of the policy consensus of two Welsh Secretaries.

Common factors concerning Welsh Secretaries

Chapter II highlighted some of the history of the Welsh Secretaries whilst in office, but what of the men themselves? Was there any commonality between Labour and Conservative Welsh Secretaries? There were six Labour and six Conservative Welsh Secretaries between 1964 and 1999 (see Table 3.3).

From the biographies of the ten Welsh Secretaries, only a few similarities were evident. They

- were all-male;
- held an average of two junior ministerial posts before becoming Welsh Secretary;
- did not hold Cabinet Office before arriving at the Welsh Office with the exception of James Griffiths and Peter Walker.

Table 3.3
Welsh Secretaries 1964 to 1999

Secretary of State	Term	Party
James Griffiths	1964–66	Labour
Cledwyn Hughes	1966–68	Labour
George Thomas	1968–70	Labour
Peter Thomas	1970–74	Conservative
John Morris	1974–79	Labour
Nicholas Edwards	1979–87	Conservative
Peter Walker	1987–90	Conservative
David Hunt	1990–93	Conservative
John Redwood	1993–95	Conservative
David Hunt (Caretaker)	1995	Conservative
William Hague	1995–1997	Conservative
Ron Davies	1997–1998	Labour
Alun Michael	1998–1999	Labour

There the similarities end. The Labour Welsh Secretaries had served longer periods in Parliament and had a far stronger knowledge of Wales and the Welsh Office than their Conservative counterparts. They held Welsh constituencies, interacted with the Welsh Office concerning the policy process, spoke fluent Welsh, all had a Welsh education, some at the University of Wales, and with the exception of George Thomas, were pro-political and administrative devolution. Their background was mainly in the legal and teaching professions and in the trade union movement. Conservative Welsh Secretaries had tended to come from the stereotypical Conservative background of the City and an Oxbridge education. Other common factors were that they:

- did not expect to be appointed to the Welsh Office; (with the exception of Nicholas Edwards)
- held a prominent position in the Conservative Party organisation before coming to the Welsh Office;
- held a constituency in England (except for Nicholas Edwards) and had no or very little knowledge of the Welsh language (excluding Peter Thomas);
- did not hold Cabinet rank after leaving the Welsh Office (except for David Hunt);
- were pro-administrative but anti-political devolution.

The fact that only Nicholas Edwards had shadowed the Welsh Office prior to his appointment also meant that Conservative Welsh Secretaries, with the exception of Edwards, had never arrived at the Welsh Office with more than one or two policy proposals in mind. They had not spent years formulating them. The majority had arrived in mid governmental term, and had therefore picked up the policies of their predecessors. As we saw in the previous chapter they had the choice to either carry them on or, if possible, reject them. Welsh Office policy would probably not had even entered the incoming Welsh Secretary's mind prior to his appointment and therefore he always started office at the beginning rather than the middle of the policy learning curve.

The policy skills of a Welsh Secretary

As we have seen with the exception of Ron Davies and Alun Michael recent Welsh Secretaries had no preconceived notions of policy for Wales and knew virtually nothing of Welsh Office policy prior to appointment. Both Conservative and Labour Welsh Secretaries were therefore appointed mainly because of their political experience or detailed knowledge of the policy process, not their administrative skills or knowledge of Wales (Rose, 1987, pp. 73–74). Professor Anthony King defined the modern Cabinet Minister as follows:

> 'Most British politicians are career politicians. Most of them are not specialists. They do not come from specialist backgrounds, and they do not devote themselves, as American congressmen do, to service on specialised committees, in the course of which they build up considerable knowledge. On the contrary, British politicians take pride in having a reasonable degree of knowledge across a remarkably wide range of subjects. They can and do talk about almost anything. They are generalists par excellence' (King, 1994, p. 204).

The later Welsh Secretaries were no exception to King's description. Three of the last four Conservative Welsh Secretaries had no prior knowledge of Wales or the Welsh Office before commencing their job. They had never served on a Welsh Select Affairs Committee nor attended the Welsh Grand Committee. All of these post holders were English born and/or bred MPs, with English constituencies. They were clearly appointed for their political skills and not for their knowledge and experience of Wales.

John Major appointed John Redwood because he believed him to be 'a man of immense intellect . . . political aptitude and . . . a formidable politician' (Major, 28/10/94). He did not appoint him because of any connection or experience of territorial administration in Wales, as Redwood had none. Peter Walker, however, was not just appointed for his political skills, it was also due to his Cabinet experience. Margaret Thatcher informed him that she valued his wide 'experience of agriculture, industry (and) environment', which she deemed suitable preparation for a Welsh Secretary (Walker, 1991, p. 202).

Welsh Secretaries had not always been appointed merely as politically capable generalists. In the period between 1964 and 1987 and post 1997 Welsh Secretaries were chosen because: they had an extensive knowledge of Wales, were regarded as shrewd political operators and also deemed by the Prime Minister to be the most effective (or loyal) MP to cover that portfolio. Sometimes the new Welsh Secretaries were not even aware of their own attributes for the post. Two of the Welsh Secretaries appointed in the 1970s, Peter Thomas and John Morris, had shadowed legal posts whilst in Opposition, yet when their parties came into office they were both allocated to the Welsh Office. Edward Heath thought that Thomas was more experienced than the then Shadow Welsh Secretary, David Gibson-Watt (MP for Hereford). Thomas had been the MP for Conwy (1951–66), and had served at both the Foreign Office and Ministry of Labour. Such experience ensured that Gibson-Watt obtained the more junior position of Minister of State at the Welsh Office (Thomas to author). John Morris's appointment as Welsh Secretary in 1974, over the head of the far more experienced George Thomas, who had already held the post (1968–70), was more a matter of political practicality than anything else. Thomas was fiercely opposed to political devolution in Wales, a major element of the Wilson government's political agenda. Morris was one of the few senior Welsh politicians who was pro-devolution. This therefore qualified him for the job of Welsh Secretary (Thomas and Tonypandy to author).

Only twice was the appointment of a Welsh Secretary a process of logical progression from Shadow Welsh Secretary to Welsh Secretary. The first of these was Nicholas Edwards' appointment in 1979. When he left his post in 1987, and the government started appointing Welsh Secretaries from English constituencies, few could even begin to accurately predict who was going to be the next Welsh Secretary until the arrival of Ron Davies, the former Shadow in 1997. With Davies' demise in 1998 and the appointment of Alun Michael, appointments were once again very much in the hands of the Prime Minister.

Getting to grips with the Welsh Office

Henderson's Law, originated by Arthur Henderson, Ramsay McDonald's Foreign Secretary, states that 'the first 48 hours (in office) decide whether a new minister was going to run his office or whether his office was going to run him' (Henesssy, 1989, p. 490). Although Welsh Secretaries put down their marker during this period it took them a lot longer than 48 hours to prove their worth. Often Conservative Welsh Secretaries had little prior knowledge of Wales, let alone the workings of the Welsh Office. They had, therefore, needed more time than Labour Welsh Secretaries to be briefed both about Wales and the complexities of the job.

The date of the Welsh Secretary's appointment tended, over the period of the Welsh Office's existence, to fit in with traditional Cabinet reshuffles. As a result, all of the Conservative Welsh Secretaries were appointed in either May, June or July (Butler and Butler, 1994, p. 64). The closer the appointment was to the end of the Parliamentary year, the gentler the start for these new Welsh Secretaries. In contrast to Wales, the Scottish Office appointments did not need to coincide with the parliamentary year's end. Scottish Secretaries, always with Scottish constituencies, had a thorough understanding of Scottish political issues, their date of appointment was therefore not so important. The last four Conservative Scottish Secretaries, for instance, were appointed in January, May, July and November (Butler and Butler, 1994). The Scottish and Northern Ireland Office's also never suffered sudden resignations in the style of Redwood's and Davies.

It took about four weeks for a new Welsh Secretary to grasp the basics of the job (Walker, 1991, p. 209). When Welsh Secretaries came from distant English constituencies, a predatory Opposition could easily expose the new incumbent's lack of policy knowledge and experience on Wales. That was why it was important for a new Welsh Secretary to be given the long parliamentary summer recess to break himself gently into the job. When the Richmond-based William Hague was appointed, in July 1995, he had just one Welsh Question Time in which his knowledge of Wales and ministerial experience could be tested, before the summer recess began. His entry was cushioned still further by an Opposition boycott of Welsh Parliamentary Question Time. This was on the grounds of his English constituency base, which they believed gave him a 'lack of accountability to the Welsh electorate'. Instead of fiery questions from battle hardened Welsh Opposition MPs, he faced empty Opposition benches and a series of friendly questions from his own backbenches; surely the gentlest arrival for any new Welsh Secretary.

The most junior Cabinet Minister

Although Welsh Secretaries biographies are dominated by recollections of their relationships with Prime Ministers, the same is not true of Prime Ministers recollections of them. There was only a fraction of mentions to Wales and Welsh Secretaries when compared to other territorial ministries (see Table 3.4.).

Table 3.4
Prime Ministers recollections of the Celtic countries
(references concerning each country/ ministry in their autobiographies).

Prime Ministers	Northern Ireland	Scotland	Wales
Wilson	87	16	6
Health	29	5	4
Callaghan	3	12	7
Thatcher	22	16	1
Major	55	8	0
Total	196	57	18

(Wilson, 1979, Heath, 1998, Callaghan, 1987, Thatcher, 1993, Major, 1999)

With Table 3.4. in mind it is unsurprising therefore that when Richard Rose undertook an extensive examination of government departments in 1987, he put the Welsh Office at the bottom, in terms of its political status as a ministry (Rose, 1987, p. 90). The post of Welsh Secretary normally carried with it the stigma of being the most junior Cabinet Minister, in one of the lowest rated government departments, unless the post holder had previously held higher ranking Cabinet post, as was the case with Griffiths and Walker. A move from this post, such as David Hunt's to the Department of Employment was regarded as "promotion" by the public, politicians and the media (BBC 21/5/93). As seen in Chapter II, only Griffiths and Walker, out of the twelve Welsh Secretaries had previously held a Cabinet Post. The media and the Welsh Opposition liked to believe that the Welsh Office's lowly ranking was because this ministry acted as a kind of kindergarten for aspiring ministers. In truth, the Welsh

Office was less of a starting block and more of a finishing line. Of the last nine Welsh Secretaries only one (David Hunt) went on to a further Cabinet appointments. Not one Welsh Secretary ever achieved one of the top four jobs, Home Secretary, Chancellor, Foreign Secretary or Prime Minister. Although Hague did become Conservative Party leader and Michael did for a short time become First Secretary of the Welsh Assembly. The Welsh Office also did not compare well with its fellow territorial ministries in respect of career progression (see Table 3.5).

Table 3.5
Posts held by Territorial Cabinet Secretaries after leaving that post (1972*– 1999**)

Territorial ministry	Number of Territorial Cabinet Secretaries	Cabinet Posts	Top Four Posts (Home Secretary, Foreign Secretary, Chancellor, Prime Minister	Average number of further posts for each ministry
Welsh Office	9‡	2	0	.22
Northern Ireland Office	11	5	5***	.91
Scottish Office	7‡	4†	1	.71

   * 1972 was the year in which the Northern Ireland Office was formed
  ** Until the introduction of the Welsh Assembly and Scottish Parliament
 *** includes two Cabinet posts for Douglas Hurd, Foreign Office and Home Secretary
   ‡ Alun Michael (Welsh Office) and Donald Dwyer (Scottish Office) became leaders of their countries devolved bodies
   † Bruce Millan went on to become a European Commissioner

As we saw earlier, apart from James Griffiths (1964–66) and Peter Walker (1987–90), no Welsh Secretary had ever held Cabinet rank before coming to the Welsh Office. This therefore put the others right at the bottom of the ministerial pecking order, the 'new boy in the Cabinet'. They were always outside of the 'inner Cabinet' (Dunleavy and Rhodes, 1990, p. 9). Although they held a middle ranking position within the Cabinet Committee system, their position in the overall Cabinet was near the bottom (Dunleavy, 1995, p. 312). This meant that these 'aspiring ministers' were sometimes unable or unwilling to stand up to their more powerful Cabinet colleagues on matters of policy determination. In 1967 Cledwyn Hughes failed to get his Cabinet colleagues to agree to a plan to establish a Welsh Senate (Assembly) [Daniel to author]. Several years later Peter Thomas was unable to prevent the establishment of an all-Wales two tier system (counties and districts) of local government in 1974. He had wished to see some of the existing unitary authorities such as Cardiff and Swansea remain in existence, instead of being reduced to district councils. He was unable, however, to resist a strong Department of the Environment, led by Peter Walker (Thomas to author). Perhaps one of the most notable examples of a Welsh Secretary's policy wishes being side-stepped by a more powerful Cabinet Minister concerned the establishment of the Welsh fourth TV channel (Sianel Pedwar Cymru, S4C).

The battle for S4C

In July 1978 the Labour government produced a White Paper which gave its blessing to a Welsh language fourth channel (Morgan, 1980, pp. 367–8). This caused great delight amongst Welsh nationalists. The Labour government was defeated at the polls in May 1979; a Conservative Party, which had always campaigned against anything thought to encourage nationalist aspirations, replaced it. It was perhaps of little surprise therefore that on 12 September 1979 William Whitelaw, the new Home Secretary, stated that the pledge to establish the Welsh language fourth channel would not be honoured (Davies, 1985, p. 146). The new Welsh Secretary, Nicholas Edwards, was himself in favour of the channel. He and his junior ministers felt unable to stand up to the heavyweight Home Secretary, William Whitelaw (Crickhowell and Roberts to author).

This decision to abandon the Welsh fourth channel reunited the nationalists behind a cause again, only a few months after the referendum on a proposed Assembly for Wales had been defeated. It acted as a lifeline to Plaid Cymru, giving them a major cause to fight for once more (Davies, 1985, p. 146). Apart from the political chorus of disapproval a number of acts of direct action were started, outside of Plaid Cymru. These ranged from the burning of the first holiday cottage in December 1979 to 'civil disobedience' by members of *Cymdeithas yr Iaith Gymraeg* (the Welsh Language Society), which led to the imprisonment of some of their members. During this period Nicholas Edwards and his junior ministers were forced to publicly back a policy to which they were privately opposed.

The situation was only resolved around a year after the initial decision had been made. In August 1980 there was a meeting between William Whitelaw and the 'three wise men' who represented the Welsh establishment. These 'wise men' were the Archbishop of Wales, the Very Rev

Gwilym O Williams, and two men with former Welsh Office credentials: Lord Cledwyn of Penrhos (former Welsh Secretary) and Sir Goronwy Daniel (former Permanent Secretary) [Evans, 1996]. Their meeting, together with a pledge by Gwynfor Evans, Plaid Cymru's elder statesman, that he would fast to death unless a Welsh language channel was brought into existence caused William Whitelaw to 'bow to pressure' (Whitelaw, 1989, p. 290). On 17 September 1980, almost one year to the day after William Whitelaw's first announcement, Nicholas Edwards declared that there would indeed by a Welsh Channel Four. This was one of the clearest documented cases of the Cabinet initially overruling the express wishes of a Welsh Secretary and his junior ministers. It also provided an example of the strength of Welsh opposition when challenged with an issue which was deemed to be close to cultural and national consciousness.

Section 3.2. The Welsh Secretary and the Prime Minister

Owing to the fact that most Welsh Secretaries were new to the Cabinet, they had, to some degree, been 'ministers on probation'. They became aware that they were being judged on their performance as departmental ministers and consequently it was rare for them to initially 'stretch their wings in Cabinet' or try to be too controversial (James, 1992, p. 118). If they had any ambition, which they invariably did, they ensured that they fulfilled their role well enough to please the Prime Minister. Peter Walker stated in his autobiography that:

> 'The only way you can move up from being Minister of Agriculture to Foreign Secretary is if the Prime Minister ordains it. The politician who keeps in favour is not being unprincipled. He or she has to recognise that the Prime Minister will decide' (Walker, 1991, p. 232).

It was of little surprise therefore that the majority of Welsh Secretaries, on the surface, had been the very model of loyalty. Welsh Secretaries since Walker, however, had remained in the bottom tranche of the Cabinet, excluded from the Prime Minister's 'inner circle' and had had little choice but to remain well behaved if they wished to progress (James, 1992, p. 118). Walker's successor, David Hunt, was consequently rewarded for his loyal service and low profile by being given the post of Employment Secretary.

Not all Welsh Secretaries had been on probation whilst at the Welsh

Office, however. The first Welsh Secretary, James Griffiths, and later Peter Walker, were already proven ministers of some years' standing when they arrived there. Both were ministers nearing the end of their careers, and therefore were perfectly willing to put their jobs on the line if things did not go their way. When James Griffiths discovered, for instance, that the 'Mandarins of Whitehall' wanted the new Welsh Office to be limited to the role of a Welsh watchdog with no executive powers of its own, he saw the Prime Minister, Harold Wilson, and threatened resignation unless these powers were forthcoming. He stated clearly that it was a case of 'all or nothing'. Wilson acquiesced (Griffiths, 1968, p. 165). Twenty three years after Griffiths' threat of resignation, Peter Walker made it clear to Margaret Thatcher that he would undertake the task of being Welsh Secretary 'his way or not at all' (Walker, 1991, p. 203). Walker was acknowledged by her as being 'a tough negotiator . . . and skilled communicator' (Thatcher, 1993, p. 340), somebody she wanted to keep in her Cabinet, so she agreed to his demands. Yet there may also had been an alternative motive for Thatcher appointing Walker to the Welsh Office. The Welsh Office's low public profile outside of Wales enabled her to keep his persona in the Cabinet, yet effectively isolate him to Wales (James, 1992, p. 122). It could therefore be said that Walker, was in essence, a kind of modern day Napoleon type figure in exile on a Welsh Elba. He was allowed to undertake his own projects and policies as long as he did not interfere with the wider UK role of the government. Walker, however, remained very much a Conservative, pioneering policies such as 'rents to mortgages', and was still subject to Mrs Thatcher's authority in both Cabinet and beyond (Walker to author).

A good working relationship with the Prime Minister was clearly important for those Welsh Secretaries who sought to create their own policy agenda (Baggott, 1990, p. 54). It was the Prime Minister after all who decided who became a member of the key Cabinet Committees, where the major policy decisions were formulated and approved. Under Margaret Thatcher, any Welsh Secretary who sought to steer the Welsh Office in a direction away from the collective norm (Walker for example) was likely to be challenged by her and forced to defend his departmental policy (Baggott, 1990, p. 54). It was therefore a test of a Welsh Secretary's character as to whether or not he was strong enough to 'hold his own ground' (Walker to author). Hesitation or lack of clarity on a policy initiative could result in that idea being discarded, as well as the reputation of the Welsh Secretary being tarnished with the Prime Minister (Walker to author).

As the personal envoy of the government in Wales, it was important for the sake of their political Party that the Welsh Secretary was seen to have a good relationship with the Prime Minister. Both had to appear together on the platform at their Party's Conferences in Wales; the Welsh Secretary often escorted the Prime Minister around Wales on their visits to the Principality. All Welsh Secretaries, therefore, claimed to have had a close working relationship with the Prime Minister (former Welsh Secretaries to author). Perhaps this was seen most closely in Tony Blair coming to Wales on a number of occasions to campaign for Alun Michael in the 1999 Labour leadership contest. Even when there were open personal clashes, such as John Major's reputed description of John Redwood as a political 'bastard' because of his Eurosceptic views (Western Mail, 28/10/94), the relationship remained publicly intact. John Redwood, himself, stated that he remained publicly loyal to John Major right up until the time of his own decision to contest the Conservative Party leadership (The Independent, 19/7/95).

Section 3.3. Cabinet Battles

Although some authors (Ham, 1992, p. 100, Kavanagh, 1995,) indicate that Prime Ministerial government has now replaced Cabinet government, there was still immense benefit to being a member of the Cabinet for a Welsh Secretary. The Welsh Secretary's resources for influencing government policy started with the fact that he had a voice in this Cabinet (Thomas, 1987, p. 155). In 1918 the Haldane Committee established the Cabinet as 'the final determiner of the policy to be submitted to Parliament' (Stanyer and Smith, 1976, p. 164). Many of the policy creation and general strategic governmental decisions were not, however, directed through meetings of the full Cabinet but instead through Cabinet Committees or subcommittees. These Ministerial Committees had a two-fold purpose. First, they relieved pressure on the Cabinet by settling the majority of business at a lower level. Second, they tried to maintain the concept of collective responsibility by ensuring that even if important questions never reached the Cabinet they were considered fully and authoritatively enough for the government to accept responsibility for it (James and Williams, 1997, p. 31).

The creation, membership, and chairmanship of these Ministerial Committees were determined by the Prime Minister (Norton, 1994, p. 184). In the Major government, for instance, there were some 28

Committees and subcommittees, none of which dealt specifically with Wales (Norton, 1994, p. 185). These Cabinet Committees were divided into two types: Subject or Standing Committees, and Ad Hoc Committees. The former category were permanent and on going. Ad Hoc Cabinet Committees were convened on a short-term or sporadic basis to consider specific issues (Dorey, 1991, p. 12).

The Welsh Secretary was a member of a large number of the Subject or Standing Committees, ranging from the Committee on Economic and Domestic Policy to European Questions Committee (Dod's, 1996, p. 124). The reason he sat on so many Committees was because his departmental remit covered part of, or the same ground as, around ten Whitehall based counterparts (Rhodes, 1992, p. 144). A Cabinet Committee had to include any minister with a direct stake in what was being discussed (James, 1992, p. 63). In theory this meant that Wales had a voice with which to contribute to and benefit from the 'Imperial policy debates'. It put the Welsh Secretary at an advantage over some of his Cabinet colleagues, who by the very nature of their own department's remit, were limited as to the number of Committees they could attend. A Committee's decisions had the same status as those of the full Cabinet, and in fact were only referred to the Cabinet if the Committee Chairman regarded there to be a significant dispute upon which the Cabinet should arbitrate (James, 1992, p. 59). In fact only Treasury ministers who were 'unwilling to accept expenditure as a charge on the reserve' had an automatic right of appeal (James and Williams, 1997, p. 31).

The Welsh Secretary had an input into the vast majority of the government's internal policy issues via the Cabinet Committees. David Hunt informed the Select Committee on Welsh Affairs in December 1992 that:

> 'As Secretary of State not only do I sit in the Cabinet but I also sit on most of the Cabinet Committees and therefore whenever policy direction/policy change is discussed then I have an immediate input into policy formulation. When policies have been taken through individual departments – the Welsh Office and individual English departments and others – obviously my officials are involved whenever Welsh interests are part of the overall picture . . .' (HMSO, 1993B, p. 89)

The Welsh viewpoint was not always listened to, howerver, Ron Davies noted that in Cabinet it was often difficult to get the 'Welsh voice' heard. In opposition it had been easier to develop a Welsh agenda (Davies to author). A study by Patrick Dunleavy, however, indicated that the Welsh

Secretary, due to his presence on a wealth of Cabinet Subcommittees, had more influence within the Cabinet than a number of his Cabinet colleagues, including the Secretaries of State for both Health and Education (Dunleavy, 1995, p. 308). However he still had less influence than the vast majority of the Cabinet including the Scottish and Northern Ireland Secretaries. None of the three territorial Cabinet Secretaries chaired any of the Committees, and it was through the chair of these that the real power was exercised (Dunleavy, 1995, p. 308).

The full Cabinet and the Committee system

Every Thursday morning the Welsh Secretary, or occasionally one of his ministerial team, attended the full Cabinet meeting. Apart from immediate or pressing issues, the bulk of the Cabinet's agenda normally concerned items referred upwards from Committees (James, 1992, p. 73). Sometimes these issues concerned arbitration exercises whereby a defeated minister was challenging a Committee's decision. This only occurred if that Committee's chairman allowed the appeal to go ahead in the first place (James, 1992, p. 69). During these exercises every Cabinet minister was, in theory, given the chance to air their views on the issue in question (James, 1979, p. 74).

When arbitration decisions involved a Welsh Secretary it was invariably about money and involved the Treasury. Nicholas Edwards sometimes believed that 'the Treasury was there to stop any money being given to government departments at all' (Crickhowell to author). Few Welsh Secretaries did not clash with the Treasury (former Welsh Secretaries to author). When Peter Walker fought John Major, then Chancellor, over the right to continuation of higher resource allocation to Wales compared to England, he only won by threatening resignation if it was not forthcoming (Walker to author). This constant pressure from the Treasury and the 'lack of political clout by successive Welsh Secretaries, relative to that wielded by their Scottish and Northern Ireland colleagues', were perhaps the main reason that some academics felt that Wales lost out in territorial resource allocation compared to Northern Ireland and Scotland (Thain and Wright, 1995, p. 325).

To try to get the necessary support to win their policy arguments in the Subcommittees and to avoid the risk of having them overturned in the full Cabinet, the Welsh Secretaries built up alliances with other government departments. Cledwyn Hughes, for instance, had a close relationship with James Callaghan when the latter was Chancellor. Later on, when Cledwyn Hughes was at Agriculture, he aided George Thomas at the Welsh Office (Cledwyn to author). Sometimes a territorial alliance was evoked, involving Welsh and Scottish Offices. Nicholas Edwards stated that he 'often supported the Scottish Secretary and *vice versa*; there was a Scottish/Welsh line with Common interests including inward investment, agriculture and forests, we only differed on steel' (Crickhowell to author).

Collective Ministerial accountability for policy output

Despite the Welsh Secretary's attendance at a wide range of Cabinet Committees and subcommittees, he did not always have an input on important policy issues. As we saw earlier, Prime Ministers sometimes used these Committees as a means of avoiding full discussion within the Cabinet. Margaret Thatcher, for instance, often presented ministers with a *fait accompli*, where they were left in the position of either having to accept the decision or resign (Birch, 1993, p. 136). It was through this method that the Poll Tax was included in the Conservative 1987 election manifesto and subsequently introduced to Wales (Baggott, 1990, p. 54). Although the Welsh Secretary was occasionally excluded from the decision making process in all but name, he still had to be 'answerable and accountable to Parliament for anything which had been agreed by the Cabinet, or one of its numerous Committees' (Dorey, 1994, p. 102). This accountability was known as the doctrine of 'Collective Ministerial' responsibility. The doctrine has been described as the 'twin facets of government unanimity and accountability to Parliament' (Ellis in Marshall, 1989, p. 46).

In 1878 the Prime Minister Lord Salisbury set out a clear definition of what was expected by each Cabinet member:

> 'For all that passes in Cabinet every member of it who does not resign is absolutely and irretrievably responsible and has no right afterwards to say that he agreed in one case to a compromise, while in another he was persuaded by his colleague. . . . It is only on the principle that absolute responsibility is undertaken by every member of the Cabinet, who, after a decision is arrived at, remains a member of it, that the joint responsibility of ministers to Parliament can be upheld and one of the most essential principles of Parliamentary responsibility established (Hansard 8/8/1878, cited in Marshall, 1989, p. 46)'.

Some ninety years later, Professor Ivor Jennings added three more points to Salisbury's definition (Jennings, 1965, p. 277 cited in Marshall, 1989, p. 46):

1. the need for a full and frank discussion in government;
2. that a minister should not disavow his own involvement in a past decision, and should give his loyal support;
3. all decisions should be considered as being made by the government as a whole.

In Cabinet there were rarely specifically Welsh views needed (Welsh Secretaries to author). Some felt that collective responsibility allowed accommodation, with lead government Ministers detailing everyone else (Michael and Thomas, G to author). Therefore in general it appeared that Welsh Secretaries abided by this doctrine of Collective Cabinet responsibility. Also this collective responsibility could be side-stepped by being applied to England and not Wales (Michael to author). No Welsh Secretary therefore ever felt the need to resign on an issue of policy because they could not support the government line.

Yet this did not mean that Welsh Secretaries were always informed on important government discussions, which they were still expected to 'collectively' support. In June 1995, John Redwood was not informed or consulted directly by John Major about the latter's decision to force a leadership contest. This lack of consultation played a major role in Redwood's decision to resign in order to contest the leadership election himself (Independent, 3/7/95, p. 2). Major himself, however, gives a different version of events which implies that Redwood left believing he was about to be sacked (Major, 1999, p. 621).

Redwood's resignation did not signal the first or last time a Welsh Secretary had not been informed about an important issue. Many of John Redwood's predecessors were not always consulted on economic policy issues either by fellow ministers or the Cabinet, even though these decisions had important policy consequences for the Welsh Office and beyond. Here are four notable examples:

1. Towards the end of the 1960s the Welsh Office had been given 'oversight' responsibilities for Energy (coal mining). George Thomas, the Welsh Secretary at the time, felt that this was in essence a case of 'responsibility without power' (Tonypandy to author). The Welsh Office was consulted about pit closures but, in reality, closures took place

only after consultations between the NUM and the Ministry of Fuel and Power, leaving the Welsh Office with little say in the matter. The Welsh Office, however, always had to deal with the economic aftermath of a pit's closure.

2. In the late 1980s Wales was receiving the vast majority of economic inward investment into the United Kingdom. Peter Walker, the then Welsh Secretary, had convinced Toyota Executives that Wales was the place to be. Then suddenly the plant was diverted from Wales to Derby in England. It transpired that Margaret Thatcher had intervened directly to divert the plant away from Wales. She had not informed her Welsh Secretary of either her decision or the reasons behind it (Walker, 1991).

3. In October 1992 David Hunt confessed that he had not been informed of British Coal's intention to close three of the four remaining South Wales deep mines (*Western Mail* 22/10/92). Although the Welsh Office was directly responsible for dealing with the economic and social consequences of these closures, the minister was allowed no input.

4. In the early 1990s civil servants under Walker and Hunt at the Welsh Office particularly the Chief Medical Officer Dame Deidre Hine gave specific warnings about the problems of BSE and the possible links to humans via vCJD. In October 2000 the Phillips Report into BSE revealed that a series of information blockages between Cathays Park and Whitehall effectively saw the Welsh Office 'stonewalled' on preventing the spread of BSE (Western Mail 27/10/00).

Ministerial responsibility for departmental policy output

The former Cabinet Secretary, Sir Robert Armstrong, stated that 'the civil service as such, had no constitutional personality or responsibility separate from the duly elected government of the day' (Shepherd, 1987, p. 69). Armstrong's statement implied that Welsh Office officials should remain loyal to the Welsh Secretary who represents the 'government of the day' and his policy output. In constitutional theory, however, civil servants should maintain a neutral stance, seeking to serve all political parties that form the government from Westminster (Shepherd, 1987, p. 78). Although academics now agree that the concept of civil service neutrality has blurred around the edges (Pyper, 1995; Dowding, 1995A), the vast majority of civil servants at the Welsh Office always retained the concept of being 'neutral, faceless and anonymous' (Pyper, 1995, p. 13).

This was something that also caused a problem when the Welsh Office became the Welsh Assembly. For the Welsh Office official, the fact that they remained anonymous meant that they were unable to speak freely in their own defence if they were subject to external criticism (Shepherd, 1987, p. 74). The minister was therefore held to be ultimately accountable for their actions and their defence. Madgwick and Woodhouse have stated that:

> 'Under the Constitution civil servants are not accountable to Parliament or in public at all. Civil servants act as delegates of ministers; their actions are made in their minister's name, not, as is the case in other countries, in their own name but on behalf of the state. The courts support this view'. (Madgwick and Woodhouse, 1995, p. 147)

This accountability by Welsh Office ministers for every action undertaken by their department is referred to as the doctrine of Ministerial Responsibility/Accountability (Dicey in Marshall, 1989, p. 22). There was much criticism in the last years of the Major government concerning ministers who had failed to accept Ministerial Responsibility for the actions of their officials (Dowding, 1995A, p. 173). Sometimes this touched the Welsh Office itself. In 1994 the Welsh Office was unable to account for some £37 million it had given to Welsh TECs and £300 million pounds on highway improvements (The Independent, 24/2/94). No Welsh Office minister offered their resignation over this huge official error. Calls by the Opposition for ministerial resignations at the Welsh Office over departmental errors, were seldom echoed outside of the corridors of Westminster and remain few and far between. John Morris considered resignation when his plans for devolution failed in 1979, as did Ron Davies when it looked as though the 1997 referendum might also fail (Morris to author, Davies, 1999). Nicholas Edwards also considered his position when the Cardiff Bay Barrage Bill failed to get through Parliament (Crickhowell to author). But just like their predecessors and successors, they did not regard the concept of Ministerial Responsibility as being the same as personal failure, so both Morris, Edwards and Davies stayed in post.

Welsh Secretaries did not always regard Ministerial Accountability as a negative concept or one which they should avoid. Ministerial Responsibility was also used by the Welsh Secretary to defend Welsh Office policy interests against other government departments. This responsibility could be used to create a strong political departmentalism, as a way of safeguarding both the ministers own position and keeping some aspects of policy making within the Welsh Office, and outside of Cabinet Committees (Dunleavy and Rhodes, 1990, pp. 12–13). Redwood, for instance, pursued health and economic policy interests in this very fashion (Williams, 1998).

Section 3.4. Defining the Welsh Secretary's Welsh policy role

Marsh et al (1998) who built upon the work of Headey (1974) identified Cabinet Secretaries with four distinct policy roles: a) Agenda setting, b) Policy initiation, c) Policy selection and d) Policy legitimisation. They noted that all Cabinet Secretaries were involved in the policy process and became much more proactive in the period after the Welsh Office's creation. In this section therefore we will take a closer look at the Welsh Secretary's exact Welsh policy role. Wales covers just over 8 per cent of the total land area of the United Kingdom and contains 5 per cent of its population (May, 1994, p. 1). In fact, it was the second smallest in terms of population of all the government's classified 'Standard Regions' (2.8m): only East Anglia is smaller (2m) (Hogwood, 1995, p. 274). In the 1990s Wales contained only around 16% of the population of largest Standard Region, the 'South East' of England (17.2m) (Hogwood, 1995, p. 274). Although the Welsh Secretary was a small player on the UK-wide stage, within the principality his power was almost absolute. David Hunt jokingly likened his position to that of a Nazi Gauleiter, (St Davids to author). Although no Welsh Secretary had the supreme power given to a Gauleiter; he was by far the most powerful political figure in Wales.

The Welsh Secretary, however, spent the vast majority of his time outside of Wales in London (Thomas, 1987, p. 165). Outside of the Cabinet, however, the Welsh Secretary also had a national (Welsh) role (Thomas, 1987, p. 165). Just as we saw of former Prime Ministers (Table 3.4) few academics ever mentioned the existence of a Welsh Secretary when they looked at the details of either Cabinet government or the UK-wide civil service (Dowding, 1995A; Pyper, 1995; Flynn and Strehl, 1996). This meant that there was no job description defining the exact policy role and function of the Welsh Secretary. The Welsh Office's Annual reports simply stated that:

'the Secretary of State for Wales is responsible for the majority of government policies as they apply to Wales . . . (these) are shared between him and the Parliamentary Under Secretaries of State who complete the Ministerial team' (Welsh Office, 1996, p. 1).

From this statement it can be assumed that the Welsh Secretary and his ministers had ministerial responsibility for the policy workings of the entire Welsh Office. From time to time, however, there were even firmer indications of the Welsh Secretary's role. In 1993 the government defined the Welsh Secretary's scope, when they declared that:

'The Secretary of State . . . (is responsible for) representing and pursuing Welsh interests in every area of government activity. The government further believes that the role of a strong Secretary of State for Wales, within the Cabinet, provides the best possible means of ensuring that the needs of Wales will be met within the framework of the broad range of government policies, while also recognising that the Secretary of State can and should, when appropriate, adapt such polices to meet the particular circumstances of Wales' (Welsh Office, July 1993, p. 2).

This declaration appeared to support the policy vision of the first Welsh Secretary, James Griffiths, of a proactive Welsh Secretary (Griffiths, 1968, p. 167). In the three and a half decades he existed at the Welsh Office the Welsh Secretary established an identified role within Wales, Figure 3.1.

Figure 3.1
The Welsh Secretary's Welsh Policy Role
(compiled from interviews with former Welsh Secretaries)

1. Ensured that the Party's manifesto for Wales and Cabinet policy was implemented by Welsh Office officials.
2. Set the timetable for the Welsh Office's internal policy agenda.
3. Experimented on personal policy initiatives provided they were approved by the Whitehall Cabinet/Prime Minister.
4. Acted as a departmental forum to receive delegations by individuals and Welsh organisations; undertook the role of a conduit to enhance the policy process.
5. Acted as an arbiter concerning rights of appeal in general policy implementation, and specifically planning, educational and environmental issues.
6. The voice of government policy in Wales to the media.
7. The voice of the Welsh Office in accountability to Parliament – appeared at Welsh Question Time, the Welsh Grand Committee, the Select Committee on Welsh Affairs and the Public Accounts Committee.

8. Defended and promoted the government's policies in Wales to the Welsh public.
9. The lead figure for his Party within Wales.
10. Moulded and created primary legislation specifically for Wales.
11. Key figure in drafting secondary legislation.
12. Wielded ultimate control over how the Welsh Block was allocated and how government institutions in Wales spent it, from the NHS to local government.
13. Appointed political and public sector administrative appointments to enable the formulation and delivery of policies.
14. The key figure behind drafting the party's 'Welsh manifesto'

As Figure 3.1. indicates, the Welsh Secretaries were at the centre of the policy making process in Wales. It was they that were responsible for the overall drafting of the Welsh elements of his party's election manifestos (Williams, 1998, p. 263).

The central role of the Welsh Secretary in the policy making process was confirmed in the author's interviews with both politicians and civil servants. They clearly stated that if the Welsh Secretary was against an internal Welsh Office policy proposal then it rarely happened. But the Welsh Secretary was not a total autocrat as far as policy was concerned. We saw earlier that the Prime Minister, the Cabinet, and his own experience, tenure in office and personal ambitions, checked his own policy determinations in respect of the Welsh Office. Despite these sometimes considerable counterweights to his own policy ambitions the Welsh Secretary still had considerable scope to determine his own policy initiatives. As we saw in Chapter I, Welsh Secretaries had used their position to try to become agenda setters rather than just policy initiators. Redwood for instance ensured that embryo Welsh party manifestos always indicated his ideas for the whole UK, even if they were outside of the Welsh Office's own remit, a case of 'for UK, see Wales' (Williams, 1998, p. 263). Major, however, tended to treat these as indications of Redwood's own personal ambition rather than being beneficial to Wales (Major, 1999, p. 621).

So at the end of this section we can see that regarding Welsh Office policy, it was the Welsh Secretary who:

• was the conduit through which any distinctive Welsh Office policy flowed, which gave him a veto over Welsh Office policy creation;
• had the ability to change the 'policy paradigm' or departmental line;

- ensured that his party's Welsh manifesto was fulfilled as far as the Welsh Office was concerned;
- sought to build up his own career through policy output;
- helped determine the autonomy of the Welsh Office's policy output;

This made him the most powerful Welsh Office figure in respect of the Welsh Office's own policy output.

Conclusion

Without doubt, the Welsh Secretary enjoyed immense power and prestige within Wales when it came to the policy process. The major determinant of whom became Welsh Secretary was the Prime Minister's personal preference. Since Nicholas Edwards left, in 1987, the appointments under the Conservatives had little or nothing to do with the new Welsh Secretary's knowledge or experience of Wales. After Peter Walker left in 1990, a new Welsh Secretary's appointment also had little to do with previous experience in Cabinet or general wide ranging ministerial experience. Their appointment had everything to do with their own political astuteness or the Prime Minister's aspiration for them to become a significant force in Cabinet, with perhaps the exception of Ron Davies who was already a member of the Shadow Cabinet. In recent years Prime Ministers were disappointed with a number of their Welsh Secretaries. David Hunt proved promising at first, and was promoted to the Department of Employment. He even came back to the Welsh Office as acting Welsh Secretary when his successor John Redwood sought the Prime Minister's job in 1995. But Redwood's leadership challenge ended in both himself and Hunt being removed from the Cabinet. Ron Davies' sudden departure also tied up his own fate, and that of Alun Michael. The fate of these men ensured that theWelsh Office's reputation as a training ground for up and coming ministers could never be proven. During the course of the appointments and dismissals of the last Welsh Secretaries, not one person in Wales was consulted or allowed to voice their opinion, not even the Conservative or Labour Parties in Wales (Purcell, Bold to author). Yet these Welsh Secretaries retained powerful positions in policy determination within Wales.

In theory, the Welsh Secretary's inclusion in a number of key Cabinet committees improved both his own and his department's input into the governmental policy process. In practice, however, the Welsh Secretary remained just one voice amongst more powerful Cabinet colleagues. Unless he could create inter-ministerial alliances he was likely to be ignored. The Welsh Secretary's adherence to Collective Cabinet responsibility ensured that even if he did not take part directly in the decision making process, he was still bound by the decisions made. The extent of official secrecy within government departments did not allow us to see how effective the Welsh Secretary had been in defending his departmental interests. Only the occasional leaks informed us of his success or failure.

This chapter defined the Welsh Secretary as the most important figure within the Welsh Office when it came to determining distinctly Welsh aspects of policy. In the following chapters we will see how the Welsh Secretary interacted with the surrounding environment in order to determine Welsh Office policy.

Notes

1. This calculation excludes Alun Michael whose term in office was fixed by the imminent arrival of the Welsh Assembly in May 1999.
2. The time scale represents the general election of 1970 until the arrival of the Welsh Assembly and Scottish Parliament in May 1999. The Nothern Ireland Office was formed in 1972.

Chapter IV

Internal Influences on the Welsh Office Policy Process:– The Office Juniors

Introduction

The Welsh Secretary did not have to carry all of the weight of determining Welsh Office policy upon his own shoulders; he had a political team from which to obtain support and advice. It was this team that Jones (1997) identified, after the Welsh Secretary, as being the most important influence on policy creation. There were two junior ministers at the Welsh Office, and between one and two Parliamentary Private Secretaries. Junior ministers and Parliamentary Private Secretaries were bound by the same Collective Responsibility as Cabinet ministers (Dorey, 1994, p. 102). This ministerial team was also aided by a political civil servant known as a Special Adviser. It was these political figures that did much to shape the Welsh Office policy agenda.

Between 1964 and 1999 there were some 21 junior ministers at the Welsh Office. The first section takes a brief look at the backgrounds and history of these junior ministers. Three-quarters of junior ministers never rise above the bottom rungs of the ministerial ladder (Theakston, 1987, p. vi). For those in the Welsh Office this figure was closer to 100 per cent. The second section assesses the reasoning behind the poor promotion prospects for Welsh Office junior ministers. It looks at the specific constraints of being a Welsh Office minister and how being a Welsh Conservative MP improved your chances of being in government, but also decreased your chance of any further promotion.

Identifying the junior minister's exact role in the Welsh Office was not an easy task. The Permanent Secretary, for example, 'was not subject to the directions of junior ministers' (Madgwick and Woodhouse, 1993, p. 39). Yet the junior ministers could play a major role in both policy creation and implementation, and therefore relied on the Permanent Secretary's advice on these issues. Section 4.3. seeks to clarify the exact role and function of the Welsh Office junior minister. It indicates the extent to which they could be classified as major players within the Welsh Office policy creation process.

Outside Wales it was said that Welsh Office junior ministers had a low profile. Parliamentary Private Secretaries (PPS) didn't have a significant profile either inside or outside Wales (James, 1992, p. 31). The Welsh Office's Conservative PPSs, like the Welsh Secretaries, did not come from Welsh constituencies. They were on the lowest rung on the ministerial ladder (Miller, 1990, p. 6). So what was the purpose of having these English based MPs at the Welsh Office? Section 4.4. examines the role and function of these aspiring MPs, and the part they played in the running of the Welsh Office policy process.

Both junior ministers and Parliamentary Private Secretaries were at the Welsh Office from the date it opened its doors in 1964 until it changed to the Welsh Assembly in 1999. The Special Advisers or political civil servants were only around for the last two decades of the Welsh Office's existence. They were not always welcome. Initially Margaret Thatcher, and later John Redwood, refused to have them. They nevertheless took a supporting role within the Welsh Office's ministerial team. The fifth section looks at their role within the Welsh Office and how they developed themselves as the 'eyes and ears' of the minister they served, regarding policy creation.

The final section looks at the mechanism which brought all of the Welsh Office's ministerial team together. In Whitehall, all of the Secretaries of State met together in the Prime Minister's Cabinet. In the Welsh Office all of the junior ministers and the special adviser met together in the Welsh Secretary's mini Cabinet. This section examines the purpose behind these mini Cabinet meetings and the implications these meetings had for the development of the Welsh Office policy process.

Section 4.1. A potted history of junior ministers at the Welsh Office

There were 21 Ministers of State and Parliamentary Under-Secretaries of State at the Welsh Office between 1964–1999. As can be seen from Table 4.1, the majority of ministers held posts at the grade of Parliamentary Under-Secretary. In the Labour governments of 1974–79 and post 1997; the first term of the Thatcher government (1979–83); and the Major Government 1994–1997; there were no Ministers of State at the Welsh Office. The four years under the Heath government (1970–74) differed from those of other periods, firstly because there was only one junior minister at the Welsh Office as opposed to the normal two, and secondly because neither Welsh Secretary nor Minister of State held constituencies in Wales.

Table 4.1
Junior Ministers at the Welsh Office 1964–95
(Wales Yearbook 1999; Butler and Butler, 1994)

Junior Ministers	Position*	Year	Party	University
Goronwy Roberts	MOS	1964–66	Lab	Wales
Harold Finch	PUSS	1964–66	Lab	None
George Thomas	MOS	1966–67	Lab	Southampton
Ifor Davies	PUSS	1967–70	Lab	None
Eirene White	MOS	1967–70	Lab	Oxford
Ted Rowlands	PUSS	1969–70, 1974–75	Lab	London
David Gibson-Watt	MOS	1970–74	Cons	Cambridge
Barry Jones	PUSS	1974–79	Lab	Bangor Normal (College)
Alec Jones	PUSS	1975–79	Lab	London
Michael Roberts	PUSS	1979–82	Cons	Wales
Sir Wyn Roberts	PUSS/MOS	1979–94	Cons	Oxford
Sir John Stradling Thomas	MOS	1983–85	Cons	London
Mark Robinson	PUSS	1985–87	Cons	Oxford
Ian Grist	PUSS	1987–90	Cons	Oxford
Nicholas Bennett	PUSS	1990–92	Cons	London & Sussex
Gwilym Jones	PUSS	1992–97	Cons	None
Rod Richards	PUSS	1994–96	Cons	Wales
Jonathan Evans	PUSS	1996–97	Cons	Guildford College of Law
Win Griffith	PUSS	1997–98	Lab	Wales
Peter Hain	PUSS	1997–99	Lab	London, Sussex
Jon Owen Jones	PUSS	1998–99	Lab	Wales

* In the Welsh Office the junior ministers were referred to either by the acronym of MOS which refers to Minister of State or PUSS standing for Parliamentary Under Secretary of State.

From Table 4.1. it can be observed that only three ministers did not obtain a university education. Of those that did, Oxbridge came out equal with the University of Wales with five each, whilst London came a close second with four. The Oxbridge domination was less evident than in either the Welsh Secretaries or the Welsh Office Permanent Secretaries. The average tenure of each junior minister at the Welsh Office, between 1964–1997 was 3 years 4 months, close to the tenure of the Secretaries of

State whom they served; their joint average was 3 years 6 months. Some other notable facts about former Welsh Office junior ministers, which provide us with some indicators of the people who helped shape Welsh Office policy, were:

- There was only ever one female minister at the Welsh Office, Eirene White 1967–70, who became Baroness White.
- Sir Wyn Roberts was the longest serving government minister in the same post this century (1979–94). He was also the only Welsh Office minister to be promoted from Parliamentary Under Secretary to Minister of State whilst at the Welsh Office. His long term in office seemed to have been aided by both his ability to speak Welsh and the fact that his experience was constantly needed by incoming English based Welsh Secretaries who lacked any real knowledge of Wales themselves.
- One junior minister, George Thomas, later became the Welsh Secretary. He was the only junior minister at the Welsh Office ever to go on to obtain any Cabinet rank.
- Michael Roberts was the only Welsh Office minister to die while in office.
- Five Welsh Office junior ministers lost their seats whilst serving at the Welsh Office, one Labour and four Conservatives.
- No Peer was ever appointed as a Welsh Office minister. During the Macmillan government (1957–1963), however, Lord Brecon served under Sir Keith Joseph (Housing and Local Government) as Minister of Welsh Affairs.
- Only three of the twenty-one junior ministers at the Welsh Office had served at any other ministry before coming to the Welsh Office (Jonathan Evans, Alec Jones and Eirene White).
- Welsh Office junior ministers also had an extremely poor record of moving on from the Welsh Office to other government departments, at junior ministerial level or Cabinet rank. This point is developed further in this Chapter.

Section 4.2. The junior minister

The number of junior ministers within government rose steadily over the course of the twentieth century. There were 31 junior ministers at the start of the century, by the mid 1990s this figure had risen to 48 (Butler and Butler, 1994, p. 66). The Welsh Office was responsible for two of these additional ministers. The Welsh Office always had two junior ministers, except for the period between 1970–74, when it had just one. These ministers were either of the rank of Minister of State, or the more often the junior level of Parliamentary Under Secretary of State. From 1994 until its demise in 1999 there were always two Parliamentary Under Secretaries at the Welsh Office. This reflected the difficulty in attracting suitable candidates to the Welsh Office at Minister of State level and the lowly status it was accorded. Their authority depended very much on the scope given to them by the Welsh Secretary. James noted that the typical junior minister:

> '(has) no formal powers: their authority is essentially informal and indeterminate, depending upon personal and political not statutory . . . they have limited authority over civil servants; in particular, the permanent secretary has in effect the right of appeal against a junior minister's decision to the secretary of state' (James, 1992, p. 29).

In the corridors of power it was perhaps of little surprise that the junior ministers were deemed to have a lowly status. They normally only dealt with ministers on their own level, and seldom with those above them (Kaufman, 1980, p. 44). The Welsh Office junior ministers, like their counterparts in Northern Ireland and Scotland, by the nature of their job came into more contact with the higher echelons of government and took on more responsibility than the majority of their Whitehall counterparts (Roberts to author). This section explores the process as behind a junior minister's appointment, the characteristics that were needed to become a minister, and the exact nature of the junior minister's policy role at the Welsh Office.

Choosing a junior minister

The Prime Minister and a handful of senior and trusted colleagues (Theakston, 1987, p. 44) appoint junior ministers. In 1979 Margaret Thatcher appointed the junior ministers with the help of William Whitelaw and the Chief Whip, Michael Jopling (Thatcher, 1993, p. 25). All were appointed within 48 hours of the general election being won (Thatcher, 1993, p. 25). The Welsh Secretary was given very little say. Peter Thomas's choice for his junior minister, for instance, was vetoed by the Chief Whip (Thomas to author). The same was apparent under the Blair government.

Ron Davies's desire to have Rhodri Morgan as a junior minister was dismissed by Tony Blair (Western Mail, 12/6/97). Outside of general elections the Prime Minister sometimes asked the Welsh Secretary if they agreed with the decision (Walker and Crickhowell to author). This was not always the case. The late Minister of State at Trade and Industry, Alan Clark, cited in his diaries that neither Cabinet Secretaries Lord Young (Trade and Industry) and John Nott (Defence) had any choice in their junior ministers. He stated that 'it was very unusual for a Secretary of State to be consulted' (Clark, 1993, p. 222). However, the precedent of appointing only Welsh MPs for Welsh Office posts made it harder to leave a Welsh Secretary out of the decision making process.

When an MP became a minister at the Welsh Office they could normally expect to stay there for the rest of their career in government. This was particularly true of Conservative MPs: not one ever progressed from the Welsh Office to another ministry. Welsh Office junior ministers did not compare favourably with those at other territorial ministries in respect of progression and promotion. Those MPs who were at other territorial ministries had a far higher success rate, Table 4.2. The evidence clearly points to the fact that those ministers who served at the Welsh Office were far more static than any of the other territorial ministries. The main reason for the lack of mobility was due to the size of the ministerial pool.

When it came to choosing a junior minister at the Welsh Office, the government was not, technically, limited by the number of MPs it had in Wales but by the number it had in the United Kingdom as a whole. By precedent, however, with just one exception (Gibson-Watt in 1970) governments always chose their junior ministers from constituencies in Wales. This meant that Conservative governments, were strictly limited by the number of MPs they had available in Wales to became junior ministers, Table 4.3. The number of Conservative MPs in Wales available to become junior ministers varied between a high of 14 and a low of 6. Labour governments by contrast never had a pool of less than 23 MPs in Wales from which to chose.

Until Jonathan Evans' appointment to the Welsh Office in 1996 it was an unwritten rule that one of the ministers must speak Welsh, something which the Conservative Central Office for Wales regarded as being of importance (Purcell to author). Wales is a bilingual nation. Welsh an official language for public administration purposes in Wales, where between 26 (1964) and 18.7 (1999) per cent of the Welsh population spoke Welsh during the Welsh Office's existence (Wales Yearbook, 1999,

Table 4.2
The career paths of territorial junior ministers between 1964 and 1994

	Home Office	Northern Ireland Office*	Scottish Office	Welsh Office
Total number of individuals holding office at junior level	48	42	37	17
% finishing career as a junior minister at another ministry	21	21	22	12
% finishing career as a Cabinet Secretary in another Ministry	19	12	16	6
% finishing career at the territorial ministry where they started	52	67	54	76
% who became Cabinet Secretary of the Territorial Ministry in which they served as a junior minister	8	0	8	6

* Starts from 1972, the year that the Northern Ireland Office was formed. Source: Butler and Butler 1994

Source: Butler and Butler 1994

Table 4.3
The Welsh Office ministerial pool 1964 – 1999

Welsh Secretary	Years in office	Party	Number in each Welsh Secretary's Parliamentary Party from which to chose Ministers
James Griffiths	(1964–1966)	Labour	28
Cledwyn Hughes	(1966–1968)	Labour	32
George Thomas	(1968–1970)	Labour	32
Peter Thomas	(1970–1974)	Conservative	7 (minister chosen from England)
John Morris	(1974–1979)	Labour	Fell from 24 to 23
Nicholas Edwards	(1979–1987)	Conservative	Rose from 11 to 14
Peter Walker	(1987–1990)	Conservative	Fell from 8 to 6
David Hunt	(1990–1993)	Conservative	6
John Redwood	(1993–1995)	Conservative	6
William Hague	(1995–1997)	Conservative	6
Ron Davies	(1997–1998)	Labour	34
Alun Michael	(1998–1999)	Labour	34

p. 357). If the government was to get its policy message across within the Welsh speaking media, it clearly needed a minister who could speak Welsh. Jonathan Evans' appointment, therefore, meant that there was no Welsh speaking minister at the Welsh Office for the first time since its creation in 1964. The failure of Tony Blair to appoint Welsh speaking Rhodri Morgan in 1997 to the Welsh Office also meant that there was no Welsh speaking junior minister until the arrival of Jon Owen Jones a year later.

With only six Welsh MPs, the Conservatives had to abandon the un-written rule concerning a Welsh speaking minister, Blair similarly ig-nored it. The Conservatives also discarded the rule governing the length of Parliamentary service prior to appointment. The latter rule indicated that at least one term in Parliament should be served before an MP gains office (James, 1992, p. 123). Of the last four junior ministerial appoint-ments to the Welsh Office by the Conservatives only one, Gwilym Jones (1992–1997), had served more than two years in Parliament before tak-ing office (Wales Yearbook, 1996, p. 135). This meant that any Welsh Conservative MP who had the slightest desire to become a junior minis-ter became one. Just like the appointment of the Welsh Secretary, under the Conservatives, a junior minister's knowledge of either government policy or the policy process had little relevance to their appointment.

From 1979 until 1999, the only junior ministerial changes that oc-curred at the Welsh Office were due to ministers resigning, losing their seats and therefore having to be replaced, or because that minister proved to be unsuitable in the eyes of the Prime Minister. The latter had only occurred three times: Sir John Stradling Thomas was removed because he did not prove to be 'a natural administrator' (Crickhowell to author), and Ian Grist was removed to make way for Nicholas Bennet. Grist had supported Heseltine in the 1990 Conservative leadership contest, whilst Bennet had been a strong campaigner for John Major (Grist to author). Win Griffiths was deemed to be a poor performer by Tony Blair and so he was also replaced in 1998 (Western Mail 18/5/98).

The only minister to 'fall on his sword' came in 1996 when Rod Richards became the first Welsh Office minister to resign because of a 'sex scandal', after having had an extra marital affair.

Section 4.3. Junior ministers and Welsh Office Policy Creation

The main policy role of the junior minister was to reduce some of the hard pressed Welsh Secretary's workload (James, 1992, p. 28). This subsequently led to a heavy workload for junior ministers. Welsh Office ministers worked extremely long hours, between 12 and 18 hours per day (Miller, 1990, p. 77). They had, due to the location of their duties and functional base in Wales, considerably more travelling to do than most of their Whitehall based counterparts. During the Parliamentary season ministers spent up to four days a week based in London, either at Gwydyr House (the Welsh Office's Whitehall base), or in their Westminster offices. Ministers also normally spent one day in Cathays Park, Cardiff or travelling around Wales. The weekend was then taken up dealing with constituency business. Family life or other non political concerns took second place until the parliamentary recess arrived. If their constituency was in North Wales they ended up travelling tens of thousands of miles each year, in a perpetual triangle: North Wales – London – Cardiff (Roberts to author).

The two junior Welsh Office ministers covered an immense portfolio of departmental policies. As there were only two junior ministers at the Welsh Office, a close working relationship was established between junior and Cabinet minister. The extent of this relationship was defined by former Welsh Office minister Sir Wyn Roberts as:

"The Secretary of State (SOS) must know everything that is going on. Therefore the SOS must take a strategic view. He must keep an eye on his colleagues. It is every minister's job to help each other out. Although key note speeches are made by the SOS, he must be backed up by his ministers in all areas." (Roberts to author)

The full policy role of the Welsh Office junior minister is detailed in Figure 4.1.

Figure 4.1
The policy role of the Welsh Office Junior minister
(Adapted from James, 1992, p. 29)

1. Advised the Welsh Secretary on policy matters.
2. Answered parliamentary questions and adjourning debates.
3. Piloted legislation through Parliament.
4. Deputised for the Welsh Secretary at Cabinet committees or the EU Council of Ministers.
5. Accountable for particular policy areas allocated to them by the Welsh Secretary.

6. Created policy within their own portfolio area.
7. Ambassadorial work - met lobbying deputations, went on visits and answered many letters.
8. For the Conservatives in Wales, acted as figureheads and the main support for Welsh Conservatives in policy creation

The junior ministers' policy responsibilities were fashioned around their ministerial portfolios, Figure 4.2. The Welsh Secretary fashioned the portfolio around the experience and interests of the post holder. In turn these responsibilities were rotated at intervals, to provide the ministers with wide ranging experience and to prevent boredom. Any portfolio changes normally occurred in line with the general Cabinet reshuffles (Roberts to author).

Figure 4.2
An example of Welsh Office ministerial responsibilities
(Welsh Office, March 1996, p. 2)

Secretary of State for Wales

Overall responsibility for the work of the Welsh Office

Parliamentary Under Secretary of State	Parliamentary Under Secretary of State
• Agriculture	• Health
• Land Use Planning	• Personal Social Services
• Housing	• Education
• Industry	• Training
• Local Government	• Small Businesses
• The Environment	• Finance
• Urban and Rural Policy	• Welsh Language
• Transport	• The Arts
• European Affairs	• Broadcasting
• Historic Buildings	• Fisheries
• Sport	• Women's Issues
• Youth	• Energy

Perhaps because the Welsh Office was one the smallest government departments, and Conservative Welsh Secretaries often had very little prior knowledge of Wales, delegation of policy responsibility was readily given to their junior ministers. Each junior minister covered the policy work of between five or six Whitehall departments, Figure 4.2. provides an example of this from 1996. This meant that they also sometimes had to represent the Welsh Office's view at various Cabinet committees and European Union Council of ministers meetings. In these meetings they mixed with the Secretaries of State for the departments they shadowed in Wales. This experience of the higher levels of ministerial life provided these junior ministers with much more political exposure, and a more varied job, than many of their Whitehall counterparts (Roberts to author).

We saw earlier that few Welsh Office ministers had any experience of other ministries before coming to the Welsh Office. This meant that they had a limited view of the operation of government. Although some had previously been either political advisers or parliamentary private secretaries the majority learnt about the policy process whilst at the Welsh Office. For the ten years from 1987–1997 they possessed one major advantage over the Welsh Secretaries there, they had a personal knowledge of Wales. As a result the Welsh Office's two junior ministers became the most visible members of the Welsh Conservative Party establishment. Welsh Secretaries from Peter Walker onwards had their background firmly rooted in the English Conservative Party establishment. These government junior ministers were the only elements of the Welsh Office which any part of the Welsh electorate could hold directly to account for any Party policy failures. Sometimes this Welsh knowledge put them in a powerful position regarding policy creation. Hywel Williams, John Redwood's Special Adviser, noted that John Major's first question on matters of Welsh Affairs was always: 'Does Wyn (Roberts) think it's important?' (Williams, 1998, p. 46). The arrival of Ron Davies in 1997, however, signalled a return to the status quo, with the Welsh Secretary once again having a knowledge of the Welsh scene.

Being seen to be a good Welsh Office minister with a good press profile was sometimes a lifeline to Welsh Conservative MPs. Nicholas Edwards increased his small Parliamentary majority of just 772 (1974 Oct) to 9,356 in his last election (1983). Sir Wyn Roberts managed to retain the highly marginal Conwy for twenty seven years. He gained the seat in 1970 with a majority of 903, and left it with a majority of 995. However, junior Welsh Office ministers were also well aware that being a Welsh Office minister had not protected an MP's seat in the past if the electorate was not satisfied. Ted Rowlands (1969–70 and 1974–75), Mark

Robinson (1985–87), Nicholas Bennett (1990–92), Gwilym Jones (1992–97) and Jonathan Evans (1996–97) were notable examples of Welsh Office ministers who lost their seats while holding office[1].

One of the most interesting roles of the Welsh Secretary's two junior ministers was the opportunity to provide the Welsh Office with its own distinct policy agenda. The Welsh Secretary allowed, and even encouraged, junior ministers to develop their own interests and policy ideas (Crickhowell and Walker to author). Sir Wyn Roberts for example helped create and implement:

- the improvements in the North Wales economy based around the A55 in the policy known as *The Road to Opportunity* (Walker, 1991, p. 209);
- the Mental Handicap Strategy in Wales, which had a foundational influence on the forming of Care in the Community for the rest of the UK (Roberts to author);
- the Conservatives' Welsh language policy (Roberts to author)
- the National Curriculum, (see Chapter IX)

If the Welsh Secretary did not agree with his junior ministers' policy ideas he vetoed them (Roberts to author). The junior minister had no right of appeal and either dropped the idea entirely, convinced the Welsh Secretary or waited for the next Welsh Secretary who came along and then tried to persuade him.

The Welsh Office had one of the lowest ministerial complements of any government department (Rose, 1987, p. 78). Although a large portfolio spread provided a junior minister with a 'more interesting job' and a chance to develop his own policy initiatives, it also raised some concerns about ministerial accountability. This was because it was difficult to see how one Welsh Office minister could cope effectively with the same areas, that were covered by around seven or eight ministers in Whitehall. This problem was enhanced with the regular swapping of portfolios from one minister to another, meaning that sometimes ministers had only around one year to deal with a specific policy area. Between March 1996 and March 1997 for instance Gwilym Jones lost the portfolios of Agriculture, Housing and Youth but gained Broadcasting, Arts, the Private Finance Initiative, the National Library and Health, on top of the twelve other portfolios he carried through (Welsh Office, 1996A, 1997). This meant that they were certainly in danger of becoming a 'Jack of all trades, and master of none'. Added to this factor was the reality that

Welsh Office ministers, like the Welsh Secretaries, often came to office during a government's mid-term and therefore played no part in fashioning the Welsh Office policies they had inherited. They therefore relied heavily on officials to fill in the gaps in their own knowledge of policy output.

The lack of ministerial experience at the Welsh Office concerning the policy process was raised from time to time. After junior minister Rod Richards resigned in June 1996, there were calls by the Welsh Liberal Democrat's Leader Alex Carlile, among others, to bring the complement of Welsh Office ministers up to four (Western Mail 3/6/96). The Welsh Office's sister departments in Scotland and Northern Ireland had five ministers each, including representation in the House of Lords (Butler and Butler, 1994, p. 45). The plea was ignored. In 1997 Tony Blair increased the Scottish Office's junior ministerial compliment from five to six in order to cope with devolution. Despite pressure from the opposition parties in Wales to raise the number at the Welsh Office, it was left at two, once again.

Lacking any effective representation in one of the two legislative Chambers (the Lords) also put the Welsh Office at a distinct disadvantage compared to its Whitehall or fellow territorial departmental competitors. In the Upper Chamber the Welsh Office only had a "Spokesman", with no official role. When they had important business in the Lords, such as passing legislation, they had to 'borrow' a minister from another department. The substitute minister then underwent an extensive briefing from the Welsh Office officials. This briefing, by its very nature, was far more extensive than what would have been needed by an existing Welsh Office minister.

During a long period of service, as was the case with Sir Wyn Roberts, junior ministers sometimes had a tremendous impact on the policy direction of the Welsh Office. They wielded far more power than the Parliamentary Private Secretary, the lowest ministerial rank in the Welsh Office.

Section 4.4. The Parliamentary Private Secretary

Parliamentary Private Secretaries (PPS) are MPs who are recruited by senior ministers to help them liaise with fellow MPs in the Commons. They do not receive any additional pay, but must instead rely on their MP's salary (NTCJ, 1993, p. 31). For their unpaid work they gain 'an insight into and experience of departmental life and the pressures of ministerial office' (Miller, 1990, p. 7). In essence they are undertaking a period of 'ministerial work experience'. The fact that a PPS is the personal choice of the minister, and not the Prime Minister as was the case with the junior ministers, means that they may be used as a 'confidante, discussing policy, political, party and even personal problems with him' (Theakston, 1987, p. 98).

An MP's appointment as PPS is traditionally seen as the first step towards ministerial appointment (Miller, 1990, p. 6). The last Minister of State at the Welsh Office, Sir Wyn Roberts, had previously been the PPS to another Welsh Secretary, Peter Thomas. William Hague began his ministerial career as PPS to the Chancellor of the Exchequer, Norman Lamont, from 1990 to 1993. Between 1995 and 1996 Jacqui Lait, then the MP for Hastings and Rye, was the PPS at the Welsh Office. This MP became one of the few women ever to experience the higher echelons of political life at the Welsh Office. But few outside Westminster were aware of her existence. PPSs tended to keep a very discreet profile; Charles Miller in his Guide to Lobbying explains the reasons why PPSs keep out of the public eye:

'(They) are by convention constrained from exercising some of the freedoms of their fellow MPs. They do not normally sign Early Day Motions, must give up their place on Select Committees, and cannot normally ask or speak on subjects covered by their own minister. For them to vote against the government would normally be regarded as incompatible with their status.' (Miller, 1990, p. 7)

An ambitious PPS at the Welsh Office therefore, sought to keep out of the public and media's view; causing embarrassment to their minister could result in both their dismissal and an end to future career hopes.

Because of their secrecy at the Welsh Office the role of the PPS in policy creation often remained an uncharted area. In the policy process the PPS's official role was to act as the 'eyes and ears' of the Welsh Secretary at Westminster. Since the Welsh Secretary was often kept away from Parliament by Welsh Office and Cabinet business, the PPS acted as the link between him and Parliament (Miller, 1990, p. 7). The power of the PPS depended on his/her personal relationship with the minister. The closer they were, the more important their role (Theakston, 1987, p. 97). Their core duties are shown in Figure 4.3.

Figure 4.3

The duties of the Welsh Office Parliamentary Private Secretary
(Adapted by Miller, 1990, p.7 and James, 1992, p.31)

---

1. Advised on Parliamentary reaction to Welsh Office policies or future measures.
2. Nurtured the minister's links with the Commons, arranged pairs for his votes, kept in touch with opinion, planted questions with sympathetic MPs at question time, and made themselves useful when the department promoted legislation.
3. Acted as a forum for complaint or enquiry by MPs, when the Welsh Secretary or ministers were not available.
4. Acted as one of the conduits for Parliamentary representations to ministers, and as a means by which outsiders could raise matters of policy concern with the minister without Welsh Office officials being involved, either as intermediaries or eavesdroppers.

From 1992–97 the PPSs at the Welsh Office, like the Welsh Secretaries they served, came from English constituencies, because the pool of Welsh Conservative MPs had ran dry. In 1997, Labour MP, Nick Anger (Pembrokeshire) became the first PPS from a Welsh constituency for five years. For the English based PPSs the lack of any evident Welsh credentials, knowledge or experience of Wales clearly made it more difficult to understand and interpret policy issues specific to Wales. Whether or not this damaged the interests of both the Welsh Office and Wales was not easy to measure. It did however lend further weight to those who argued that politicians at the Welsh Office lacked direct accountability to the Welsh electorate for the policies they helped create.

Section 4.5. The role of the Special Adviser

Lawton and Rose (1994) saw the special adviser as the civil servant who was most clearly identified with the creative part of the policy process. Although strictly speaking they were civil servants, few would see them themselves as such. The origin of the special (or political) adviser (SA) went back to the Labour government of the 1960s. Initiating from a recommendation in the Fulton Report in 1968, they were used as a counterbalance to advice given by officials (Butler, 1986, p. 4). Initially a few SAs were appointed in order to advise some ministers on their departmental work. The number of SAs grew under the Heath government of 1970–74 and the Labour government of 1974 to 1979. Although the Labour Party made use of SAs whilst in office, their only SA at the Welsh Office was Gwilym Prys Davies. He was appointed by John Morris (1974–79) to advise upon the political complexities of devolution (Butler, 1986, p. 7). Initially Margaret Thatcher did not approve of this patronage given to non-elected politicians, but later changed her mind when they proved to be useful to the general election campaign in 1983 (James, 1992, p. 214). As a consequence they found their way back into the Welsh Office (Dunleavy and Rhodes, 1990, p. 10).

If the Welsh Secretary or one of the Welsh Office ministers desired a special adviser, he first got the personal approval of the Prime Minister. The SA, like the PPS, was purely the choice of the Welsh Secretary. There were two types of SA: experts and generalists. The expert gave briefings which a minister could then use to check or challenge Welsh Office advice. The generalist, had some expertise but was normally re-cruited as 'political aide de camp' (James, 1992, p. 214). The fact that a number of SAs followed their masters to new portfolios after they left the Welsh Office tends to indicate that most SAs at the Welsh Office were generalists rather than experts.

The extent of a SA's influence with the Welsh Secretary over policy was difficult to measure, because they were only one of many voices seeking to influence any one issue (James, 1992, p. 215). The closeness between the Welsh Secretary and his SA was easier to gauge. Michael McManus followed his master, David Hunt, to the Department of Em-ployment in 1993 and then on to the Duchy of Lancaster in 1994 (McManus to author). John Redwood's SA, Hywel Williams, similarly left the Welsh Office to help him contest the Conservative Party leader-ship. Not all Welsh Office SAs sought to solely serve their master, how-ever. Some had political ambitions of their own. One of Nicholas Edwards' Advisers, Chris Butler, resigned his position to contest the 1985 Brecon and Radnor by-election. Peter Walker's SA, Rod Richards, left to contest the Vale of Glamorgan by-election in 1989. Both lost but later became MPs. The role of these SAs was to be Prospective Parliamentary Candi-dates (PPCs), or Conservative MPs in waiting. They were, in effect, PPCs being trained and subsidised by the tax payer.

Just as the PPS acted as the Welsh Secretary's 'eyes and ears' within Parliament, so the SA fulfilled this role in the political environment out-side of Westminster. The role and function of SAs, however, varied de-pending on the relationship developed between the adviser and minister

(James, 1992, p. 215). Charles Miller defined them as mini 'Policy Units', acting as providers of political advice and a buffer between a minister and his officials (Miller, 1990, p. 12). Chris Butler, a former Welsh Office SA himself, defined the basic role of a SA as 'Keepers of the Ark of the Manifesto' (Butler, 1986, p. 5). In essence, they ensured that civil servants did not dilute or avoid implementing manifesto promises. SAs also had a host of other policy duties which are defined in Figure 4.4.

Figure 4.4
The role of the Welsh Office special adviser
(Butler, 1986, p.5, Williams, 1998, p.46)

1. Took forward and then developed their minister's 'half-formed ideas'.
2. Provided a balance to civil service arguments.
3. Acted as a 'roving commission', warned on departmental difficulties or political 'banana skins.
4. Wrote some political speeches, this depended on the minister.
5. Liaised with Central Office, and tested the political waters concerning new policy initiatives.
6. Oiled and cajoled the wheels of government rather than being adversarial.

To the Welsh Office official, the role of the SA was often unclear as there was no job description. Even their legal status was questionable. Sometimes the adviser needed to obtain the specific permission of both their minister and the Permanent Secretary to look into a particular area or at certain papers. With these problems in mind, the SAs were therefore left to carve out their own 'niche' within the Welsh Office (Butler, 1986, p. 6).

Section 4.6. Bringing the Welsh Office's political actors together – The mini-Cabinet

Although the Welsh Office's political actors often had quite independent roles there was also a great deal of policy interrelationship between them. There were almost daily meetings during the parliamentary season between the Welsh Secretary and his junior ministers. The Welsh Secretary had a meeting with his Director of Information every morning, and junior ministers were often called into this as well (Press Office to author). Here they were briefed on contemporary policy events affecting the Welsh

Office. On other broader policy issues, especially prior to Welsh Parliamentary Question Time, the ministerial team received its briefing direct from Welsh Office officials. In fact, civil servants supplied the ministerial team with virtually any type of policy briefing they desired (Dowding, 1995, p. 124).

Scottish and Northern Ireland Secretaries had likened themselves to a 'mini-Prime Minister presiding over a team of colleagues' (Kellas, 1989b, p. 41 and Hennessy, 1989, p. 472). Simon James' description of the Prime Minister's role in a UK-wide context could apply equally to the Welsh Secretary in a Welsh context. James stated:

> 'He (the PM) is the leader and the figurehead, the government's main spokesman. The Cabinet takes from him its tone and style. Yet he depends heavily on his colleagues. He co-ordinates their efforts, arbitrates between them at moments of conflict, encourages some and restrains others' (James, 1992, p. 90).

The Welsh Secretary presided over a similar but much smaller set up. The Welsh Office mini-Cabinet contained all of the Welsh Office's political actors, from the Welsh Secretary to the special adviser. The meetings of the mini-Cabinet were often ad hoc affairs. They took place when either prior planning or opportunity meant that all of the Welsh Office's political players found themselves together in the same location (Press Office to author). It was these mini-Cabinet meetings which discussed issues, ranging from new policy ideas to strategic planning decisions within the Welsh Office. The policy decisions of the Welsh Office mini-Cabinet were limited by three factors, however:

- their own legal resources, and the expertise the department had built up (Rhodes, 1992, p. 148).
- the Whitehall Cabinet, in that it would not allow them to differ too publicly from the national policy norm (former Welsh Secretaries to author).
- the normal rules governing ministerial and Cabinet responsibility (former Welsh Secretaries to author).

The mini-Cabinet was well aware that differences between policy in Wales and the wider UK were accepted more readily if it could be argued that there were Welsh economic, cultural or social peculiarities (Thomas, 1987, p. 145). So the mini-Cabinet also consolidated and then presented

arguments concerning their case to the larger Whitehall Cabinet committees. It was also within these mini-Cabinet meetings that the political
culture of the Welsh Office was defined (Dowding, 1995, p. 112). The
mini- Cabinet could determine whether the Welsh Office pursued either
interventionist policies, as it did under Peter Walker, or a more Thatcherite
agenda, as it did under John Redwood.

Conclusion

This chapter has noted a number of distinctions between ministers at the
Welsh Office and other government departments. Firstly, those entering
the Welsh Office ministerial team knew by precedent that they had little,
if any chance of moving on to another government department. There
was a twenty three year gap between Ted Rowlands becoming a Minister
of State at the Foreign Office in 1976 and Peter Hain moving there in 1999.
In the intervening twenty three years every Welsh Office's junior ministerial career ended at the Welsh Office. The Conservatives' small minority
of MPs within Wales ensured that they had little scope for manoeuvre.
The government could not afford to move these junior ministers elsewhere. Who would replace them? The only way out for a junior minister
was: dismissal (Griffiths, Grist, Owen Jones and Stradling Thomas) death
(Michael Roberts), resignation through scandal (Richards), loss of their
Parliamentary seat (Bennett, Evans, Jones and Robinson) or retirement
(Wyn Roberts). Whilst in office these ministers could only take comfort
in the fact that the Welsh Office provided them with extensive opportunities to develop their own policy interests within Wales. If, like Sir Wyn
Roberts, you remained in post for fifteen years, it was perhaps only the
regular changing of policy responsibilities that prevented the minister
becoming a part of the fixture and fittings of the Welsh Office. No other
government department seemed to put such career restraints on those
junior ministers that served within it.

Secondly, for a decade (1987–97) the Welsh Office's junior ministers
became crutches for incoming English-based ministers to rely on for policy
advice and general advice on Wales. They also became the most visible representatives of the Conservative Party's policy output within Wales at a grass-
roots level. These ministers knew from precedent that, unlike their boss, the
Welsh Secretary, they were unlikely to gain further promotion and therefore
their futures lay in Wales. This pushed them much more into the Welsh
public eye. These ministers remained the only element of the Welsh Office
directly accountable to sections of the Welsh electorate.

Ministerial policy ambitions, however, were curtailed by the degree of autonomy they were given by their Welsh Secretary. Policy discretion was also governed by the fact that they often came into office in the mid term of a government which had fixed policy objectives, and by their own ability to come to grips with an often changing policy portfolio.

Thirdly, at least one of the two Welsh Office ministers was normally required to speak Welsh. Such linguistic requirements were not made the prerequisites of appointments at any other government departments. They were often vital to the functioning of the Welsh Office and the presentation of the government's policy agenda to the twenty per cent of the Welsh population who speak Welsh.

Finally, Welsh Office ministers were given a very large policy portfolio to cover. Although those in the Scottish and Northern Ireland Offices had similar policy remits, those at the Welsh Office had slightly more. This enabled them both to have a far greater input on policy matters than the majority of their Whitehall counterparts, it also allowed them to experience the higher levels of government in a more direct fashion. It was not unusual for a Welsh Office junior minister to pilot through a government Bill alongside a Cabinet Secretary or even to attend Cabinet subcommittee meetings. This was unusual in other government departments.

The policy distinctiveness of the Welsh Office was also enhanced by the Parliamentary Private Secretary(s) and Special Adviser who supported the Welsh Secretary and occasionally his junior ministers in their policy duties. The holders of these Parliamentary and political posts remained very much in the background. Just like the Welsh Secretary they served, they often had very little prior knowledge of Wales or the Welsh Office before they were appointed. Their advice to the Welsh Secretary and his ministers remained as secretive as the reasons for their original appointment. The extent of their influence on the Welsh ministerial team remains unknown. Their direct accountability to the Welsh populace was non-existent. We know that all of the ministers, PSS(s) and their adviser(s) met for regular meetings as a 'mini-Cabinet'. We do not know what they discussed or how significant it was, who influenced who on policy or how policy decisions were ultimately made. We do know, however, that nearly three million people within Wales lived with the consequences of their policy output for three and a half decades.

Notes

1. Only Gwilym Jones did not seek office again.

Chapter V

Internal Influences on the Welsh Office Policy Process:– The Civil Service

Introduction

During the Welsh Office's period of existence the major theory on how civil servants interacted with the policy process was called the Whitehall model of policy making. This indicated that civil servants either originated major policy or so altered it, as it passed through their hands, so as to make it substantially different (Jones, 1997, p. 450). This Chapter examines the extent to which civil servants within the Welsh Office shaped government policy either around the Whitehall model of policy making or any other model.

This chapter starts by identifying how the Welsh Office was structured to deal with the policy process. It examines the formal structures and the extent to which the Welsh Office official could truly be regarded as a policy expert. Between 1945 and 1979 there were six Conservative and six Labour governments. Between 1979 and 1997 there was only a Conservative government. This single party rule meant that the Conservatives had an unparalleled opportunity to restructure the civil service. The second section examines how civil service reform altered the policy process at the Welsh Office. It explores two of the most important changes to affect the structure of the civil service: The Next Steps agencies and the policy of 'Market Testing' service provision. The extent to which both of these policies affected the extent of Welsh Office policy output is assessed.

The previous chapters identified those closest to the policy process as being the Welsh Office politicians. The Welsh Office administrative machine had a key civil servant who worked closely with those politicians, the Permanent Secretary. As the senior 'permanent' civil servant at the Welsh Office his/her task was to ensure that policy ideas became policy reality. Section 5.3. explores the type of individual that became a Permanent Secretary at the Welsh Office. It goes on to identify their role in the policy process and, perhaps more importantly, their relationship with the Welsh Secretary and how this influenced policy making.

The final section examines one of the key questions about policy making at the Welsh Office: Was it the Minister or the Mandarin who determined Welsh Office policy output? The section looks at two schools of thought concerning the Minister – Mandarin debate.

Section 5.1. The Welsh Office's internal departmental structure and the policy process.

As is the tradition with the vast majority of the civil service, most Welsh Officials were policy 'generalists' and not 'specialists' (Pyper, 1995, p. 24). Alder indicates that these civil servants have the following functions (Alder, 1994, pp. 231–232):

1. to advise ministers on policy matters;
2. to manage the use of government resources;
3. to make decisions in individual cases under powers conferred on ministers by particular statutes;
4. to carry out the day-to-day administration of government departments.

The Welsh Office had been structured in order to fulfil Alder's four functions. Chapter II stated how the Welsh Office's internal departmental structure evolved. It was mainly due to the assimilation of the Welsh branches of existing government ministries, and the creation of new internal departments around fresh government policy. The continual change in government policy ensured that the Welsh Office's internal structures constantly changed. Over the last ten years of its existence, however, the Welsh Office became a little more settled. The Welsh Office's internal structure finally represented, in essence, a mini Whitehall in Wales. Its departments were based around functional policy areas, mainly modelled on UK policy issues, rather than any specifically Welsh concerns. Normally only at a divisional or sub-divisional level was there any concession to specific matters concerning Welsh issues, either geographically or culturally (Welsh Office, July 1995).

Despite the general settling down in the Welsh Office's internal structure, new government policies always dictated the continued evolution of the internal structure. Thus, if you examine the Welsh Office's internal structure between 1964 and 1999 you will see that barely six months went by without either a new division emerging, or an internal department being merged or split to form another new department.

The government created new policy ideas all the time. The internal structure therefore adapted to the government's policy making cycle. The need for structural flexibility was therefore essential to ensure the effective implementation of government policy. In March 1997, for instance, there were 13 definable departments within the Welsh Office (see Figure 5.1.). These in turn were sub-divided into a further 64 divisions. Of all the departments, only the Establishment Group was concerned solely with the internal Welsh Office administration. The Finance Group and the Legal Division also had a significant input in internal administrative matters. The remaining departments dealt with external policy creation, implementation and monitoring (Welsh Office to author). An addition to these 13 groups/departments was the Office of Her Majesty's Chief Inspector of Schools in Wales (OHMCI). Not formally part of the Welsh Office, the OHMCI was nevertheless required to keep the Welsh Secretary informed about educational standards and fiscal matters relating to Welsh schools (Welsh Office, 1997).

Many of the Welsh Office's internal divisions interrelated with each other over issues of policy to form what could be described as a quasi-matrix organisation (Lawton and Rose, 1994, p. 132). The most obvious example of this was when several departments created a project group in which individuals from a number of different divisions worked together on a specific policy area. A group set up to look at the issue of poverty, for example, could involve the Health Strategy Division, Social Services Policy Division and Housing Division, creating their own joint policy group in the process.

Policy expertise was vital if the Welsh Office was to develop its own policy, or shape Whitehall policy to its own agenda. Civil servants were therefore allocated to specialist divisions in which they were trained up to a level of policy expertise. To a large degree policy expertise depended on the size of each Welsh Office internal department, which varied enormously. In the last decade of its existence, the largest two of these were the Agriculture Department with some 471, and the Transport, Planning and Environment Group which had 418 civil servants. At the bottom of the scale were the ministers and Senior Staff Support (Private Office) with only 33 civil servants. When these extremes were eliminated there was an average staffing number per department of around 164 (Welsh Office,

Figure 5.1
An example of the Welsh Office Departmental/Group
Organisation Structure (March 1997)

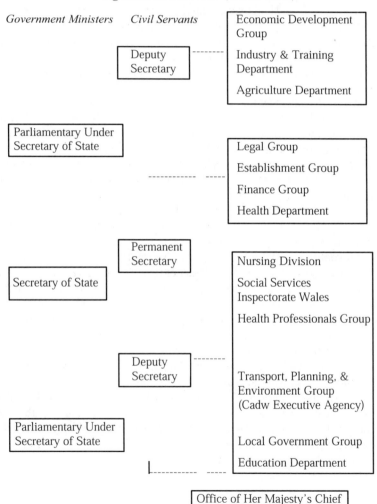

March 1997, p. 5). This meant that Welsh Office civil servants could provide only a fraction of the expertise compared to their far more numerous Whitehall colleagues.

Civil Servants achieved expertise in the Welsh Office by being trained for the task in hand and by creating the mystique of the 'master of knowledge' though controlling 'access to the knowledge stored in the files' (Lawton and Rose, 1994, p. 87). They were aided by the fact that they had a virtual monopoly of all relevant information, which ensured that ministers, and those outside the department, normally accepted their policy expertise with minimal questioning.

Civil Servants may not always have been the policy experts they were assumed to have been however. They couldn't simply be switched from one policy area to another. As in most government departments, when civil servants started a new job at the Welsh Office their training often involved a learning curve, ranging from about six months to two years. This meant that there were a significant number of partially trained administrators throughout the Welsh Office at any one time. Supervisory mechanisms normally ensured that the semi trained did not cause too many problems. But as the Welsh Office staffing net was spread ever more thinly, it stretched to breaking point in places, creating a ministry sometimes unable to fulfil its own policy role (Welsh Office officials to author). In a number of policy areas where expertise was thin, Welsh Office officials frequently relied on a 'lead' Whitehall department to help them deal with unfamiliar queries (Welsh Office to author). In 1995 for instance a Welsh Affairs Select Committee report on 'Wales in Europe' expressed concern over how just six civil servants were able to co-ordinate the department's response to the massive influx of European Union policy documentation. In 1994 alone, they had received: 3980 telegrams, 597 Official Journals, 421 European Parliament documents and 8260 European Commission documents (Welsh Select Affairs Committee 25/10/95); a substantial amount of which needed a co-ordinated departmental response. The demands of being within the European Union were clearly immense for a small department, such as the Welsh Office. The Welsh Select Affairs Committee noted the weaknesses of the Welsh Office compared to other Whitehall departments in this respect and indicated that the Welsh Office probably suffered as a result.

Identifying Welsh Office policy output

James (1992) and Marsh et al (1998) indicate that there was often a departmental view on policy. This was a 'compound of ethos, experience and outlook' (James, 1997, p. 90). The clearest way to discover the Welsh Office's view on policy is to examine their former Departmental Management Plans (DMP). Every division within the Welsh Office was required to produce an annual management plan (Central Management 2 to author). It covered their programme expenditure and running costs, and contained:

• the setting of divisional and policy objectives;
• an outline of objectives against available fiscal and management resources;
• a setting of targets against which performance could be measured;
• a basis for forming decisions about the allocation of current and future resources.

Such logical planning was part of the Weberian model of the civil service (Dowding, 1995A, p. 26). The progress of these plans was formally monitored within the Welsh Office at six-monthly intervals by the Permanent Secretary and the two Deputy Secretaries. The divisional plans were then used to form the basis for Group plans, which in turn were collated to form the DMP. Each DMP stated in great detail what the 'departmental view' was on each aspect of government policy. With a careful eye the seasoned observer could also pick out where policy in Wales differed from that in England.

The DMP sought to provide an indication of the key personnel, past achievements and projected output of the Welsh Office over the forthcoming three year period. There was no doubting that the Welsh Office's DMP was an extremely useful piece of documentation for those wishing to identify Welsh Office policy output. All government departments produced one, yet the Welsh Office's DMP was the only one to be produced in two languages (English and Welsh).

Section 5.2. Civil Service Reform and the Welsh Office policy process

Thatcherism dismissed political devolution for Wales. It accepted that there were only two levels of government: central (represented by Whitehall and Westminster) and local government (Bulpitt, 1983, p. 236). The Welsh Office was central government's direct link to local government. This meant that there were few concessions given to Welsh nationhood, as seen earlier. In Figure 5.1. we can see that no internal Welsh Office department appeared to be modelled directly around unique Welsh policy considerations. The word 'Welsh' did not appear before any internal department title and the word 'Wales' only twice (Welsh Office, 1997, p. 3). This was in sharp contrast to the Scottish Office where every department had either 'Scottish' or 'Scotland' in the title (Scottish Office, 1996, p. 6). At the Welsh Office, internal departments merely state their functional title, emphasising clearly which Whitehall ministries they shadow, Figure 5.1.

Individual groups and divisions in Wales were shaped around the implementation of the government's policy agenda within Wales. Over the last two decades of its existence these government policies had been dominated by the ideology of Thatcherism and the philosophies of the New Right (Griffith, D, 1996). In brief, Thatcherism disapproved of nearly 'anything public' and sought to 'roll back the frontiers of the state' (Davies, 1995, p. 60). Yet interventionist Welsh Secretaries, such as Nicholas Edwards and Peter Walker acted contrary to some aspects of Thatcherite policy, and expanded the role and size of the Welsh Office. Despite this softening of Thatcherism, the central core of the philosophy was still implemented within Wales. Although these policies were often alien to a traditionally socialist Wales, they came from southern England, it had been the Welsh Office's responsibility to introduce them (Griffiths, D. 1996, p. 74).

The policies of the New Right had a more direct impact on the policy process within the Welsh Office itself. New Right policies sought to increase both competition and savings in the civil service. Rhodes (1990) described this as the 'hollowing out of the state', the process of pushing the governance of the state further away from the centre. During the 1980s various measures associated with increasing the civil service's 'economy, efficiency and effectiveness' resulted in minor changes to the Welsh Office's management, internal budgetary mechanisms and organisational structure. The most significant of these measures to affect the British civil service in the 1980s was perhaps the 'Next Steps Initiative'. This involved transforming those sections of the civil service that were involved in service delivery into semi autonomous agencies. It originated in the 10 Downing Street Efficiency Unit's report: *Improving Management in Government: The Next Steps* (1987). This initiative was made to mark a clear distinction between 'the policy making work of advisers to ministers and the day to day work of service deliverers' (Lawton and

Rose, 1994, p. 142). Policy implementation would be transferred from government departments to semi-autonomous bodies, known as Executive Agencies. A chief executive, who could be appointed from outside the civil service, would head each body. The idea behind this change was to allow ministers to concentrate on policy creation rather than the day to day humdrum of policy delivery (Flynn and Strehl, 1996, p. 69). It would also inject into the civil service a 'freedom of self management', away from the policy core, and hence the ability to adapt to 'an entrepreneurial, output and customer-led culture' outside of the civil service (Lawton and Rose, 1994, p. 143). The agencies produced annual reports and sought to follow set Key Performance Indicators (KPIs).

Although the Treasury and civil service committee endorsed the concept of the Next Steps agencies in 1994, they did express some concern over the lack of accountability of some of these agencies, although no direct problems were found at Welsh Office agencies (Butcher, 1995, p. 42). Talbot detailed a number of faults about Next Steps agencies, including continually moving KPIs, secrecy over resource allocation and general concerns over issues of 'accountability, equity and probity issues' (Talbot, 1997, p. 29). However, the extent to which these concerns applied specifically to the Welsh Office was never examined.

By 1997 around 75 per cent of all civil servants were in executive agencies (Talbot, 1997, p. 3). Only around 15 per cent of civil servants under the Welsh Secretary's responsibility were in agencies (Welsh Office, 1997). By contrast some 81 per cent of civil servants at the Home Office and 27 per cent of civil servants under the Scottish Secretary were in executive agencies (Talbot, 1997, p. 14 and Scottish Office, 1996, p. 107). Of the three agencies directly connected to the Welsh Office, only one of these, Cadw (Welsh Historic Monuments), was solely within the Welsh Office's remit. The other two agencies, the Farm and Rural Conservation Agency (FRCA) and the Planning Inspectorate Agency [PIA], (Welsh Office, 1997, p. 8), were jointly shared with the Ministry of Agricultural Fisheries and Foods (MAFF) and the former Department of the Environment (DoE). Thus, the Welsh Office was only slightly affected by what was designed to fundamentally alter the structure of the civil service. This meant that policy making and policy implementation had been kept mainly within the Welsh Office.

There were perhaps two main reasons why the Welsh Office had so few agencies compared to other government departments. Firstly, it was one of the Home civil service's smallest ministries (Dowding, 1995A, p. 47). One of the main objectives behind the Next Steps was to reduce the civil service to smaller 'more manageable' units (Fry, 1995, p. 103). It could hardly be said that the Welsh Office, with only around 2,500 civil servants, was a vast government department. In 1995 a review of the Welsh Office's internal management structure reinforced this point; it noted that 'individuals had more wide-ranging responsibilities than their counterparts elsewhere' (Welsh Office, 28/3/95). The second reason behind the Welsh Office having so few agencies was that it was much more of a policy enabler than a policy deliverer. In 1988, when the Next Steps programme was introduced some 95 per cent of the civil service were concerned with the delivery of services (Talbot, 1997, p. 5). In the Welsh Office the vast majority of its civil servants were far closer to the policy making centre of government than their counterparts in the rest of Whitehall; as a result very few Welsh Office officials were involved in direct policy delivery. Those few Welsh Office officials who were involved in operational matters became part of the 'Next Steps' agencies.

Many within the Conservative Party, such as former Chancellor Nigel Lawson, saw the 'Next Steps Initiative' as being inadequate, preferring full scale privatisation instead (Fry, 1995, p. 99). Within a few years of the Next Steps being established, it was complemented by a series of policies with the more direct aim of increasing the civil service's, and hence the Welsh Office's, internal 'economy, efficiency and effectiveness'. This affected the Welsh Office in its policy delivery. The measures ranged from decentralised budgeting to 'market testing' and the Citizen's Charter initiative.

From 1989 onwards the Welsh Office was required by the government to make targeted efficiency (Welsh Office, 1993, p. 106). This figure started at around 2 per cent of running costs, and by 1996 had reached 8.2 per cent. According to the Welsh Office's own statistics, this target was always met (Welsh Office, 1997, p. 6). The methods of achieving this efficiency target included divisional expenditure control by decentralised budgeting, previously mentioned, and by following the recommendations of the work of a number of internal/external efficiency related bodies (Welsh Office, March 1994, p. 115–116). Whereas the efficiency scrutinies often led to a decrease in staffing numbers, especially on temporary staffing, it did little to reduce permanent staffing numbers. This was to change in the November 1991 with the publication of a White Paper entitled: *Competing for Quality*. This set out plans for the expansion of competitive tendering throughout the public sector. Importantly, however, we should note that like Next Steps, market testing had spared the Welsh Office policy core and this therefore did not affect policy creation. The same cannot be said, however, of the staff cuts that came from the government's White Paper: *Continuity and Change*, which is reviewed in 5.4.

Section 5.3. The Permanent Secretary and the policy process

The lead (civil servant) on policy implementation at the Welsh Office, as in other government departments, was the Permanent Secretary. They sought to maintain the semi-detached neutrality traditional to the civil service. Unlike their political masters, their future was not generally determined by who won or lost the general election. The appointment of a Permanent Secretary was in the hands of the Prime Minister. They were advised by other senior Permanent Secretaries (who formed a Senior Appointments Selection Committee) and the Welsh Secretary (Kavanagh, 1995, p. 318). Little was known or was revealed about the Welsh Office Mandarins (Permanent Secretaries). While in office, they were both discreet and secretive. Their faces often remained hidden, not only to the Welsh public and media, but also to the majority of Welsh Office civil servants who worked under them even though this role had been deemed to be 'an unusually public and political role for a civil servant' (Williams, 1998, p. 50).

The Welsh Office had seven Permanent Secretaries up until 1999 and, with the exception of Rachel Lomax, all were male. All shared the fact that they had been born in Wales and were of Welsh parents. Until late in the Welsh Office's life it was not known whether the Permanent Secretaries were Welsh by precedent or design. In April 1996, however, the Welsh Office placed an advertisement in the *Western Mail* for a new Permanent Secretary. The job description indicated that they should have had an "understanding of and preferably some experience of and connection with the special character of Wales" (Price Waterhouse, 1996). But these links were often tenuous, as can be seen from three of the last four post holders at the Welsh Office. Sir Trevor Hughes, Michael Scholar and Rachel Lomax were born in Wales but until their arrival at the Welsh Office as Permanent Secretaries, their careers were undertaken wholly outside of Wales. The educational and administrative backgrounds of the Permanent Secretaries are given in Table 5.1.

Table 5.1
The Welsh Office Mandarins 1964– 1999*

Permanent Secty.	Department before appointment	Age on Appointment	University	Capacity at Univ. of Wales	Served on a Welsh quango after leaving the Welsh Office
Sir Goronwy Daniel (1964–69)	Fuel and Power	50	Aberystwyth	Principal Vice-chancellor University of Wales	Numerous
Sir Idwal Pugh (1969–71)	Housing and Local Government	51	Oxford	Vice president Swansea	Chairman Development Corporation for Wales
Sir Hywel Evans (1971–80)	Welsh Office	51	Liverpool	Court of Governors	Several
Sir Trevor Hughes (1980–85)	Transport	55	None	None	None though served on English ones
Sir Richard Lloyd Jones (1985–93)	Welsh Office	52	Oxford	Vice President Cardiff	Chairman Staff Commission, Welsh Arts Council
Michael Scholar (1993–1996)	Treasury	51	Cambridge, Berkley, Harvard	N/A	N/A
Rachel Lomax (1996–1999)	World Bank Washington	50	Cambridge, London School of Economics	N/A	N/A

* John Shortridge the very last Welsh Office Permanent Secretary has been excluded because his tenure was only a few months before the Welsh Assembly arrived.
(Welsh Office information to author; Who's Who 1980 and 1996)

There were a large number of similarities shared by the majority of Permanent Secretaries, (Table 5.1). These included:

1. of those who attended university the majority went to Oxbridge;
2. they obtained the post between the ages of 50 and 52;
3. many went on to obtain a prominent position within the University of Wales;
4. after retiring from the civil service many obtained a chair(s) on a Welsh quango(s)

Three Permanent Secretaries, Sir Idwal Pugh, Michael Scholar and Rachel Lomax did not end their civil service careers at the Welsh Office. All went on to prominent positions in Whitehall departments. Rachel Lomax, the first female Permanent Secretary, was also the first to arrive at the Welsh Office from outside of the civil service. She came from the World Bank in Washington, USA, though she had previously been at the Treasury.

In June 1996 the appointment of Rachel Lomax shed some light on the policy role of the Permanent Secretary at the Welsh Office. The recruitment process was undertaken by Price Waterhouse and not the Welsh Office directly. For the first time candidates were not limited to the civil service, as had been the case with all previous postholders. The job description and person specification clearly stated the role of the Welsh Office Permanent Secretary, Figures 5.2. and 5.3. The Permanent Secretary and the Welsh Office had to be able to serve any Secretary of State, whichever political party he belonged to (Pyper, 1995, p. 12).

Figure 5.2
Duties of the Permanent Secretary

---

1. The Welsh Secretary's principal adviser on policy.
2. Advised the Welsh Secretary on appointments to, management and organisation of public bodies.
3. Dealt directly with the those who chaired and managed the public bodies in Wales, in addition to the Chief Executives of the 22 Welsh unitary authorities.
4. The department's senior manager.
5. The Principal Accounting Officer, in which role they were personally responsible to Parliament for ensuring propriety, regularity and value for money in relation to the department's expenditure.
6. Played a significant role in relation to any constitutional issues that arose concerning Wales and its relationship to the rest of the United Kingdom.
7. Chief representative of the department at an official level to the outside world.
8. Co-ordinated major aspects of work with other central government departments in Wales.
9. Represented the Welsh Office in Wales and London - made speeches, hosted occasions, and attended functions.
10. The usual Parliamentary and other representation responsibilities of a Permanent Secretary.
11. Responsible for maintaining the core civil service values of integrity, political impartiality, objectivity, and selection and promotion on merit.

12. Upheld the standards of work and conduct, and met the requirements of government security.
13. Developed and implemented the department's responsibility to equal opportunities, Citizen's Charter and Investors In People standard.

Source: Price Waterhouse, 1996.

As seen in Figure 5.2., the Permanent Secretary's key role was to ensure the Welsh Office administered government policy 'efficiently and effectively'. They also had to make sure that the public bodies for which the Welsh Office was responsible, namely the Executive Agencies and the quangos, did likewise. The Permanent Secretary chaired the key internal departmental committees that co-ordinated the department's internal and external affairs. They were also the Department's Accounting Officer. It was s/he who signed the department's accounts at the end of the financial year and was therefore directly accountable to Parliament for them, when appearing before the Public Accounts Committee. At the same time, however, they made sure that the Welsh Office did not become politicised and that it retained its neutral stance. Maintaining a political balancing act whilst running a government department, and in effect governing an entire country, needed a person with immense skills. The Permanent Secretary also had to defend the department in dealings with other government departments. At the Wednesday morning meetings of all Permanent Secretaries, in the Committee Room of the Cabinet, the Welsh Office's administrative head sought to ensure that their department held its own when dealing with other government departments (Kemp, 1994, p. 595).

Few details concerning the Welsh Office's input into these meetings has ever been revealed. We do know, however, that the Welsh Office has been overruled by Whitehall on a number of occasions. In the 1960s one of the Permanent Secretary meetings voted resoundingly to reject Sir Goronwy Daniels proposal for the establishment of an elected all-Wales regional body.

In May 1990 the Welsh Office pressed the Department of Health (DoH) with its concerns over the outbreak of BSE in Wales. It was seen as a source of irritation by the DoH. In response to one such letter from the Deputy Chief Medical Officer for Wales, Ruth Jacobs, the DoH principal medical officer, Dr Hillary Pickles, said: 'I am surprised you feel it necessary to put so much effort into challenging the views of colleagues at DoH who are more senior, more experienced in the area, devote a higher proportion of their time to the topic and have frequent access to the real experts in the field' (Western Mail, 27/10/00). The Phillips Report on BSE in October 2000 indicated that the Welsh Office rather than the DoH was right about BSE but its junior status meant that it was ignored.

What else Whitehall rejected or amended remains a secret but undoubtedly the Welsh Office's case was often strengthened or weakened by both the power, personality and career ambitions of its Permanent and Welsh Secretary. It was not unsurprising therefore that the Welsh Office's person specification, Figure 5.3, called for substantial leadership and management skills.

Figure 5.3
Welsh Office's Person Specification for Permanent Secretary

Suitable candidates will ideally have:

1. Shown leadership ability and skill at or near the top of a large private or public sector organisation, and have a commitment to and experience of excellence in top level management.
2. Sensitivity to political issues and the ability to work effectively and impartially with ministers and others at all levels.
3. The ability to lead and motivate staff and deliver results.
4. A proven record in managing large-scale financial resources, and a knowledge of and familiarity with strategic planning and financial systems.
5. Understanding of and preferably some experience of and connection with the special character of Wales.
6. Proven experience in strategic policy development and implementation, particularly where implementation will be carried out by third parties.
7. Understanding of, and preferably some direct experience of, constitutional issues and Whitehall and Westminster.
8. Outstanding personal and representational qualities, including integrity, rigorous and creative intellect, flexibility, stamina, resilience, and communication skills.
9. Knowledge of the Welsh language (desirable but not essential).

Source: Price Waterhouse, 1996.

We can note from Figure 5.3. that the government required any Welsh Office Permanent Secretary to have a far greater knowledge of Wales than the Welsh Secretary. Welsh Secretaries such John Redwood and William Hague had no prior knowledge of either the Welsh language or the 'character of Wales', whereas this was a desired requirement for any Permanent Secretary at the Welsh Office (Price Waterhouse, 1996).

The Permanent Secretary and the Welsh Secretary

In the Welsh Office's job description for the Permanent Secretary there were only three references made to how they could deal with the Welsh Secretary. It stated that they should:

1. advise the Secretary of State on a wide range of public appointments within Wales, and on the organisation and management of public bodies in Wales;
2. have sensitivity to political issues and the ability to work effectively and impartially with ministers and others at all levels;
3. advise the Secretary of State . . . and then act on his behalf to implement policies' (Price Waterhouse, 1996).

The rule book produced by the Cabinet Office on ministerial conduct, *Questions of Procedure for Ministers*, also made it clear that the Permanent Secretary had a duty to advise him on matters of policy (Pyper, 1995, p. 81). The civil service, through the offices of the Permanent Secretary, was seen as the counterbalance to political impatience, the 'voice of caution' (former Welsh Secretaries to author). Nicholas Edwards thought that the reason for this caution was that 'civil servants tend to want to avoid disaster and are therefore constantly coming up with reasons for a thing not to be done' (Crickhowell to author).

The relationship of a minister to his Permanent Secretary has been defined as being 'like that of husband and wife in a successful marriage' (Hennessy, 1989, p. 485). If this was the case, then the Welsh Office appeared to have had successful marriages on the whole. No Permanent Secretary was ever dismissed, suspended or publicly admonished while serving at the Welsh Office. Good relationships between Minister and Mandarin were sometimes enhanced by the fact that they had both already known each other prior to their appointments to the Welsh Office. Goronwy Daniel (1964–1967) for example, was at Aberystwyth University with Welsh Secretary, Cledwyn Hughes (1966–68) which greatly helped strengthen their working relationship (Daniels to author). Sometimes, however, this factor made little difference. Michael Scholar (1993–1996) had played in the same cricket team as John Redwood

(1993–1995), and they had both worked, in differing capacities, for the Prime Minister, Margaret Thatcher, at 10 Downing Street where Redwood had admired him (Williams, 1998, p. 50). When they worked at the Welsh Office, however, Scholar fell well below Redwood's expectations. Redwood was said to regard him as 'a courteously fainéant Cambridge Wittgensteinian who, it seemed, had succumbed to the Whitehall form of life' (Williams, 1998, p. 50). On the whole, however, the relationship between the Welsh Secretary and his Permanent Secretary remained one of confidentiality and great secrecy (Welsh Secretaries to author).

Section 5.4. Policy determination within the Welsh Office: Ministers v Mandarins

Welsh Office officials were servants of the Crown, not the government of the day; they were therefore likened to the monarch, above party politics (Flynn and Strehl, 1996, p. 51). This meant that they could not stand for political office or publicly express opinions on political matters. Sir Edward Playfair (1965) wrote that:

> '. . . civil servants who work for months on a policy come to their own conclusions about the best way forward: it was a bit much to ask of any group of intelligent people to devote their minds to an issue for a long time without coming to some personal conclusion about it. This is not so much a matter of imposing their own political beliefs as drawing the conclusions to which they think the evidence points. If they say to ministers 'Policy x will not work' it will not be because they believe it to be morally wrong but because, having worked through all the details, they think it will achieve results A, B and C, of which A and B are undesirable.' (Playfair, 1965, cited in James and Williams, 1997)

Miller stated that: 'ministers, in theory, had absolute power over policy formulation. However, the balance between ministers and officials invariably tilts towards the servants rather than their masters' (Miller, 1990, p. 91). Whereas James (1992) indicates that between ministers and mandarins:

> '. . . there is little argument over policy, and where there is argument it rarely develops into open warfare. The two most important

requirements are for a minister to recognise a good practical argument from his officials when he sees it and to demonstrate sufficient political weight and judgement for officials not to waste time arguing with him when he says "It shall be so".' (p. 91)

With differing views on whether it was ministers or mandarins who were the ultimate determinants of policy output, ascertaining who controlled policy creation in the Welsh Office is a difficult task. Although there is substantial literature on policy creation and the role of civil servants, there is little on the nature of these processes at the Welsh Office. Former Welsh Secretaries always claim to have had ultimate control but had always needed the support and advice of their civil servants (former Welsh Secretaries to author). Civil servants never talked openly about their ability to shape policy, although they would often comment privately; these unattributed conversations however became little more than office gossip and cannot be used in any academic study. The question therefore remained: who were the real policy makers at the Welsh Office? This study has defined two schools of thought: the 'Yes, Minister school', which believes in the notion that the civil service was really in charge of the government, and the 'Minister in Charge School' which took the opposite view. This section deals with both schools of thought.

The 'Yes, Minister' School

The 'Yes, Minister' School takes its name from the fictional 1980s TV series of the same name. It was clear from the TV show that when a civil servant said 'Yes, Minister' they really meant 'No Minister . . . The 'Yes, Minister' School indicated that officials were the real holders of power (Benn, 1980; Hennessy, 1989; Miller, 1990; Clark, 1993; Jones and Kavanagh, 1995, Marsh et al, 1998). The minister was merely a temporary outsider. A bureaucracy such as the Welsh Office could therefore lead to the 'dictatorship of the official' (Lawton and Rose, 1994, p. 38). According to Miller, officials tend to dominate ministers because (Miller, 1990, pp. 91–92):

Knowledge is power: ministers relied on their officials for information in order to make decisions. Civil servants selected the information that ministers had and could choose what to put in and leave out (Kavanagh, 1995, p. 324). Indeed one former Welsh Secretary (upon his arrival at the post) commented that:

'. . . . they suffocate you with papers. Though the only relevant information they include was a sheet that contains a summary from the
Permanent Secretary. But how many meetings or different arguments
have been held before this conclusion was reached? What opinions
have been left out?' (Tonypandy to author)

Ministers had limited access to any alternative advice and were reminded
by experienced civil servants at the Welsh Office that their manifesto
commitments needed to be altered in order to comply with reality
(Lightman, 1995, p. 17).

Ministers are overburdened. This reduces their time available for personal deliberation on, and drafting of, policy. The Scott Inquiry into the
supply of arms to Iraq (1993–4) made it clear that ministers did not have
time to see every paper passing through the office, and relied on officials
to filter information (Madgwick and Woodhouse, 1995, p. 147). The less
time ministers had, the more they needed to rely on civil service advice
to fill-in their knowledge and experiential gaps. Williams indicated that
Welsh Office officials from the Permanent Secretary downwards 'always
wanted the minister to take the rap' (Williams, 1998, p. 50). Ministers
were also considerably out-numbered by senior civil servants. In 1995
they were outnumbered by 65 to 1 (Kavanagh, 1995, p. 324).

Pressure of work. Ministers had not only their departmental work but
also parliamentary, party, and constituency demands on their time. Ministers were therefore required to delegate (Kavanagh, 1995, p. 324).

The interdepartmental net. If ministers rejected the advice of their
officials, the latter often enlisted the support of other departments connected with the issue. The pressure from other, larger, Whitehall departments' ministers would then theoretically force the more junior Welsh
Secretary to reverse or adapt his policy decisions to his own civil servants' preferred choice. To this effect they often enlisted the help of Number
10 and the Cabinet Office in order to control their minister's 'hauter and
energy' (Williams, 1998, p. 50).

Access to departmental papers was restricted. By convention ministers were unable to review the papers of previous administrations. They
could not therefore learn from their opposition predecessors' mistakes.
Thus when local government was restructured in Wales in 1994 the Welsh
Secretary was unable to review the work undertaken by his Labour counterpart on this issue in 1978.

Ministers were temporary outsiders in the Welsh Office. Tony Benn
saw the civil service as deeply committed to the benefits of continuity

politics and reluctant to adapt to the changing policies of incoming ministers (Benn, 1980). In Chapter III we saw that the last three Conservative Welsh Secretaries' tenure was only 27 months. Although some Welsh Office ministers were characterised by longevity in their posts, Nicholas Edwards stayed 8 years and Sir Wyn Roberts remained for 16 years, the majority were only there for a few years. They therefore lacked policy expertise and relied on the civil servants for advice. Civil servants as 'old hands' could therefore steer the minister in their desired direction (Lightman, 1995, p. 17).

Civil servants were not directly accountable to the public but ministers were. Alun Michael noted that: 'the officials of the Welsh Office had no sense of being accountable directly to the public and the elected representatives of the public.' (Michael, 2000, p. 3). This accountability was left to the Minister.

Case study that supports the 'Yes Minister' School

In July 1994 the government published a White Paper entitled: *The Civil Service: Continuity and Change* (HMSO 1994B) which set out its policies on the future of the civil service. This was part of the government's *Citizen's Charter* initiative. The Cabinet Minister responsible for the civil service, William Waldegrave, stated that the aim of this reform programme was to 'map a way forward for the civil service to the end of the century and beyond' (Butcher, 1995, p. 40). The White Paper covered everything from the creation of a new senior level of civil servants, to the greater delegation of responsibility for pay and grading to government departments. Although *The Economist* felt that *Continuity and Change* would have little overall impact on the civil service (The Economist, 13/7/94, p. 23), other commentators saw it as nothing less than a revolution (Fry, 1995, p. 130). Sir Peter Kemp, the former Whitehall Mandarin saw the White Paper as recognition that the civil service was 'an enormously diversified set of services . . . and finally buries the idea of the old monolithic civil service' (Kemp, 1994, p. 49). This White Paper in effect implied that the Welsh Office would be able to determine its own future and would grow apart from the traditionally Whitehall structure. However as will be seen later, little change had in fact occurred in the actual management structure.

After a period of consultation, to which Welsh Office civil servants and their trade unions contributed[1], the government produced its final

White Paper: *Taking Forward Continuity and Change* (HMSO 1995A). The Welsh Office was set a number of aims and objectives in this White Paper including the review of its Senior Management Structure (Grade 5 and above). This review's objective was to provide an 'improved senior management structure not driven by a Whitehall-wide grading system' (Welsh Office, 28/3/95). It was undertaken by an internal enquiry aided by the Treasury and Sir Peter Phillips, chairman of the Principality Building Society. Although they recommended that the 72 most senior posts be reduced to just 10, the actual change introduced by the Welsh Secretary was far more conservative in nature.

The Philips Report recommended a Board of Directors of four, in number, supported by six other Directors. The Welsh Office settled on a Board of Directors of six supported by ten other Directors (Welsh Office Personnel Management Division to author). This, therefore, left the existing management structure virtually intact. These post holders were meant to be referred to by their new titles i.e. Board Director or Director. In reality only the deputy secretaries were referred to by these titles; the remainder had kept their old titles such as Chief Nursing Officer or Principal Establishment Officer.

The major aim of Philips' changes was to 'Produce a leaner, flatter management structure' by 'matching the structure to the needs of the organisation' (Welsh Office, 28/3/95). In practice the post-Philips organisation chart of the Welsh Office looked virtually identical to the pre-Philips Welsh Office. The change should have mirrored the slim-line management structures of the private sector (for example, a Board of Directors) it did not. It can be concluded that the Welsh Office evaded the changes envisaged by the Philips Report. The Welsh Office had managed to continue with its existing structure remaining virtually intact and the Mandarins had preserved their own positions. The senior civil servants had managed to avoid implementing a change that would have been detrimental to their own future.

The 'Minister in Charge' School

The 'Minister in Charge' School claimed that it was the government and not the civil service who had ultimate control. A number of former ministers had stated that the minister was firmly in charge (Kaufman, 1980; Walker, 1991). They were supported later by academics who pointed to the decline of the power of the civil service (Pyper, 1995,

Dowding, 1995A). This meant that the civil service became more 'managerial' than 'administrative' in terms of achieving government policy (Alder, 1994, p. 240). Those academics in the 'Minister in Charge' school point to the fact that three overriding factors had destroyed civil service power. These are:

Ministers set the policy agenda, civil servants advise in private, ministers decide and take the public credit or blame (Kavanagh, 1995, p. 324; Lightman, 1995, p. 17). Even when policies had been immensely unpopular in Wales they had still been implemented by Welsh Office officials. The opting out of schools and hospitals were both extremely unpopular policies inside and outside of the Welsh Office, but were still implemented. If the civil servants were in control, these policies would clearly not have been implemented.

The radical and determined nature of the Thatcher government which set a precedent for the ministers serving under Major. The first Welsh Secretary in a Thatcher government, Nicholas Edwards, served eight years, nearly twice the length of all but one of his predecessors. This length of service gave ministers a sense of permanence and a subsequent chance to adapt the Welsh Office to their own design.

The sheer length of time of the Conservative administration, during which they implemented a wholesale restructuring of the civil service. They 'promoted men who did not try to find fault with radical plans but instead went ahead and executed them' (Dowding, 1995A, p. 124). Nearly two decades of Conservative government meant that civil servants had little opportunity to 'remind (ministers), from time to time, that they are there to serve all political parties' (Tonypandy to author). Instead the ministers could remind the officials that the government had both the time and durability to change them. This could explain why when Ron Davies took over he sensed that the civil service wanted a Welsh agenda (Davies to author).

Ministers during the Thatcher period became far more willing to take alternative sources of advice outside of existing departmental structures (Marsh et al, 1998, p. 32). Think tanks and special advisers often bypassed the traditional civil service advisers on policy issues, the role of the special adviser was particularly relevant to Wales, see Chapter IV.

Case study that supports the Minister in Charge theory

The years between 1965 and 1994 saw an eleven fold increase in civil servants employed at the Welsh Office (see Table 5.2.). The vast majority of this increase could be put down to the assimilation of civil servants into the Welsh Office. Between 1970 and 1980, these came from the Welsh branches of existing Whitehall departments, when they transferred their responsibilities directly to the Welsh Office. Much of the increase in Welsh Office numbers in the period from 1974 to 1979 was in preparation for serving a Welsh Assembly that did not arrive for another two decades. Over the course of the 1980s and 1990s the Conservative government's reforms of the civil service had a great impact on the Welsh Office structure. Initially the Welsh Office benefited from the radical agenda undertaken in the Thatcher period. The changes undertaken to the economy, local government and the health service in Wales led to nearly 2,600 Welsh Office civil servants by 1990 (Butler and Butler, 1994, p. 123). The Major government's plans for the future of the civil service had been described as a compromise 'between the requirements of ministers and others to modernise in the image of the private sector whilst maintaining core values integral to the legitimacy of the civil service' (Butcher, 1995, p. 43). The completion of the Next Steps programme (see Section 5.2.), which had little effect on the Welsh Office administrative machine, increased the Major government's desire for further efficiency and management change (Butcher, 1995, p. 43). The Major government's aim to have under 500,000 civil servants by the late 1990s had an effect on the Welsh Office (Pyper, 1995, p. 3). Between 1994 and 1997 Welsh Office civil service numbers were reduced by nearly twenty per cent (Welsh Office, 1999, p. 4); this was slightly less than the planned reduction of a quarter (Welsh Office, 1996, p. 6).

Table 5.2
The number of Welsh Office civil servants 1965–97

Year	Civil Servants[2]
1965	225
1970	903
1980	2324
1990	2562
1994	2500
1995	2350
1996	2265
1997	2035

(Butler and Butler, 1994; Welsh Office, 1999)

The number of Welsh Office civil servants remained virtually static between 1980 and 1994 – whilst those at the Scottish Office, grew by 9.5 % (Butler and Butler, 1994, p. 57). While Welsh Office staffing numbers had remained relatively static, administrative functions continued to be delegated to the Welsh Office. Hogwood saw the changes of the Thatcher era as a general civil service move towards 'rationalisation and consolidation of functions, with the additions of responsibility to the Scottish and Welsh Offices being important territorial exceptions' (Hogwood, 1992, p. 175). This rise in policy duties and lack of subsequent increase in civil servants makes an interesting comparison. During the period between 1979 and 1995 the Welsh Office obtained the following additional policy functions and duties: (Civil Service Year Books, 1980–1996):

- the total expenditure within the various Welsh Secretaries responsibilities increased from £1,790 million in 1979/80 to £6,804 million in 1996/97 (Welsh Office, 1982, and 1996). This increase of some 151% in expenditure (in real terms) had dramatically extended the importance of the Welsh Office's fiscal monitoring duties;
- the participation in, drafting of, and subsequent enforcement of some 50 new Acts of Parliament, which directly affected the Welsh Office's administration of government policy in Wales[3];
- the reorganisation of the NHS in Wales; from the merging together of the District Health Authorities and Family Health Services Authorities to the creation of the regulatory and legislative framework involved in the NHS internal market (1990 onwards);
- local government reform, the restructuring of Welsh local government, monitoring of local government spending and compulsory competitive tendering (1980 onwards);
- local government revenue changes, the creation or dissolution of: rates, community charges, council tax and some aspects of business rates (1989 to 1993);
- increased economic development programmes, administration of European Funding, and the establishment and monitoring of the Training and Enterprise Councils (1980 onwards);
- the introduction of the National Curriculum, opting out for schools, funding for further and higher education and the Welsh universities (1988 onwards);
- environmental protection and European inspired agricultural funding changes (1986 onwards);

- increases in Welsh Office spending and patronage of Welsh language usage and Welsh culture (1980 onwards);
- the need to monitor and co-ordinate responses to the massive influx of European Union documentation (1980 onwards);
- the introduction of the Citizen's Charters and subsequent increase in collation of statistics relating to this exercise (1992 onwards);
- the creation and monitoring of some 22 major Welsh quangos (and a whole host of minor ones) including responsibility for board appointments. Fifteen of Wales' twenty two major quangos were created since 1979 (Wales Yearbook 1999).

This large rise in responsibilities, without a subsequent rise in staffing numbers, often resulted in much of the administration for the Welsh Office's new duties being devolved to Welsh quangos. This loss of control had implications for the Welsh Office in policing the expanding Welsh quangos. Some of these concerns were highlighted in reports or hearings by the National Audit Office, the Public Accounts Committee (The Independent, 19/5/94 and 24/2/95) and the Welsh Select Committee and internal Welsh Office studies such as those by KPMG Peat Marwick on Welsh quangos (The Observer, 29/1/95). Despite these fears Redwood and Hague did not protect the Welsh Office civil servants from the civil service cuts demanded by the Treasury. John Redwood announced in 1994 that Welsh Office staff would be reduced by some 400 civil servants from 1995/96 onwards (Western Mail, 15/12/94). He saw it as a way of purging the old establishment civil servants who had been left there since the devolution era of the late 1970s and allowing the 'brighter, younger and frustrated' the ability to emerge into the higher grades (Williams, 1998, p. 50). This staff cut was followed by William Hague announcing, in December 1995, a further reduction in Welsh Office staff by 200 for 1996/97 (Welsh Office to author). Some saw Hague as pursing this policy in order to undermine political devolution by ensuring that the Welsh Office was too overstrecthed to pursue such an ambitous plan. After losing around 20 per cent of its total staff the Welsh Office struggled to cope, with the majority of its most experienced staff over the age of 55 (Welsh Office source to author). If the Mandarins were in charge they would surely not have allowed their own administrative machine to be so drastically reduced.

Which theory best reflects policy making in the Welsh Office?

It is difficult to test which of the two schools applied to the Minister – Mandarin relationship in the Welsh Office. There is some anecdotal evidence from former Welsh Secretaries to indicate that Welsh Office civil servants maintained some power, although other former ministers made it clear that they were firmly in charge (former Welsh Secretaries to author). Redwood for instance replaced the 'cold, unfriendly' staff in his Private Office and went on to build a core team around his Special Adviser and Principal Private Secretary (Williams, 1998, p. 48). Civil servants have never commented publicly on who held the power balance, with the exception of Ivor Lightman the former Welsh Office Deputy Secretary whose work was cited earlier. Privately they indicated that the ministers were firmly in charge, often ignoring their policy advice (Welsh Office officials to author). Some important evidence indicates that it was the ministers and not the mandarins who were in charge of the Welsh Office. This primary evidence perhaps concerns the staffing cuts, discussed earlier. Although the mandarins were able to preserve their own positions from change they were unable to prevent the main civil service body from being severely cut. Between April 1992 and April 1998 the Welsh Office lost around a fifth of all its staff (Welsh Office, 1999, p. 4). It was difficult to imagine any 'budget maximising bureaucrat' (Niskanen, 1973) or 'Yes, Minister's', Sir Humphrey Appleby (Lynn and Jay, 1984) ever allowing a fifth of their staff to be lost. Thus, we must conclude that the Welsh Secretary, if not fully in charge, had a very firm hold over his Welsh Office civil servants. This did not mean, however, that a mixture of the two Schools did not also exist on occasions, with both Ministers and Mandarins determining the policy output depending on both the interest and determination each had in relation to the policy issue in question.

Even if the civil servants did not have the ultimate power in the Welsh Office, the Welsh Secretary's seat in the Cabinet could provide a beneficial boost to their status in the wider civil service. They had direct access to the highest echelons of government decision making. This ensured that the Welsh Office was treated by Whitehall as being more than a 'concentration of regional offices' (Thomas, 1987, p. 158).

Perhaps the last word in this section should be left to Richard Crossman, the former Labour government Cabinet Secretary who was asked whether it was ministers or Mandarins who determined government Policy. He replied:

'If the Labour government has made mistakes and suffered failures, would I attribute these failures and mistakes to the civil service? My answer is 'no' . . . I would say that normally when a government fails it is not because the civil service blocks its plans, but because the government team has not had a clear enough sense of direction. A government which really knows where it is going, a government which has a series of measures ready, prepared, well thought out, has to hand . . . an instrument which will enable it to carry out all it wants.' (Cited inTheakston, 1992, p. 44).

Conclusions

The reason that the Welsh Office was unique among government departments was firstly because of the Welsh language issue and secondly, that the small size of the department brought civil servants much closer to the policy core. These two matters aside, the Welsh Office did not differ significantly from the other territorial departments. The Welsh Office administrative structure was based on the Whitehall model, with only a few minor internal differences. The Welsh Office, therefore, remained a strongly bureaucratic organisation in the Weberian tradition. The internal management structure was based around policy output. On the whole this bureaucratic model seemed to work well, with policy being implemented in Wales without the appearance of significant problems[4]. The Welsh Office administrative machine was there in order both to implement policy created in Whitehall and by the Welsh Office itself. Changes during the Thatcher period had little effect on the policy core, during the Major government and periods of Welsh Secretaries: Redwood and Hague, large cuts were made to the Welsh Office administrative machine. These cuts added to the fact that Welsh Office policy expertise was restricted (because of the size of the department) to only a fraction of the expertise available in Whitehall. Civil servants were therefore increasingly thinly spread over the Welsh Office's policy remit. This made it harder to determine distinct Welsh Office policy on a wide range of areas without having to rely heavily on Whitehall departments.

The Welsh Office's Permanent Secretaries were required to have an 'understanding of and preferably some experience of and connection with the special character of Wales' (Price Waterhouse, 1996). Despite this, only two of the seven Permanent Secretaries had a background in Welsh public administration and only one of the seven had received a Welsh university education. The Permanent Secretaries were very much influenced by the environment outside of Wales. Assessing the power of the Permanent Secretary over policy determination is a difficult task to undertake. The Permanent Secretary did, however, have a clearly defined role within the policy process. Although they were 'the Welsh Secretary's principal adviser on policy' finding out exactly what they advised upon was not an easy task. Welsh Office Permanent Secretaries often took or have taken a lifelong vow of silence, which was encouraged by lucrative quango positions after leaving their post. The little evidence there is tends to support the view that they fulfilled their role effectively and enjoyed a good relationship with the Welsh Secretary they were serving at the time.

Just as the power of the Permanent Secretary over the policy process is hard to determine so is the overall Minister-Mandarin relationship. Knowing whether it was the minister or the Mandarin that was responsible for policy output (for those of us outside of the Welsh Office machine) often depended on which school of thought one supports. Undoubtedly it was not always clear cut and in some cases it may have been the civil servants who determined a particular policy, but at other times it may have been a minister. However, official secrecy ensures that the exact state of play remains hidden. Civil servants virtually never made any public comment on Minister-Mandarin relations. And ministers made little comment on their former officials. Both sides were keen to ensure that there was never any public discord visible between them. The evidence indicates, however, that although Welsh Secretaries could have survived without the advice and administrative support of there officials, it was they, and not the civil service that were the ultimate determinants of their policy output.

Notes

1. Their details are listed in Taking Forward Continuity and Change (1994).
2. These figures do not include those additional 'hidden staff': casual employees (on less than one year contracts), secondments from other ministries, student placements and overtime equivalents. This normally equates to between 110 to 200 additional employees over any one year (Welsh Office source). Nor did it include Next Step Agency staff or those from NDPBs, which the Welsh Office listed at some 2233 in March 1997.

3. Between 1980–1994 there were over 50 Acts of Parliament which the Welsh Office had to implement, these included: 11 concerning local government, 8 Acts concerning housing, 7 concerning education, 4 concerning child welfare, 4 concerning health, 2 concerning Social Security issues related to local authorities. The remaining Acts were Welsh Office derived e.g. Welsh language or Cardiff Barrage; dealt with internal Welsh Office changes e.g. Executive Agencies to Transport & Highways, Environmental protection; or Planning issues: (Butler and Butler 1994).

4. During the course of this study the majority of those interviewed, who had regular contact with the Welsh Office, expressed satisfaction with the administrative service they received from it.

Chapter VI

External Influences on the Welsh Office Policy Process:– Parliament

Introduction

It was through Parliamentary mechanisms that the Welsh Office came into existence, gained its powers and was eventually abolished. To the Welsh Office therefore Parliament was the giver of live and death. Jones (1997) saw Parliament as being the third most important influence on government policy making. Parliament was also a mechanism through which Welsh Office policy output could be clearly identified either in a legislative or procedural context. In theory Parliament is the ultimate source of power in British government. Jones and Kavanagh (1994) noted that: 'A majority vote . . . could make or change any law; there is no written constitution to place limits to this power' (p. 137). It also had the theoretical power to hold the Welsh Office/Secretaries to account for their actions. According to Michael Allen, Parliament (commonly known as Westminster) has three major functions (Allen and Thompson, 1996, p. 271):

1. *Providing the personnel of government.* By convention ministers are drawn from Parliament.
2. *Legitimisation.* Parliament gives its assent to government policy.
3. *Scrutiny and influence*, which is conducted through the legislative process, Parliamentary Questions and the Committee structure.

Chapters IV and V examined Allen's first point. This chapter looks at his second and third points. It was noted in Chapter I that the power of Parliament to amend government policy became far more limited in the twentieth century that in the nineteenth. Despite these drawbacks Parliament still played an important role in the policy process by sustaining a government, acting as a 'sounding board of the nation', scrutinising the government's and its part in the legislative process (Jones and Kavanagh, 1994, pp. 141–145). This chapter identifies those areas of Parliament that were of particular relevance to the Welsh Office policy process. The first section in this Chapter, therefore, deals with the legitimisation processes by which the Welsh Office created its own policy through legislation or contributed to the legislative policy process of other government departments.

Apart from the legitimisation of government policy, Parliament was also there to scrutinise and influence policy. In the case of the Welsh Office there were five major parliamentary occasions in which policy output were scrutinised. These were:

- *Welsh Question Time* – this was held every four weeks during the Parliamentary session
- *The Welsh Grand Committee* – this committee consisted of all Welsh MPs, and it discussed Welsh affairs, either at Westminster or in Wales itself.
- *The Public Accounts Committee* – this committee examined government expenditure to ensure that no sums had been spent that had not been previously authorised by Parliament.
- *Standing Committees* – there were six of these and they were set up to examine legislation while it passed through Parliament.
- *The Welsh Affairs Select Committee* – this had been formed purely to scrutinise the work of the Welsh Office.

The second section of this chapter examines the influence of those occasions listed above on Welsh Office policy output. The chapter makes use of interviews from parliamentary officials, the former Chairman and members of the Select Committee on Welsh Affairs (WASC) and former government ministers. Some of the more relevant Select Committee on Welsh Affairs reports are also reviewed.

Section 6.1. The Welsh Office, the legislative process and policy output

James (1997) noted that 'Many policy decisions can be taken using ministers' existing powers. But many significant initiatives require legislation' (p. 5). The Welsh Secretary, as a member of the Cabinet, had a right to instigate original policy or intervene on the formulation of non-direct Welsh Office policy if he considered that there was a Welsh dimension, Figure 6.1. (Patchett, 1996, p. 16). But the numbers of opportunities to do so were limited. Between 1992 and 1996, for example, the Welsh Office had direct involvement in just seven per cent of all legislation passed (Davies, 1996, p. 21). The vast majority of the Acts of Parliament were for 'reserved matters'. This meant that they dealt with matters that were not devolved to the Welsh Office, such as matters related to Home Affairs, Defence or Scotland and Northern Ireland.

Figure 6.1. illustrates the interaction between the Welsh Secretary and the Welsh Office at various points during the law-making process. The breadth of the Welsh Secretary's powers of intervention were commensurate with his Cabinet position and the status accorded to it. In the case of secondary legislation his powers became almost total.

Figure 6.1
The Welsh Office's Influence on the Law-Making Process

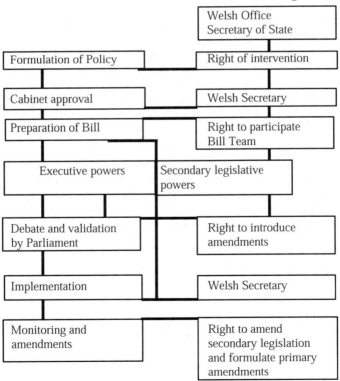

Source : Adapted from Patchett, 1996, p. 16.

The distribution of legislation over the four completed parliamentary sessions of 1992 to 1996 that affected the Welsh Office is shown in Table 6.1.

Table 6.1
Distribution of Legislation Between 1992–96

Parliamentary tion	Total Session Bills	Wales Only Bills Number of	Bills with Delegated Legisla- for Wales
1992/3	71	Cardiff Bay Barrage Act Welsh Language Act	Agriculture Act 1993 Education Act 1993 Health Service Commissioners Act 1993 Leasehold Reform, Housing & Urban Development Act 1993 Non-Domestic Rating Act 1993
1993/4	44	Local Government (Wales) Act	Education Act 1994
1994/5	56	0	Environment Act 1995 Health Authorities Act 1995
1995/6	24	0	0

Source: Davies, 1996, p. 21.

As there was little primary legislation, the Welsh Office had a far greater involvement in the creation and use of secondary legislation as a method of determining policy output. The legislation was not scrutinised to any great extent by Parliament, but was instead compiled by Welsh Office officials outside of both the public and parliamentary gaze. Often this legislation gave the Welsh Secretary sweeping powers which he could use to fill gaps in the legislation. Section 16(2) of the Education Act 1994, for instance, provided the Welsh Secretary with the 'power to confer or impose on the Higher Education Funding Council for Wales such functions supplementary to its functions as a funding agency as he thinks fit.' The Health Authorities Act 1995 enabled the Welsh Secretary to initiate secondary legislation to vary, abolish or create a Health Authority. This power was readily used to disband Wales's nine authorities and replace them with five in 1996 (Davies, 1996, p. 18). On the whole, however, secondary legislation was used for more mundane matters. In 1994, for instance, the Welsh Office issued 64 statutory instruments (SIs) ranging from the establishment of NHS Trusts to prescribing Welsh forms (Constitution Unit, 1996A, p. 49). The Welsh Office's legislative abilities also allowed it to develop its own unique policy agenda. In 1996 the Constitution Unit noted that over the previous decade 'Welsh Office ministers had shown a growing confidence to develop separate policies for Wales', via secondary legislation (Constitution Unit, 1996A, p. 48), see Chapter I.

The Welsh Office policy, primary legislation and the law making process

Between 1543 and 1996 there were only thirteen major Acts of Parliament that applied to Wales. Eight of these had occurred since the establishment of the Welsh Office (Griffiths, P., 1996, pp. 63–64). Despite there being little primary Welsh legislation, the Welsh Office still had a role to undertake in any Parliamentary Bill sponsored by another department that affected Wales. Various Welsh Office departments were involved in the legislative process, from the analysis of the original policy ideas, right up to the implementation and subsequent monitoring of the legislation. When this legislation passed through Parliament, a number of Welsh Office officials from the appropriate department were located in London. They were referred to as the Bill Team (Welsh Office to author). The team's purpose differed depending on whether the legislation affected only Wales or was a joint England – Wales Bill. When it came to legislation that was not specifically Welsh in its origin, the Welsh Office Bill Team acted in a sub-ordinate role to the government department that was leading that legislation through the House of Commons. Its main purpose was to ensure that any clauses specific to Wales were dealt with in the Parliamentary consideration of the Bill.

A purely Welsh Bill involved even more detailed policy work by the Welsh Office. The preparation for this started with the Welsh Office's administrative division most concerned with the legislation, drafting the Green and/or White Papers. It was then involved in the consultation process which surrounded the new Bill, and provided the Welsh Secretary with the results of that consultation. It was he who then decided on the exact legislative content of the Bill. The Bill Team's task was then to ensure that Parliamentary Counsel wrote his policy wishes into the correct legal format. It was the Counsel, and not the civil servants, who translated the Welsh Secretary's policy preferences, into a wording that would be legally enforceable in English and Welsh Law (Welsh Office to author).

The Standing Committee

The bulk of the Welsh Office Bill Team's work occurred in Standing Committee. It was within the Standing Committee that the essence of the Bill was shaped, and therefore civil servants were constantly supplying new briefings to ministers. The Standing Committee was one of six, which had been specifically created to amend and scrutinise legislation. For purely Welsh legislation Wales should theoretically have benefited from House of Commons Standing Order Number 86. This allowed for the Standing Committee to be 'so constituted as to include all members sitting for constituencies in Wales in order to effectively scrutinise this legislation (Osmond, 1995, p. 19). This same Standing Order provided for the Committee not to exceed 50 members. Because there were 32 Opposition MPs in Wales, in the last Conservative government (1992–97) and they had just 6, it meant that they could never obtain a majority in such a Committee. The Conservative government suspended Standing Order Number 86 on all occasions that Welsh legislation was considered between 1979 and 1997. The Standing Committee for the Local Government (Wales) Act 1994, for example, was limited to 28, with 15 members being drawn from the government.

The Committees which considered Welsh Bills always included the Welsh Office minister responsible for that Bill, his PPS, if he had one, and a government Whip. Governments of any persuasion ensured that there was little opportunity for any other party to alter their desired policy outcomes on legislative matters. In the Committee stage of the Local Government (Wales) Act 1994 the government was defeated on 4 out of 25 divisions but reversed all of this in the House later on (Boyne et al, 1995, p. 65). The opposition were normally lucky to get any amendments passed at all (Livsey, Morgan to author). As far as the government was concerned the time for policy adaptation was during the Green and White Paper stage, not during the passage of the Bill. This did not mean, however, that they would not amend their own Bill in order to alter the desired effects of the policy outcomes. Occasionally amendments were used to buy off rebellious MPs who wished to see the policy altered to suit their own personal or constituency interests (Boyne et al, 1995, p. 61).

Section 6.2. The Welsh Office and the Parliamentary policy account-ability mechanisms

Section 6.2.1. Welsh Parliamentary Question Time

The most regular mechanism of announcing Welsh Office policy output to Parliament was during Welsh Question Time. The regularity of Welsh Parliamentary Question Time was fixed: it was normally held every four weeks (on a Monday) in the House of Commons. At Question Time the Welsh Secretary or his deputies could theoretically be asked probing Parliamentary Questions (PQs), either in an oral or written form. These PQs 'could be factual and seek information rather than give it' (Dub's, 1989, p. 37). In the adversarial political world of Westminster, however, they were more often than not used for party political point scoring or by the government to give policy statements or hints of policy reversal or adaptation.

The use of a Question Time as a mechanism for scrutiny was limited. In theory there was scope for a maximum of 30 oral questions at Question Time, but in practice only around 12 to 15 questions could be asked and answered in the 40 minutes allotted (Welsh Office Parliamentary Officer to author). After an oral question had been asked and answered, the MP who asked it was allowed to address the minister with a further 'supplementary question'. Although the 'supplementary' had to relate to the subject matter of the original question, it was the MP's main chance to put the minister on the spot (Dub's, 1989, p. 40). But the Welsh Secretary didn't always need to give a reply. The Welsh Office could refuse to answer a specific question if the costs of gathering that information were over a certain amount (£450 in 1996). In reality, however, they only refused to answer those questions which involved a 'considerable amount of research' (Welsh Office Parliamentary Officer to author). Ultimately it was the Welsh Secretary who decided what went in an answer: he approved the wording of all answers before they were made public (Welsh Office Parliamentary Officer to author).

Over the last years of the Major government there was an increasing tendency for the Conservatives to ensure a large number of their own MPs, with English constituencies, submitted questions at Welsh Question Time. From 1995 to 1997 this meant that sometimes the majority of oral questions asked were not in the form of probing questions from the Opposition parties, but instead friendly questions from John Redwood or William Hague's own colleagues. They had little direct interest in Wales but instead acted to promote Conservative Party policy in Wales (Aaronovitch, 1996, p. 2). During the 1995/6 Parliamentary Session, up to two-thirds of the first 24 questions at Welsh Question Time were asked by English based Conservative MPs (Constitution Unit, 1996A, p. 51). Such tactics did much to discredit Welsh Question Time as a mechanism of accountability but it still remained a useful device by which the Welsh Office could give publicity to its own policy agenda.

Welsh Question Time, however, remained both the most frequent and rapid method by which Parliament could try to hold the Welsh Office ministers to account for their policy output. Yet Welsh MPs had to take part in a lucky dip with their Conservative colleagues in England in order to get their questions through. It was of some relief therefore that Parliamentary Questions weren't the only way of obtaining information about the activities of the Welsh Office. There was also the Welsh Grand Committee and the Select Committee on Welsh Affairs.

Section 6.2.2. The Welsh Grand Committee

In 1946 an annual Welsh Day debate was introduced to the House of Commons to examine specifically Welsh issues. Held on or around St David's Day each year this debate had an open agenda, within which matters of a fiscal or administrative nature could be debated. This Welsh Day Debate was followed some 14 years later by the introduction of the Welsh Grand Committee (Wales Yearbook, 1996, p. 129). The Conservatives established it as a method of trying to undermine the Labour Party's proposals to introduce a Welsh Office (Osmond, 1985, p. 24). Initially it consisted of all Welsh MPs, with up to 25 other MPs to reflect the balance of parties in the House of Commons (Jones and Wilford, 1983, p. 6). By 1997 the number of Welsh MPs had risen to 40, but the number of other Members had been scaled down to five. Two of these additional MPs were normally the English based Welsh Secretary and his PPS (Dod's, 1994, p. 360).

The role of the Welsh Grand Committee was to consider 'such matters relating exclusively to Wales that were referred to it by the House of Commons' (Cornock, 1995, p. 8). In essence the Grand was there to debate issues that concerned Welsh Parliamentary members. The Grand also had the power to 'take on' the Second Reading of a Bill, though this had not happened again after 1976. The obvious reason for not allowing the Grand to review Welsh legislation was that the Labour majority within it would halt or drastically alter any Conservative legislation destined for Wales. Labour was also reluctant to use the Grand as it allowed militant Labour voices to be raised equally with pro-government views.

When the Conservatives were in office both they and Labour had to agree any agenda with them before the Grand could be held. Between December 1995 and December 1996, the Labour Party refused to agree an agenda for the Welsh Grand and it did not meet. This was because they believed that the Conservative government was 'trying to manipulate the agenda of all meetings to its political advantage by arranging the timetable in such a way as to give prominence to the contributions of government ministers' (Western Mail, 9/11/96). Until more time was given to their spokesmen, Labour would not allow the Grand to meet. Therefore the Grand was unable to meet to discuss such issues as the Clwyd Child Abuse Scandal and the Sea Empress Disaster (Carlile, Davies and Wigley to author).

When the Welsh Grand Committee did meet, its four hour meeting was taken up mainly by speeches either from the Welsh Secretary or his Shadow. In one meeting in February 1995, for instance, John Redwood spoke for 59 minutes, and was followed by his shadow, Ron Davies, who spoke for a further 40 minutes. Although they both gave way to interventions from other MPs, they nevertheless dominated almost half of the proceedings between them.

Although a variety of questions could be raised in the Welsh Grand Committee, it only met very infrequently, just 10 hours per year (Western Mail, 17/5/95, p. 6). In 1993 it held its first meeting outside of Westminster in the Chambers of Cardiff City Council. This first meeting ended in somewhat of a farce as MPs left early to return to the true centre of political power, Westminster, to take part in a critical vote. The second meeting in Wales in 1994 was also poorly attended by both MPs and members of the public (Western Mail 2/2/95, p. 8).

It is interesting to note that the word 'Grand' was in the title not because the Committee was deemed to be so, but because it was the French for 'large'. The Grand has never enjoyed much praise; only a few years after its establishment it was already being dismissed as 'a talking shop for Welsh members rather than an effective committee of scrutiny' (Borthwick, 1967, p. 276). Few non-Conservative MPs had much respect for the Grand. Liberal Democrat Wales Leader, Alex Carlile, boycotted the Grand's first meeting in Cardiff because he regarded it as 'a toothless talking shop' (Western Mail 2/2/95). The Labour Party and Plaid Cymru did not regard it as a significant mechanism for holding Welsh

Office policy to account (Labour Party Wales, 1995, 1996 and Plaid Cymru, 1995). Former Shadow Welsh Secretary Ron Davies made it clear that it would be abolished once an Assembly came into operation, although this did not in fact occur (Davies to author). And the *Western Mail* referred to it as the 'Welsh Bland . . . the political megastore of talking shops . . . weaker than a little community council' (Western Mail 2/2/95). The Grand had no power to censure the government on issues of policy or even compel it to act on its recommendation or motions. Sometimes a vote was taken at the end of a debate, but the result merely registered the Opposition's protest and was not binding in anyway on the Welsh Secretary and did not alter Welsh Office policy output.

The extent of the criticisms made against the Grand, the move of the Welsh Opposition towards accepting political devolution, and the Scottish Office's increased role for its own Grand Committee, made the conservative government strive to improve the status of the Welsh Grand. Shortly after the devolution defeat in 1979, the new Welsh Secretary Nicholas Edwards proposed a new forum for Welsh debate. Edwards' proposals were aimed at quietening nationalist calls for greater political devolution. In November 1995, some sixteen years later, William Hague announced plans for the Welsh Grand to meet six to seven times year, three times in Wales. One Labour MP, Donald Anderson (Swansea East), described the changes as the 'longest recorded gestation period of a mouse' (HTV 3/12/95). These proposals, like those of Nicholas Edwards, were aimed at tackling growing calls for greater Welsh political devolution by being seen to do something. The Grand, like its counterpart in Scotland, had the power to summon UK ministers, including the Prime Minister, before it for questioning, although it never did so. It could be conducted through the medium of Welsh, even though during the Conservatives' last few years in office there was no Welsh Office minister who was able to reply in Welsh. These changes did nothing to reduce the Opposition's criticisms of the Welsh Grand or deter calls for a proper Welsh Assembly to debate issues relating to Wales (Wales Labour Party, 1995, Plaid Cymru 1995 and Liberal Democrats Wales, 1996).

Section 6.2.3. Select Committees and the Welsh Office

The role of Select Committees

Select committees are a method by which backbench members of Parliament attempt to influence and control the policy agenda of the government of the day (Hawes, 1993, p. 1). Each committee chooses their own subjects for investigation, and then produces a series of reports after taking evidence. This evidence can be taken from ministers, officials, other MPs and interest groups. Although the majority of modern day Parliamentary Select Committees were formed in 1979, a few have origins going back the 1950s and 1960s (Jones and Wilford, 1986, p. 5). Until 1979, however, the presence of Select Committees and the reports they produced did not attract the attention they do today (Jones and Kavanagh, 1994, p. 152). It was in 1979 that a 'new Parliamentary broom' abolished most of the old committees and established 14 new ones. A Select Committee has tremendous power in calling people to appear before it, or to order the production of papers. A request to appear before a Select Committee has the same power as a subpoena; it cannot be refused (Miller, 1990, p. 39).

The role of the Parliamentary Accounts Committee

Welsh Office policy output were often related to, and limited by, the department's own expenditure. Parliament's major control over the allocation of the Welsh Office's budget was by a Parliamentary Vote undertaken on the Welsh Office's individual Supply Estimates. This was, in effect, Parliament's way of granting the Welsh Office its own budget. It was normally a foregone conclusion that the government would ensure that this was passed, but it was sometimes subject to certain accounting conditions (Welsh Office to author).

The Public Accounts Committee (PAC) undertook the major scrutiny of the Welsh Office's expenditure. This is an extremely powerful committee. In the last decade of the Welsh Office's existence it was supported by 900 staff and had a £28 million a year budget (Hawes, 1993, p. 213). It was this committee which examined government expenditure, often via the National Audit Office (NAO), to ensure that no sums had been spent by the Welsh Office that had not already been authorised by Parliament (Miller, 1990, p. 38). The PAC was a cross-party Select

Committee chaired by an Opposition MP and with the Financial Secretary to the Treasury in attendance. Like almost every other select committee, the PAC had an in-built government majority.

The PAC worked very closely with the National Audit Office (NAO), directing its examinations into the Welsh Office. It could summon the Welsh Office's permanent secretary, the Chief Accounting Officer, to stand before it. The permanent secretary was the Accounting Officer responsible for the Welsh Office accounts, and was therefore questioned by the Committee on any wasteful expenditure or irregular commercial contracts (Miller, 1990, p. 38). The PAC was sometimes very critical of Welsh Office accounting procedures. The PAC could cause the Welsh Office to alter its policy implementation process if it identified fiscal concerns. For example in 1987 and 1992 it criticised the Welsh Office's monitoring of the DBRW, stating that 'there was a major lesson to be learnt from this case' (Morgan and Ellis, 1993, p. 28). The DBRW was later merged into the WDA. In 1994 it made similar criticisms concerning the poor monitoring of the Welsh TECs (The Independent, 19/5/94). Each time these negative reports were issued, the Welsh Office was forced to produce a reply stating how it intended to solve the problems highlighted and improve its own financial regulatory procedures.

The Select Committee on Welsh Affairs – its origins

It took 15 years after the establishment of the Welsh Office in 1964 before a specific Parliamentary mechanism was established to examine its policy creation and implementation role and function. In 1975 John Morris, Labour's Welsh Secretary, stated that:

> 'On an All-Wales level of authority we already have a host of nominated bodies exercising enormous powers. Other decisions, some of them in great detail were taken by myself and while I am answerable to Parliament no one would pretend that Parliament's scrutiny of the Welsh Office's activities was adequate' (Jones and Wilford, 1986, p. 4).

John Morris's solution to his lack of accountability for policy output was the establishment of a Welsh Assembly. Political devolution failed at that time, however, and on the 26 June 1979 the Wales Act (1978) was repealed and the Select Committee on Welsh Affairs was created instead.

It was both an acknowledgement that the Welsh Office needed greater Parliamentary scrutiny and, at the same time, a concession to greater Welsh political autonomy (Jones and Wilford, 1986, p. 19).

The policy role of the Select Committee on Welsh Affairs

The main role of the Select Committee on Welsh Affairs (SCWA) was as a policy analyst and evaluator (Hawes, 1993, p. 58). The SCWA had the power to scrutinise and examine any area of work undertaken by the Welsh Office but only within the same remit as the Welsh Office. Gareth Wardell, the SCWA Chair (1983–97) defined how the SCWA set its agenda:

> 'Work normally starts from an individual member's problem, which has developed, into a big issue. Sometimes it was already a big issue. This issue then becomes the subject of a SCWA investigation. Because Wales is a small country issues can be readily identified. There were no no-go areas within the SCWA's remit (Wardell to author)'.

Unlike the Standing Committees (which deal with legislation), the MPs who serve on Select Committees are not chosen by the Whips, but instead by a Committee of Selection (Kavanagh, 1990, p. 67). The majority party in Wales holds the Chair of the SCWA, which has been the Labour Party for the last 75 years. The position of Chair was therefore decided amongst members of the Welsh Parliamentary Labour Party. One of the key advantages of being Chair of a Select Committee is that you are exempt from serving on other Select Committees and Standing Committees (Dafis, Wardell to author).

Between 1979–1997 there were only three Chairs of the SCWA, with Gareth Wardell holding the Chair from 1983 to 1997, Table 6.2. Gareth Wardell spent his entire Parliamentary career, some fourteen years, as Chairman of the SCWA.

The SCWA had one unique characteristic. It was the only select committee not to have had an in-built government majority during the Conservative government of 1979–1997 (Dafis, Wardell to author). The Committee of 10 MPs was split 50:50 between Conservatives and Welsh opposition parties; neither side therefore had a majority. The lack of a government majority was a reflection of the fact that there were so few Conservative MPs in Wales. When the SCWA was established in 1979 the Conservatives had 11 MPs in Wales, by 1992 they only had six, three of whom were soon serving in the government. The consequence of a decline in Parliamentary numbers meant that the Conservative government found it ever more difficult to find Welsh MPs from its own party to sit on the SCWA. In 1979 all six of the Conservatives on the SCWA held Welsh constituencies. By 1996 only two of the five Conservative MPs on the SCWA held Welsh constituencies. Prior to 1997 no government majority on SCWA meant that Committee reports and investigations had to be undertaken by consensus if permanent deadlock was to be avoided.

Table 6.2
Chairs of the Select Committee on Welsh Affairs 1979–99

Name	Party	Commencement Date	End date
Leo Abse	Labour	December 1979	November 1981
Donald Anderson	Labour	December 1981	October 1983
Gareth Wardell	Labour	October 1983	May 1997
Martyn Jones	Labour	May 1997	to date

The primary function of the Select Committee on Welsh Affairs

The Committee's remit was to 'scrutinise the work of the Welsh Office' (Wales Yearbook, 1996, p. 130). This could involve a large number of policy areas because of the wide range of functions the Welsh Office covered. The Committee looked at any policy it wished within the 'oversight' of the Welsh Office, or any other policy that affected Wales directly. Although these investigations were normally carried out in Westminster, they could be and were undertaken throughout Wales.

The Committee had the power to call for 'persons, papers and records'. It also had the power to summon a named Welsh Office official to give evidence. After the Committee had heard all the evidence put before it a report of its findings was produced, which included the minutes of meetings explaining how these findings were arrived at. Once this was produced the Welsh Secretary was then compelled to reply to its findings, if necessary citing what action would be undertaken to overcome any shortcomings. The reports issued varied between those designed to investigate specific policy proposals, and short enquires aimed at looking at immediate concerns.

The Committee's first major inquiry, 1979–80, was undertaken on *The Role of the Welsh Office and Associated Bodies in Developing Employment Opportunities in Wales* (Englefield, 1984, p. 247). It flexed its powers from an early stage by summoning before it both Welsh and Trade and Industry Secretaries. Over the following decades the SCWA looked at innumerable topic areas, often in the heat of controversy. In 1980, for example, it examined and recommended a Welsh language TV channel at the same time that the government was refusing to commit itself to one. Over the next decade and a half the SCWA examined a large number of topic areas ranging from health and privatisation to heritage and the environment. In 1995 the SCWA examined the subject of Wales in Europe when Wales was being governed by one of the most Eurosceptic members of the Cabinet, John Redwood. It was often controversy that provided the SCWA with moments of glory. Their report on the RECHEM chemical processing plant in Gwent, for instance, was one of its shortest but most well received. It led to an independent inquiry which went on to vindicate the plant's existence after years of local protest about the alleged dangers of the plant (Dafis, Wardell to author). Similarly the SCWA examined the issue of 'nursery vouchers', while the legislation was being considered. It came out against them.

The effectiveness of the Select Committee on Welsh Affairs in altering Welsh Office policy output

The SCWA had a proven track record in altering Welsh Office policy output. This record owed much to its longest serving Chairman, Gareth Wardell [1979–1997] (Dafis to author). It was through him that the SCWA had been stewarded to scrutinise the Welsh Office more effectively. The SCWA had a significant influence on changing government policy, because it was able to persuade ministers to change their mind on issues outside of the glare of publicity. As was noted earlier, ministers often altered or amended Welsh Office policy without appearing to have backed down.

The SCWA had a number of distinct advantages over other Select Committees, the most prominent of these were (Carlile, Dafis, Wardell to author):

1. There was a great deal of behind-the-scenes work between the SCWA and Welsh Office ministers, which led to the smooth production of reports.

2. The SCWA members worked effectively as a team often going together as a group to visit Wales. Through 'hands on personal involvement' they were more aware of the socio-economic environment in Wales and could therefore follow issues up locally.
3. Despite the fact that members of the SCWA were from different parties they tended not to be partisan on issues. Only occasionally, on topics such as Wales in Europe, did the views of members diverge significantly.
4. The lack of an in-built government majority between 1979–1997 ensured that a Welsh consensus had to be reached on most issues.

There were also some significant failings of the Select Committee on Welsh Affairs. The SCWA, like the Welsh Grand Committee, was not always able to scrutinise to the full extent of its ability, the Welsh Office. This was not because the members of the Committee did not desire this to be so, or did not work sufficiently hard on the issues in hand. The reason was that the Welsh Select Committee could only consider one issue at a time and was therefore unable to respond to day to day events. In addition to this, the remit of the Welsh Office became so large that it was almost beyond the scope of any one committee to investigate it properly. As a result some areas of the Welsh Office's responsibility remained untouched by the Committee either for years, or were never investigated at all. This led to calls for the SCWA to set up subcommittees on some issues (Du Cann, 1984, p. 39).

Gareth Wardell found the following problems with the Committee:

1. The Welsh Office tended to be too protective over supplying information to the SCWA. This sometimes strained relation ships.
2. The Public Accounts Committee had a virtual monopoly of the National Audit Office (NAO). The NAO, it was felt, should have been available also as a resource to the SCWA.
3. It was almost impossible to persuade another committee to pursue a Welsh Office subject area.
4. Reports given by the SCWA were seldom, if ever, debated within Parliament, which tended to lead to them being sidelined after the initial publicity given to them died down. This point was also seen a as major disadvantage of the whole Select Affairs system (Jones and Kavanagh, 1994, p. 64 and Miller, 1990, p. 40).
5. From 1992–1997 the Conservative's inability to fill the places on

the Select Committee proved a problem. Those English MPs who were drafted in tend to have very poor attendance records. Although, Plaid Cymru MP Cynog Dafis believed that this factor was an advantage in that it allowed the Committee to draw up reports that were much more critical of the government than usual (Dafis to author).

Wardell also noted that the Welsh Office had the tendency to delay replying to SCWA recommendations in order to portray the department in a better light (HMSO, 1993A, p. 1). By delaying its replies it could implement recommendations before the Parliamentary response was given. One example of this concerned the administration of the European Social Fund. The SCWA recommended on 25th October 1995 that the Welsh Office should take over control of the European Social Fund from the Department of Employment (Wardell, 1996). In its reply to this recommendation some three months later, the Welsh Office stated that administration of the European Social Fund had already been transferred to the Welsh Office, from the 1st January 1996 (Wardell, 1996).

Some Welsh MPs dismissed the Welsh Affairs Select Committee as a waste of time. Ian Grist, the former Welsh Office minister, refused to serve on it after losing his ministerial post at the Welsh Office in 1990. He stated that it was 'lightweight and of direct interest only to a minority of Welsh MPs' (Grist to author). Grist had, however, served on the SCWA before becoming a junior minister. On the whole, however, most Welsh MPs appeared to be keen to serve on it, though individual MPs attendance rates did vary dramatically (Osmond, 1992, p. 16).

Conclusion

Westminster did have an important role in acting as a formal outlet for the Welsh Office in making policy output public and in testing the opposition and the public's reaction to policy ideas. It was less open, however, to allowing the Opposition to shape or alter its policy. Chris Ham noted of Parliament that:

'It is important to distinguish the formal power of Parliament from its effective role. Although formally Parliament passes legislation, examines public expenditure and controls the government, effectively it carries out these functions within strictly defined limits. As long as there is a House of Commons majority to support the government, then Parliament has few significant powers within the system of central government' (Ham, 1992, p. 101).

Bearing Ham's point in mind it is unsurprising that the government, opposition or even its own MPs had little effect on Welsh Office policy during the legislative phase. The only significant defeats of Welsh Office policy at the legislative stage were for the 1970s devolution proposals, in the Scotland and Wales Bill 1977, and the 1980s Private Members' Cardiff Barrage Bill in 1986. Both Bills were central planks of the government's Welsh policy agenda, and both were defeated in Parliament. Even these Bills, however, came back to Parliament once again and were successfully passed. These two instances apart, there is very little evidence to support the view that Parliament had anything but the smallest impact on Welsh Office policy during the legislative phase.

Opinion is split as to the degree of influence westminster had over Welsh Office policy output. The Select Committee on Welsh Affairs and the Public Accounts Committee undertook numerous probing studies on Welsh Office policy output. These Committees, however, suffered from weaknesses that meant that the Welsh Office was not always held to account for its policy output as effectively as the democratic process required. Much work, however, was undertaken outside of the public gaze. Beyond of the glare of publicity, important aspects of Welsh Office policy were adapted to comply with Westminster scrutiny. The process of co-operation rather than conflict tended to dictate the Welsh Office's relationship with the Westminster Committee structure.

A Welsh Secretary did not have total political power. He found himself constrained by constitutional safeguards such as Collective and Ministerial responsibility, as was seen in Chapter III. These constitutional safeguards, however, became less effective as time passed. The Prime Minister could remove him if he over stepped the mark but this never happened. There was also Parliament to hold him to account. Welsh Question Time and the Welsh Grand Committee collectively were designed to put him on the spot. They were there to make him accountable for his actions and to inform the public of his future plans and how they would affect the people of Wales.

However, the mechanisms that were meant to enhance democracy often proved very ineffectual in its defence during the Conservative period in government. The government became adept at avoiding Parliamentary scrutiny. Welsh Question Time was packed with English-based Conservative MPs asking government-friendly questions, with little space left for the Welsh Opposition parties. The Welsh Grand was granted more effective powers in the 1970s, but it seldom met and its motions were readily ignored by the Welsh Secretary. The Welsh Office consequently remained a department in which policy output were only effectively checked by the ministers' reaction to the media, the extent of the Welsh Office ministers' own ambitions or ego, occasionally by their fellow Cabinet ministers, and ultimately by the Prime Minister.

Chapter VII

The Remaining Major External Influences on the Welsh Office Policy Process

Introduction

Decades before the arrival of the Welsh Assembly, the Welsh Office was already determining distinctly Welsh policy. Chapter V indicated how the Welsh Office acted as a conduit through which government policy ideas flowed and were rejected or modified and eventually implemented. The very presence of the Welsh Office had forced each political party in Wales into creating policy that was often unique or, at the very least, fashioned for Welsh Office implementation. For Plaid Cymru and for the Liberal Democrats (who have a federal structure) there was the regular production of policies created specifically for Wales, many of which covered the Welsh Office's remit. The two main UK political parties, the Conservatives and Labour also produced a limited amount of specifically Welsh policies. Even within the Conservative Party, which controlled the Welsh Office for two-thirds of its life, there was clear evidence of distinct policies for Wales. The first section of this chapter therefore deals with the policy making process of the Conservative Party, with specific reference to the evolution of the party's proposals on Welsh local government.

The chapter's second section examines the largest political party in Wales, the Labour Party. It was the only political party, apart from the Conservatives, to have controlled the Welsh Office. Section 7.2 examines the degree of Welsh (Wales) Labour Party policy making during the Welsh Office's period of existence. It concentrates on the role and function of the Shadow Welsh Secretary, a post which the Party held for two thirds of the Welsh Office's existence.

The third section briefly examines the interaction between the former third parties and the Welsh Office. This section assesses the more limited impact of Plaid Cymru and the Welsh Liberal Democrats on the policy direction of the Welsh Office.

The final section in this chapter explores the other influences on the Welsh Office policy process that have not been covered in earlier chapters. These elements were acknowledged to have an important influence of the policy creation process of government (Jones, 1997). They were the media, UK-wide and Welsh, policy think tanks, Committees of Inquiry and the European Union. Each are assessed in turn, in the context of their influence on the Welsh Office policy process.

Section 7.1. Internal Conservative Party policy creation mechanisms in Wales

The process of policy creation in any political party can be tortuous and lengthy. Burch and Wood (1990, p. 15) define three phases in the creation of this policy:

1. *Initiation*: the source, generation and early development of a policy proposal.
2. *Formulation*: the development of a policy in detail and its outline as a concrete set of proposals.
3. *Implementation*: the carrying out of the policy once formally agreed to or approved.

Over the course of the Welsh Office's existence both Labour and the Conservative Party were involved in all three elements of Burch and Wood's policy creation process. The Welsh Office was the administrative machine through which their Welsh policy was mainly created, adapted and implemented. The incumbent political party therefore made great use of it, both in aiding their own process of policy creation, and in implementing policy output.

The Conservatives were the governing party for the majority of the Welsh Office's existence. The distinctiveness of the Conservative Party policies while at the Welsh Office can be gauged in Chapter I. This section briefly analyses the Conservative Party's policy creation in the context of the Welsh Office.

Conservatives in Wales

It was fair to say that Wales was not a natural Conservative domain. Since their first Welsh Secretary took office in 1970, the Conservatives' best Parliamentary period for elected representatives in Wales was between 1983 and 1987, their worst period was between 1992 and general election of 1997, Table 7.1.

Table 7.1

The Conservative Party's best and worst Parliamentary period between 1970 and 1997[1]

Period	Percentage of total Welsh MPs	Number of MEPs	Percentage of councillors
1983–1987	37	1 from 4	12.9
1992–1997	16	0 from 5	3

(Wales Yearbook, 1997; Rawlings and Thrasher, 1993; Deacon, 1995)

Even in their best period (1983–1987), the Conservatives never surpassed the number of seats held by their Labour rivals at any government level within Wales.

The structure of the Conservative Party organisation in Wales dates back to a major overhaul of the party structure in 1948. Unlike Scotland, Wales did not have its own Central Office. Instead it had a Regional Office, (one of seven Regional Offices in England and Wales) [Tether, 1996, p. 117]. The Party tried to adapt itself to a Welsh setting, after an internal Conservative Party market research poll in the 1960s indicated that it was perceived as being the 'English party in Wales' (Butler, 1985, p. 160). Although it was true to say that the vast majority of Conservative policies that affected Wales had their origins outside of Wales, on closer inspection a notable Welsh dimension was apparent in the policy of the Welsh Office.

The Welsh Conservative Party, however, was kept at some distance from the Welsh Office and the government in general. When the Prime Minister appointed a Secretary of State for Wales, for instance, the Welsh Conservative Party was only aware of this at the same time as everybody else (Purcell to author). The Conservative Central Office for Wales had no officials dedicated to policy creation (Purcell to author). Unlike the Wales Labour Party, there was no senior post devoted to policy. The officers who supported the Conservative Party Central Office for Wales were virtually all connected to 'campaigning'. This may well have been because the party placed such a strong emphasis on the Union within the United Kingdom that it did not wish to be seen to internally devolve policy-making within the party (Aughey, 1996, p. 233). The Party's political policy creation role, therefore, fell mainly on the work of two amateur groups plus the Welsh Secretary and his mini Cabinet. All were aided by an official from the Number 10 Policy Unit (Purcell to author). This gave us three groups in total:

1. *The Welsh Secretary and his mini cabinet*; this involved ministers and their political advisors. They originated and expanded their own policy ideas with the help of both the Welsh Office and the Conservative Party policy machinery. Their role in the policy process was dealt with in Chapters III and IV.
2. *The Welsh Policy Unit*; this consisted of a selection of Welsh Conservative Party members representing the professions, industry, farming and women (Williams, 1998, p. 263).
3. *Elements of the Wales Conservative Party membership*; when the Welsh Conservative Party compiled its manifestos for Wales it contacted some of its Welsh members for their opinions.

The annual Conservative Conference in Wales, attended by the Leader, Welsh Secretary (or Shadow Welsh Secretary) and his juniors, acted as the formal seal of approval on policy. It did not, however, act as a policy originator and any resolutions on Party policy passed there were not binding on the Welsh Secretary.

The majority of Conservatives Party policy distinctive to Wales came from the incumbent Welsh Secretary, with considerably less from the wider Welsh Party (Williams, 1998, Crickhowell, 1999). Despite this general lack of policy from the Conservative Party in Wales, the party did have a significant impact on Welsh Office policy from time to time. Perhaps the clearest ever case of the Conservative Party in Wales creating and then influencing a distinct Welsh policy concerned the 1994 Welsh local government changes. Here the party helped determine a system of unitary authorities for Wales (Deacon, 1997). David Hunt, Sir Wyn Roberts and Nicholas Bennett (the three Welsh Office ministers at the time the unitary authority proposals were announced), Conservative Party officials, Conservative councillors and political advisers interacted in order to provide Wales with a system of unitary authorities.

During the policy creation process of the new local government structures there was little, if any, interference from outside Wales. Local government changes in Wales were ultimately subject to Cabinet approval, which was true of all legislative changes. These changes were not, however, Cabinet driven. The impetus came from within the Welsh Office, the Conservative Party in Wales and the Welsh local government establishment. While these changes took place, Welsh Office officials recall little contact with the Department of the Environment and Scottish Office over the reforms (Welsh Office to author). Instead they remember a process that was constructed and conducted almost totally within the Welsh Office and the Welsh local government establishment, having originated with Welsh Conservatives. The restructuring of Welsh local government in Wales provides us with perhaps the clearest example we have of the Welsh Conservatives' role in the Welsh Office policy process (Deacon, 1997).

Section 7.2. The Wales Labour Party and the Welsh Office

Although academics such as Pelling, Smith and Spear (who have produced significant studies on the Labour Party) make numerous references to the Scottish Labour Party, no reference was ever made by them to the party in Wales. At the time of writing the subject of the Wales Labour Party remains, to all intents and purposes, hidden. Outside of the area of Welsh devolution, academic studies on the Wales Labour Party are limited almost exclusively to those historical studies undertaken by K. O. Morgan. Contemporary academic studies on the Wales Labour Party are non existent.

The extent of Wales Labour Party policy differences

The Labour Party established a regional office in Wales in the 1920s. In the late 1930s Wales was acknowledged as a separate regional council within the Party. The regional office, however, became part of the Party's central office in Wales rather than part of the regional council (Lynch, 1997, p. 9). Over time, however, there was increasing pressure from the nationalists within the Labour Party in Wales to regard Wales as a nation rather than just a region of England. The modern Wales Labour Party has therefore grown out of the former South Wales Regional Council for Labour and the Welsh Council of Labour (Balsom and Burch, 1980, p. 11).

The significance of Wales being regarded as a nation rather than a region came about in 1949 with the establishment of the Welsh Council. This meant that the Labour Party now recognised Wales as a distinct geographical unit. This Council (made up of MPs, councillors and businessmen) advised the government on a variety of matters relating to Wales. It had the power to contact the Cabinet directly about issues that concerned Wales. The Council also had the effect of making the Party in Wales focus more clearly on Wales. From 1964 onwards the Welsh Party also had one of its MPs as a Cabinet or Shadow Cabinet Member by right (the Welsh or Shadow Welsh Secretary). This put the Party in Wales on a par with Scotland and ahead of the English regional councils.

Although the Wales Labour Party is integrally linked to the other eight regions of the Labour Party, it has the ability to perform a number of autonomous actions that have not been enjoyed by the English regions. It has its own Executive Structure and policy creation process just like the other regional councils, but there are differences. It had a Shadow Secretary of State (for Wales) who could argue for Wales in the Shadow Cabinet. In addition, the Wales Labour Party as a regional council also drew up its own general election Manifesto. It did this for nearly every general election from 1950 when it produced: *Labour is Building a New Wales*.

During the 1960s and 1970s, a succession of Labour Welsh Secretaries had the opportunity to shape Wales Labour Party policy so that it differed from that in England. This was often diluted in Cabinet or Westminster, however, so that it did not make Wales too distinct from England. Cledwyn Hughes attempted to introduce a Welsh Assembly and reform Welsh local government into a system of unitary authorities in the 1960s, although this came to nothing. John Morris' attempts to do exactly the same ten years later also failed. Apart from these endeavours at devolution, Labour Welsh Secretaries' only efforts at unique or differing Welsh policies concerned some elements of industrial policy, such as the creation of the Welsh Development Agency, and support for the Welsh language via the first *Welsh Language Act* in the 1960s. In Wales it was often economic issues that united the party more than anything else. The Labour Party attacked the Conservatives for their neglect of regional development and promised that, with planning and economic growth, they could do better (Jones and Keating, 1985, p. 107).

Although the Labour Party designed its own devolution policy for Wales it had problems if it wished to decide any policy area that would also be present in Wales. For a number of years the Wales Conference was barred from discussing any British policy issues (Lynch, 1997, p. 12). This severely limited the role of Conference in Wales. Later on the party in Wales was given a little more scope to discuss, but not adapt or change, British policy matters. In the mid to late 1990s Welsh

Conferences were able to approve a small number of uniquely Welsh policies. The Welsh educational policy *Excellence for All*, for example, was approved in May 1995, the devolution proposals *Shaping the Vision* were approved in May 1995, and *Preparing For A New Wales* in May 1996. But even on issues such as Welsh devolution, which would seem to be mainly a Wales Labour Party matter, policies passed by the Welsh conference were then passed on to the party's National Executive Committee (NEC). It was the NEC which then put its seal of approval on them. Although the NEC had the power to stop any Welsh policy in its tracks it never saw fit to do so (Bold to author). Perhaps this is evidence that the Welsh party was not very revolutionary or even proactive in policy making.

How different were Wales Labour Party policy output therefore from those of the British Party as a whole? The evidence tends to prove that it was not very different at all. In their 1987 and 1992 general election manifestos, few Wales Labour Party policies differed to a great degree from those of the Party's British Manifesto apart from on the issue of devolution. In 1987 the Wales Labour Party's distinctive Welsh policy areas were limited to a few issues: (Wales Labour Party, 1987):

1. a Welsh Economic Planning Council;
2. encouragement of the use of the Welsh language;
3. a separate Arts Council for Wales.

In 1992 Welsh issues revolved around (Wales Labour Party, 1992):

1. an Assembly for Wales within the lifetime of the next Parliament;
2. a Welsh arm of the Environmental Protection Agency;
3. a new Welsh Language Act and
4. the introduction of unitary authorities into Wales.

These were issues with which their main opponents, the Conservatives, could find little fault because they had the same policies in their manifestos. By 1994 the Conservatives had introduced legislation or policies for all but two of Labour's 1987 and 1992 Welsh Manifesto pledges. The Conservatives had only ignored the issue of the Assembly and its forerunner, the Welsh Economic Planning Council. The Labour Party on the surface had very few uniquely Welsh policy differences from the Conservatives, who were regarded as the strong Unionist Party.

Those few Wales Labour Party's policies that were unique were always centred on the work and operation of the Welsh Office. In fact, there was never a solely Welsh initiative by the Wales Labour Party outside of the Welsh Office's remit between 1970–1997 (Wales Labour Party Manifestos 1970–97). It was unsurprising therefore that the Welsh Office always examined any Wales Labour Party manifestos in great detail. In fact, as soon as a general election was called, the Welsh Office ordered well over a hundred copies of the manifestos of each of the four main parties in Wales. It then set about drawing up 'briefs' on how the Welsh Office would be able to implement any future government manifesto commitments (Welsh Office to author). A practice that was to be useful training for the arrival of the Welsh Assembly.

The Ron Davies era

Before examining the influence of the Shadow Welsh Secretary, the origins and purpose of this post will be looked at. The Shadow Welsh Secretary was the political counterpart of the Welsh Secretary, the post was created as an automatic response to the establishment of the Welsh Secretary in the Cabinet in 1964. The occupier normally gained his post by being elected or appointed to the Shadow Cabinet, and in turn being allocated that portfolio by the Party Leader (Shaw, 1994, p. 112). Just as in the Cabinet proper, Shadow Secretaries were aware that they owed their position and status very much to their Leader. They were therefore bound by the same doctrine of collective responsibility as the government. Breaking this responsibility could lead to their sacking (Kavanagh, 1990, p. 223). There were just eight Shadow Welsh Secretaries as opposed to eleven Welsh Secretaries, Table 7.2. After the Conservatives lost all of their seats in Wales in 1997, William Hague, as the new leader, scrapped the very post he had just held.

Shadow Welsh Secretaries, excluding Ann Clwyd and William Hague, had an average time of just over five years in post. This was two years more than Welsh Secretaries, see Chapter II. The extra time they had in post ensured that they were able to develop policies more fully than their counterparts at the Welsh Office. In 1979 and again in 1997 the new incoming political parties brought in their Shadow Welsh Secretaries (Nicholas Edwards and Ron Davies). They remained the only two Shadow Welsh Secretaries ever to become Welsh Secretaries. The six other ex-Shadows either:

- moved on to other areas whilst remaining an MP (Ann Clwyd, William Hague, Barry Jones);
- ran out of time and therefore retired before gaining office (Alec Jones);
- were rejected by their Leader either before or after their party had won the general election (David Gibson-Watt and George Thomas).

Table 7.2
Shadow Welsh Secretaries 1964–1997

	Party	*Term*
David Gibson-Watt	Conservative	1964–70
George Thomas	Labour	1970–74
Nicholas Edwards	Conservative	1974–79
Alec Jones	Labour	1979–83
Barry Jones	Labour	1983–92
Ann Clwyd	Labour	1992
Ron Davies	Labour	1992–97
William Hague	Conservative	1997*

* Post was abolished in 1997 by William Hague

The policy role of the Shadow Welsh Secretary

Ron Davies defined the role of the Shadow Welsh Secretary as being 'shaped almost solely by the occupant' (Davies to author). Thus the post carried with it a fair degree of both autonomy and variety. The Shadow Welsh Secretary had an interest in a variety of Shadow Cabinet interests, ranging from constitutional reform to agriculture and health. They also had one of the most important roles in establishing what their party's policy agenda was (Crickhowell, 1999, p. 62). The ranking of ministers within the Shadow Cabinet, just like the Cabinet proper, depended upon the personality of the individual, the amount of time they had already spent in Shadow Cabinet, and their place in Shadow Cabinet elections (Davies to author).

Over the years, the Welsh Secretary developed a distinct policy role Figure 7.1. The Shadow Welsh Secretary also had a wider national role as the policy voice of the Welsh Party inside the Shadow Cabinet. Within the Shadow Cabinet there was a degree of co-ordination between Welsh and Scottish Shadows. Both sat next to each other in Cabinet, and George Robertson (Scottish Shadow) and Ron Davies formed a close working relationship (Davies to author). Although there were no institutionalised arrangements between Scottish and Welsh Shadows, they both followed events in each other's country very closely. They shared communality over a number of issues, the most notable being devolution (Davies to author).

Figure 7.1

The role of the Shadow Welsh Secretary on policy issues
(Source: Morgan and Griffiths to author)

1. Acknowledged head in terms of policy creation
2. The dynamo behind Welsh policy creation.
3. Determined terms of reference for the Policy Standing Committee
4. Facilitator of policy decisions through the Executive Committee
5. Ensured that wider UK policies did not impinge on Welsh policy.
6. Monitored and corrected statements by other Shadow colleagues on issues concerning the Welsh Party's policies e.g. on education and health.
7. Ensured that Welsh MPs continued to publicly support Labour Party policies.
8. Sat on appropriate Standing Committees and responded to ministerial speeches during the various Parliamentary stages of legislation

The replacement of Ann Clwyd by Ron Davies in 1992 led to the most proactive Shadow Welsh Secretary since Nicholas Edwards. Ron Davies (1992–97) was acknowledged by his fellow Labour Party MPs as having created a distinctly Welsh Labour agenda on issues ranging from devolution to the Welsh rural economy (Morgan, Griffiths and Wardell to author). Ron Davies was aware that the Wales Labour Party had a great deal of scope to create its own policy initiatives, independent of the English regions. Over his period in office the Wales Labour Party increasingly developed its own agenda. This more independent Welsh policy making process was enhanced by three factors:

• Firstly, 'quite a lot of policy autonomy already existed in the Welsh Office. This made Wales distinct from the English regions' (Griffiths to author). The fact that Welsh Secretaries such as Walker and Redwood pursued different policies to those in England (on issues such as health care and the economy) encouraged the Wales Labour Party to create its own policies. Although this process was often more reactive than proactive. Labour's *Rural White Paper* in 1996, for instance, was a response to the Welsh Office's own version. Nevertheless the Wales

Labour Party had created its own distinct Welsh alternative policy, without the need to merely adapt policy from England.

- Secondly, there was a history of forming a political consensus in the smaller Welsh political community. In the 1980s, Labour councils and the Wales TUC co-operated with the Conservative controlled Welsh Office over inward investment. Some of this co-operation or acceptance of good ideas continued in later years. On the environment for example, the Countryside Council for Wales originated the *Tir Cymen* environmental stewardship scheme, a variation of the Countryside Stewardship Scheme that occurred in England. This linked environmental payments to the whole farm, not merely a field or two as occurred in England (Welsh Office to author). The Wales Labour Party actively supported the Conservative government's scheme, as did Plaid Cymru and the Liberal Democrats (Morgan to author). Thus a 'good idea' was not always rejected merely because it came from the 'Tories'.

- Thirdly, the role played by the Shadow Welsh Office team. The Shadow Welsh Secretary was, without doubt, the most important figure behind policy creation in the Wales Labour Party. As a member of the Shadow Cabinet he was linked directly to the Party at the highest level. He sat as an Ex Officio member of the Welsh Executive Committee, and helped determine the composition of the Policy Standing Committee. Although the Shadow Welsh Office ministers did not sit on the Welsh Executive Committee or its subcommittees, they often acted as the policy dynamos of the Wales Labour Party.

The role played by the Shadow Welsh Office Team is important enough for further consideration. In the matter of rapid policy creation it was the Shadow Welsh Office Team which was the most important. Although Wales Labour Party policy usually differed only between 10 to 15 per cent from that concerning England or the wider UK (Morgan to author), some issues were much more distinct. Clear examples of these differences could be seen in Welsh agriculture and education Wales Labour White Papers, or the unique endorsement of Welsh language or devolution issues. In education for example, the Welsh's party's *Educational Excellence for All* highlighted in-service training for teachers while in teaching. In contrast the English document highlighted training before starting work (Griffiths to author).

Section 7.3. The third parties and the Welsh Office policy process

For the duration of the Welsh Office's existence both Plaid Cymru (Party of Wales) and the Welsh Liberal Democrats remained the 'third political parties' in Wales. The Labour Party being the first and the Conservatives the second. We should therefore note that during the life of the Welsh Office Plaid Cymru had not yet made the political breakthrough that was later to make them the second party of Wales.

Plaid Cymru

Plaid Cymru founded in 1925, is one of the oldest nationalist parties within Europe (Lynch, 1996, p. 52). It developed initially as a linguistic and cultural movement and then into the sole party dedicated to Wales. It was politically active throughout the period of the Welsh Office's existence. In fact from 1958–1973 successive governments kept a Top Secret file on Plaid Cymru code-numbered BD 25/59. Its contents remain secret but were added to by Welsh Office officials until it was closed in 1973 (Wales on Sunday, 23/7/00). Consecutive Welsh Secretaries were concerned at Plaid Cymru's increasing appeal. During the 1970s the party took on the radical tradition in Welsh politics and some of the 'Welsh' perspectives of the Liberals (Balsom et al, 1983). Its President, Dafydd Wigley, pushed his party on a course that would turn Wales into an 'independent nation within Europe' (Lynch, 1995, p. 209). The Welsh Office would clearly have played a central part in any Plaid plans.

Although Plaid Cymru could never have gained a majority at Westminster Parliament in their own right (they only contested 40 of the 657 seats), they could gain Labour or Conservative seats in Wales. This could have prevented either the Conservative or Labour Parties gaining an overall majority. The appeal of their policies therefore became a direct threat to the other major political parties in Wales. Plaid Cymru's campaign for an independent Wales also led the Liberals to re-emphasise their own commitment to political devolution (Roberts, 1985, p. 87). As seen earlier, Plaid's increasing success was a major factor in Labour expanding its own political devolution proposals in 1974 (Davies, 1985, p. 136 and Dorey, 1995, p. 147) and increasing the Welsh Office's autonomy over land use planning (Tewdwr-Jones, 1997, p. 58). It also contributed to the Conservatives' decision to increase Welsh cultural funding and their establish a Welsh Fourth Channel in 1981 (Davies, 1985, p. 147).

Thus, both political parties which controlled the Welsh Office were unable to ignore the presence of Plaid Cymru and its appeal to the nationalist agenda when determining policy in Wales.

Welsh Liberal Democrats

In the general election of 1906 the Liberals took 33 of Wales' 35 seats; in the general election of 1992 the Liberal Democrats took just one of Wales' 38 seats. Liberal fortunes in Wales, like much of the rest of the UK, had been dramatically reversed. For much of the twentieth century Wales acted as a refuge for the Liberal Party. In 1945 over half of the total Liberal MPs in the UK were representing by Welsh constituencies (Graham–Jones, 1993, p. 328). Ironically, when the Liberal Party was in its ascendancy little attention was paid to delivering administrative or political devolution to Wales. It was only when Emlyn Hooson became leader of the Welsh Party in the early 1960s that the party started to take Welsh policy seriously (Graham-Jones, 1993, p. 344). The Welsh Liberal Party separated from the English Party on 1 September 1966 (Roberts, 1985, p. 98). It has been responsible for determining its own policy creation every since. The vast majority of its policy creation, approved at its annual Spring Conference, related to issues which were within the Welsh Office's remit (Burree to author).

It was during the Labour administration that the Liberals were able to obtain their strongest influence over the Welsh Office. The Lib-Lab Pact and devolution referendum of the 1970s, and the 1997 devolution campaign brought the Welsh Secretaries closer to the Liberals than at any other time. The party, however, never became close to the Conservative Welsh Office. During this era the Liberals fought the Conservative Party for three of their own four key seats in Wales (Brecon and Radnor, Conwy and Montgomeryshire), which soured relations between the two parties and kept them apart. The party's lack of resources also meant that it couldn't monitor and interact with the Welsh Office as much as it would have liked.

Section 7.4. The other influences on the Welsh Office policy process: the media, think tanks, European Union and official inquiries.

This section looks at the remaining influences on the Welsh Office policy process. No one area is represented as being a greater influence than the others were. It does not seek to study the influence of public opinion on the Welsh Office mainly because there is no literature on this area. We know that some of the political parties shaped their policies according to opinion polls which they conducted, or through the use of Focus groups, most notably with Labour. There was no evidence to indicate that any of the political parties used these methods to shape uniquely Welsh policies, however. These appear to have been determined by other factors. Politicians claimed to take public opinion into account when determining policy and often met protest groups or responded to public concerns (Welsh Secretaries to author). But the shortage of research undertaken in this area means that it is impossible to determine to what extent public opinion influenced policy issues. The existence of policies such as the closure of the coal mines, the Poll Tax, nursery vouchers, and the opting out of schools and hospitals which appeared to be against the majority of Welsh opinion indicated that public opinion was not considered too highly when determining Welsh Office policy, at least by the Conservatives.

Section 7.4.1. The media and the Welsh Office

The Welsh Office and the UK media

The mass media is a vital part of the political system and therefore few politicians make policy without first considering a media strategy as well (Negrine, 1994, p. 9). Jones (1997, p. 452) indicates that the role of the media in the policy process is threefold:

1. influencing the climate in which policy is created through articles, debates, general coverage and editorials;
2. provision of ideas from columnists to the government;
3. providing crucial information to the public on policy development.

The interaction between the Welsh Office and the media, however, was limited on a UK-wide scale. At a UK-wide TV and radio level there was only a very occasional mention of it. Only in the print media could the Welsh Office's existence be measured at all. In 1969 the Welsh Secretary generated by far the least national publicity of any of the Cabinet ministers (Headey, 1975, p. 237), just 4 per cent of that generated by the Prime Minister and 64 per cent of that generated by the Scottish Office (Headey, 1975, p. 237). Twenty-five years later little had changed. Table 7.3.

illustrates that the Welsh Office, on the whole, had a far lower media profile than its territorial sisters. Over the five year period covered in Table 7.3, 1991 marked the period of lowest coverage for each territorial ministry in respect of their Secretary of State. By 1995 the coverage of stories concerning the Welsh Secretary had almost doubled, those concerning the Scottish Secretary had increased by 25 per cent, and those concerning the Northern Ireland Secretary had risen by 35 per cent. Despite the large rise in stories concerning the Welsh Secretary, he still only had 38 per cent of the coverage of his Scottish counterpart and 47 per cent of that of his Northern Ireland counterpart. *The Times/Sunday Times* coverage of Welsh Secretaries tended to increase when the personality holding the post was of a more forceful character. John Redwood in his first year in office achieved around 75 per cent more coverage than his predecessor, David Hunt. This exposure, however, did not significantly increase the amount of attention paid to the Welsh Office, only to its leader, Table 7.3.

Table 7.3
Number of stories relating to the three territorial departments in
The Times and Sunday Times (1991–1995)

Year	1991	1992	1993	1994	1995
Number of stories containing the word...					
Welsh Office	41	31	40	50	46
Welsh Secretary	42	67	81	73	82
David Hunt	58	84	18	N/A	N/A
John Redwood	N/A	N/A	132	150	70
William Hague	N/A	N/A	N/A	N/A	51
Scottish Office	197	204	220	231	224
Scottish Secretary	168	186	115	139	213
Ian Lang	166	226	151	162	115
Michael Forsyth	N/A	N/A	N/A	N/A	179
Northern Ireland Office	47	46	60	69	78
Northern Ireland Secretary	128	132	131	131	173
Peter Brooke	155	65			
Sir Patrick Mayhew		75	173	166	249

Table 7.3. excludes references to Conservative leadership election in 1995 in which John Redwood took part. Adding in these figures more than doubles those stories which mention either John Redwood or the Welsh Secretary.

By examining the average coverage of stories between 1991–1995, Figure 7.2, it can be seen that the Welsh Office had by far the lowest national media exposure, of any the three territorial ministries. Within the set period it received only 19 per cent of the coverage of the Scottish Office and 68 per cent of that of the Northern Ireland Office.

Figure 7.2
The Territorial Ministries share of Times/
Sunday Times territorial coverage (1991–1995)

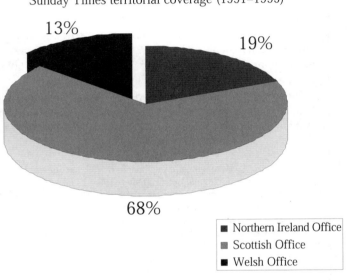

■ Northern Ireland Office
■ Scottish Office
■ Welsh Office

Occasionally a Welsh Secretary made the national headlines not because of Welsh Office news management, but because of his own policy agenda and news management. In 1985, for instance, Nicholas Edwards was threatened with a writ when he publicly criticised GEC's 'cash mountain' (Crickhowell, 1999, p. 69). Perhaps the largest public row, however, occurred in the summer of 1993. It was during this period that the Conservative government was in the middle of its 'Back to Basics' policy campaign. The policy centred on a return to 'family values'. John Redwood made a speech at the then University College of Wales, Cardiff entitled: 'There Aren't Many Fathers Around Here' (Redwood, 1994, pp. 69–72). The speech condemned the proliferation of single mothers on Cardiff's St Mellon's Housing Estate. It shot both the housing estate and Welsh Secretary onto the national media stage. A whole nation-wide debate on the issue of single mothers started. It was a deliberate attempt by Redwood to boast his national profile despite reservations from Number

10. Yet Welsh Secretaries under Questions of Procedure for Ministers (QPM), Paragraph 87 were required to:

> 'ensure that their statements are consistent with collective Government policy and . . . should exercise special care in referring to subjects that are the responsibility of other ministers' (Williams, 1998, p. 272).

It was therefore perhaps not surprising that the Welsh Office did not receive much national coverage in the London based media. Even Redwood could only break QPMs so many times without incurring the wrath of the Prime Minister. Welsh Secretaries, however, did seek to cultivate relationships with the national press in London, with special briefings for prominent journalists (Williams, 1998, p. 55).

The Welsh Office and the Welsh media

Of all the London based paper media, only the Financial Times had a Welsh correspondent during the Welsh Office era (Mackay and Powell, 1997). Even they were based in Bristol. Hume (1983) indicated that 'there is little in the English language press . . . particularly the weeklies . . . which offers any support to the idea that Wales is a distinct nation' (p. 231). The Welsh Office had, therefore, to rely on the Welsh media to sell its policies. In the television and radio media it was relatively simply with both the BBC Wales, S4C, ITV and independent radio having regular news items to fill, often with Welsh Office news items. These programmes, however, often lacked the close scrutiny or resources given by the national media. The relationship between the BBC Wales and the Welsh Office was so close, however, that in 1995 and 1997 they allowed access to a series of 'fly on the wall' documentaries. Welsh Office news items, often led the Welsh news agenda. Penetrating the news media based outside of Wales, however, remained a rare occurrence.

The Welsh Office had little difficulty getting its news items reported in the Welsh print media but this amounted to limited coverage, even within Wales. In 1997 the highest penetration of the paper media was *The Sun* (22.5 per cent of Welsh households). This was followed by *The Mirror* (12.5 per cent), *The Daily Mail* (9.8 per cent) and then the two Welsh newspapers: *The Western Mail* and the *Daily Post* both at 6 per cent (MacKay and Powell, 1997, p. 15). Only 13 per cent of papers read in Wales were, therefore, produced there, as a opposed to some 90 per cent in Scotland, resulting in the vast majority of the Welsh population obtaining little coverage of Welsh political affairs [Institute for Welsh Affairs, 1996, p. 11]. Similarly a third of the population lived in areas where they could pick up English television transmitters (Mackay and Powell, 1997, p. 9). This meant that no one area of the media in Wales had a monopoly or even a full coverage of Wales. Similarly ownership of the Welsh media, with the exception of a few independent radio stations, was outside of Wales (Mackay and Powell, 1997, p. 9). This further enhanced the general lack of media interest in the Welsh Office policy agenda.

This meant, however, that the Welsh based media did have a regular interest in looking at Welsh Office policy output. Newspapers such as the *Western Mail* and *Daily Post* regularly led with stories associated with the Welsh Office or Welsh Secretary. And editorials, articles and sometimes even campaigns by the media itself sought to shape the Welsh Office policy agenda. The Welsh Office in turn supplied the Welsh media with daily Press Notices and media briefings in order to fill its air space or column inches.

With few exceptions the Welsh Office was usually able to set their own news agenda. The Welsh media had little impact on the Welsh Office policy agenda (Welsh Secretaries to author). In fact the media in general had little direct impact on the Welsh Office policy process. This was because it rarely came under the powerful probing gaze of the London media.

But what did this low media coverage mean in practice for Welsh Office policy creation? It could in fact have been beneficial for a Welsh Secretary's own policy autonomy. As we saw earlier, Anthony King (1994) noted that the Welsh Office enjoyed policy autonomy by virtue of its low profile within the government. This autonomy could also be enhanced by the department's low profile within the national media. If the media was not concerned with what was happening in Wales, then the Welsh Secretary could escape the intensive probing that his other Whitehall counterparts were subjected to over their policy output. There was only a much weaker Welsh media to hold the Welsh Secretary to account or lobby for policy change. He could subtly bend Collective Cabinet responsibility or deviate from government policy norms, without anybody outside of the Principality being any the wiser. This ensured that he enjoyed far greater autonomy than his more public Cabinet colleagues who were scrutinised more closely by the London media.

Welsh Office ministers egos, and political ambitions however, dictated that they often desired significant press coverage. Hunt and Hague were happy to rely on the Welsh Office to provide this whereas Redwood's desire for publicity was so great that he provided an open door policy with the media (Williams, 1998, p. 97).

There appears to have been no empirical studies undertaken on the effect of even the limited Welsh media on Welsh Office policy output. The fact that the Welsh Office and various Welsh Secretaries sought to maintain good relations with the press, however, indicates that they may have had some influence even if it was merely by acting as a sounding board to the general public on policy ideas.

Section 7.4.2. Think tanks

In Sections 7.1. and 7.2. we saw that the political parties established their own internal think tanks in Wales to develop policy ideas. Jones (1997) stated that Margaret Thatcher was particularly fond of these think tanks because she thought that the 'civil service was constitutionally incapable of generating the policy innovation which the Prime Minister craves' (p. 455). Her own Number 10 Policy Unit was headed at times by the Welsh Lord Griffith and by John Redwood. The Unit, however, did not design policy that was specific to just Wales.

The major UK think tanks, such as the Centre for Reform, Centre for Policy Studies and the Institute of Economic Affairs were located in England. The only specific Welsh issue they tended to look at was devolution. The Institute for Public Policy Research produced a report on Welsh devolution in 1995, the Constitution Unit produced one in 1996, and the Electoral Reform Society also produced one in same year. The conclusions and recommendations of these studies were not taken up by any of the political parties in Wales that did not already advocate their recommendations previously (Deacon, 1996B).

Wales had only one major think tank of its own, during the Welsh Office era, the Institute of Welsh Affairs (IWA). With the appointment of the writer John Osmond as director in 1995 the IWA started producing regular studies on a variety of topics with decisions related directly to Wales, on issues as diverse as Wales In Europe, devolution and the Sea Empress disaster. The papers it produced and the conferences it held were aimed at influencing key decision makers on Welsh Office policy. No study, however, was undertaken to ascertain the influence of the IWA. It had former senior Welsh Office civil servant, Ivor Lightman, on its board and its reports were often cited in Parliamentary debates. The fact that a number of prominent politicians and decision makers connected with the Welsh Office wrote regularly for its journal, *Welsh Agenda*, may indicate that they took IWA's policy suggestions seriously.

Section 7.4.3. Committees of inquiry

Committees of inquiry are a mechanism by which raw material can be gathered for new policy (Brown and Steel, 1979, p. 248). Perhaps the most important form of inquiry is the Royal Commission. A Royal Commission can be the precursor to major policy changes (Jones, 1997, p. 455). Only a few Royal Commissions had any influence on Welsh Office policy making. During the Thatcher and Major governments (1979–97) no Royal Commission had any impact on the Welsh Office.

The Royal Commission on Local Government (1966–9), which looked at specifically English local government did influence the Labour government's proposals for Welsh local government reform. This was because Welsh Office ministers lost the nerve to 'go it alone' without seeing what was going to happen to English local government first (Tonypandy to author). Perhaps the most significant Royal Commission to impact upon the Welsh Office was the Royal Commission on the Constitution which reported back its draft recommendations in April 1969. Its federalist recommendations on Welsh devolution, however, were totally rejected by the anti-devolutionist George Thomas (Jones, 1983, p. 23).

The Welsh Office from time to time established its own advisory or internal commissions to determine policy. In 1965 James Griffith got his Permanent Secretary Sir Goronwy Daniel to look at local government reform in an internal commission, see Chapter II. More recently, in 1995, Sir Peter Phillips chaired an advisory committee into the Welsh Office's internal management structure, see Chapter V. Both of these commissions' recommendations were side stepped by either the Welsh Office or outside government forces. Not all commissions' recommendations can be so readily ignored, however. In 1996 the Sea Empress oil tanker disaster off the coast of Pembrokeshire resulted in another inquiry being set-up. It brought forward recommendations which the Welsh Secretary was obliged to accept. Commissions provided a channel through which information and ideas could be fed into the government machine from outside (Brown and Steel, 1979, p. 249). On the whole, however, there were few commissions at the Welsh Office in which to influence its policy creation process.

Section 7.4.4. The impact of the European Union on the Welsh Office

Treaty obligations and the growing power of Union institutions imposed increasingly powerful constraints upon the freedom of Welsh Office policy making (Jones, 1997, p. 459). The Welsh Office was responsible for an increasing range of responsibilities related to European policy-making and implementation (Pyper, 1995, p. 163). Some areas of Welsh Office policy making, such as regional development grants or agriculture, were either determined directly from Brussels, or the Welsh Office needed their approval before policy implementation was undertaken (Welsh Office to author). The Welsh Office's interpretation of the rules caused some friction with Welsh local government, which tried to bypass the Welsh Office through integration in European policy networks, although this did not always prove to be very successful (Rhodes, 1997). There were few areas within the Welsh Office which were not affected by European Union policy decisions. The Welsh Office Agriculture Division, which employed the largest number of civil servants at the Welsh Office had almost its entire policy agenda determined by Europe (Welsh Office to author). It was clear therefore that Europe had an important influence on Welsh Office policy making and that the Welsh Office spent a great deal of time either responding directly or giving its own opinion on issues through the lead Whitehall departments (European Affairs Division to author).

Some Conservative Welsh Secretaries resented the loss in policy sovereignty to Brussels. The Europhobe Welsh Secretary John Redwood reacted to Brussels policy influence by putting the Welsh Office firmly behind a British rather than Welsh outlook on policy issues. John Osmond, in his book *Wales in Europe*, noted that:

'John Redwood ordered the Welsh Development Agency to drop the marketing theme 'Wales in Europe' from its promotional literature. Instead, in accordance with his Unionist and Europhobic outlook, he insisted the WDA print brochures emphasising that Wales was an integral part of the UK. The Union flag rather than Y Ddraig Goch was to be given pride of place in the literature. This was on the grounds that foreign investors were supposedly confused by material emphasising that Wales was a dynamic small nation in a borderless European Union' (Osmond, 1995, p. 70).

Whereas Hywel Williams, Redwood's Special Adviser, noted:

'Redwood spent much of his time during his last few months in office trying to remove the signs on Welsh roadworks stating that the European Union was responsible for the grants that paid for the work. Every time Redwood spotted the twelve stars he detected a propaganda coup masking the reality that the lion's share of the cost came from the British taxpayer. Hours of meetings and several yards of frayed official nerves later yielded the conclusion that the triumphalist signs had to stay.' (Williams, 1998, p. 96).

Similarly William Hague showed his anti-European colours when, in the BSE crisis in 1996, like his Scottish counterpart, Michael Forsyth, he refused to fly the European flag over the Welsh Office (Hague, 5/6/96). But the most damaging factor on the Welsh Office's attempts to influence the European Union's policy agenda was the refusal of Welsh Office ministers to attend the European Union's Council of Ministers meetings. The Council was the key legislative and decision making body of the European Union (Cole and Cole, 1993, p. 26). It was here that the appropriate minister presented Wales's case. In the past, the appearance of a Welsh Secretary at a Council of Ministers meeting was a rare occurrence. Redwood went to just one in his two year stint at the Welsh Office (Western Mail, 22/3/96).

In October 1995, the Select Committee on Welsh Affairs Report on 'Wales in Europe' recommended that, where the decisions of the Council of Ministers affect Wales, a Welsh Office minister should be present (SCWA, 1995). The Select Committee on Welsh Affairs Report resulted in William Hague restating the Welsh Office's commitment to influencing European policy agenda. He stated:

'I have a seat in the Cabinet as Secretary of State for Wales and I am a member of the Cabinet's European Committee. I ensure that Wales' interests are not overlooked' (Hague, 22/3/96).

William Hague's record on attending Council of Minister's Meetings, however, remained little better than Redwood's (Welsh Office to author). The European Union became ever more important for the Welsh Office over matters of policy, from issues such as the ban of Welsh beef exports to the issue of European structural funds. As Europe became ever more important, however, the Welsh Office own existence was drawing to an end.

Conclusion

The incumbent political party's politicians in Wales helped control an administrative machine, in the form of the Welsh Office, which had to be supplied with policies to implement. Either these policies came from the party's London power base, or they were fashioned by the party's own apparatus in Wales. As the Welsh Office expanded so the political parties in Wales, often led by the Welsh Secretary himself, altered or even created policy with a heavy Welsh slant. The Welsh Office helped in ensuring that all government policy within its remit was tailored to Welsh circumstances.

For the opposition parties in Wales there was very little formal or even informal contact between them and the Welsh Office. This was partly because of the existence of a neutral civil service. This meant that whatever happened within the Welsh Office, it remained out of sight for the vast majority of time from those who had been elected to scrutinise the workings of government. All opposition parties, however, still determined policy that would be implemented by the Welsh Office should they have ever gained power. Although both the Liberal Democrats and Plaid Cymru had their own plans for how they wanted the Welsh Office to develop as part of a Welsh civil service, political circumstances dictated that they would never get their own way. Only Labour and the Conservatives ever possessed the power to shape the Welsh Office; it was these party's policies that most concerned the Welsh Office official.

Distinct Wales Labour Party policy output was limited. Historically the Party in Wales had viewed itself as almost totally integrated with the Party in the rest of the UK. Those in Wales felt that they would be sidelined from important national policy creation and decision making if they allowed the Party in Wales to become more autonomous. Major Labour Party politicians with a Welsh base, such as Callaghan, Foot and Kinnock, saw both their own and the Wales Labour Party's future in Westminster and Whitehall not in Cardiff. They saw the Welsh Office as merely a branch of Whitehall in Wales. Due to the desire to be British, distinctly Welsh policy was very rarely allowed to occur. Shadow Welsh Secretaries and their front bench team tried to enhance the element of Welsh policy distinctiveness, but were often overwhelmed by the sheer volume of policy this had to be applied to.

Many of the factors that played a significant role in influencing UK-wide government policy, such as the media and Inquiries had a more limited impact in Wales. The UK-wide media tended to ignore the Welsh Office on the whole, and the more limited Welsh media, by its very nature, was patchy in influencing the Welsh Office policy process. National inquiries in Wales were a rarity and therefore had little relevance to the Welsh Office. Think tanks, like the Welsh media were limited in Wales to almost a token presence. The Institute of Welsh Affairs was the most prominent example of a Welsh think tank. It increased its role in latter years but its influence was untested. The impact of the European Union on the Welsh Office was also an unknown quantity to a large extent. The last few Conservative Welsh Secretaries, however, saw it as a serious threat to British policy determination and consequently sought to shield the Welsh Office from interacting with the European policy process.

Notes

1. Although the Conservatives lost all of their Westminster seats in the 1997 general election which made them even worse off 1992–1997 was the last complete Parliamentary term of the Welsh Office's existence.

Chapter VIII

Completing the Policy Jigsaw:–
The Territorial Policy Community

Introduction

In the previous chapters we have examined the major internal and external influences on the Welsh Office policy process. Yet there is still one significant element missing from our policy creation jigsaw. This element was a major influence on the policy process that also brought with it elements of the other external influences on the policy process we have already discussed, together with some new ones. This final all encompassing influence on the policy process was the territorial policy community that surrounded the Welsh Office. In 1985 Osmond indicated that 'since the creation of the Welsh Office, there had been a progressive evolution of a consultative network of policy making' (p. 233). This large territorial policy community (consultative network) developed over the course of the Welsh Office's existence. Much of this community did not exist prior to the Welsh Office's creation and increased as a result of the Welsh Office's role in the policy field. It was this policy community that brought together the policy actors we have seen in the previous chapter. It was this community that sought to shape and fashion Welsh Office policy and in turn was used by the Welsh Office as a major resource in aiding its policy shaping. And it was this community that mainly represented the power of the non-Conservative majority in Wales in the policy-making of the Welsh Office during the Thatcher and Major eras.

The first section of this chapter examines the extent and nature of the Welsh territorial policy community. It looks at the theoretical nature behind this community and the scope of the community in Wales. This theme is developed in the second section, which seeks to clarify the identities of the occupants of the Cathays Park Village and the exact nature of the interrelationship between them, and the Welsh Office.

The territorial policy community was not a perfect consultative body however. The final section examines the extent to which the Welsh Office in its final years was increasingly able to manipulate elements of the community, namely the Welsh quangos. This manipulation had caused increasing concern, and evidence suggests that the Welsh Office had become less open to the community and more apt at forcing its own policy mandate through regardless of the policy community's opposition.

Section 8.1. The Welsh Territorial Policy Community: The Cathays Park Village[1]

In Chapter I it was seen that Wales did indeed have a number of distinctive policy differences from England. But the Welsh Office was often unable to produce or drive through its own policies without the help of its policy community. It had developed this community in order to enhance both its relations with the Welsh establishment and its independence from the Whitehall policy machine. Heclo and Widavsky (1981) pointed out that civil servants recognise that their policy desires cannot prevail unless they maintain a community to support them because they must face a confederation of departments with similar support. Jordan and Richardson (1979) indicated that:

> "The policy-making map is in reality a series of vertical compartments or segments – each segment inhabited by a different set of organised groups and generally impenetrable by 'unrecognised groups' or by the general public" (p. 74).

To this extent the Welsh Office through legislation, internal powers or merely its presence in Wales built up a policy advisor/service provider community with a remit unique to Wales.

Britain has been described as a 'post-parliamentary democracy', in which policies were developed in negotiation between government agencies and pressure groups organised in policy networks outside of Westminster (Ham and Hill, 1993, p. 27). Benson defines a policy network as 'a cluster or complex of organisations connected to each other by resources dependencies and distinguished from other clusters or complexes by breaks in the structure of resource dependencies' (Benson cited in Ham and Hill, 1993, p. 176). Dowding saw these policy networks as the 'personal relations of small groups of political actors' (Dowding, 1995B, p. 140). Rhodes noted that in Northern Ireland, Scotland and Wales these smaller 'issue networks' were encompassed into what he defined as the larger 'territorial policy communities' (Rhodes, 1992, p. 281). It is the contention of this chapter that the territorial policy community that existed in Wales enhanced Welsh policy differences and this factor is explored in the following pages.

The Welsh Territorial Policy Community

Although Whitehall and Westminster, as seen in Chapters II, VI and IV, by their nature, had the greatest sway on policy creation and implementation carried out by the Welsh Office, there was also a distinct Welsh policy network within Wales. Whitehall's policy network became known as the Whitehall Village (Heclo and Wildavsky, 1996, p. 35). It was a network so powerful that the territorial departments also had offices in London which devoted a major part of their time in take part in this network. Similarly in Scotland, a policy community had developed around the Scottish Office's New St Andrew's House base (Brown et al., 1996, p. 96). In Wales the territorial policy community (Rhodes, 1997, Rhodes and Marsh, 1992, p. 185) was drawn to the Welsh Office's headquarters in Cathays Park, Cardiff. As well as being a home for the Welsh Office, Cathays Park acted as the political, cultural, academic and administrative heart of Wales. In the last five years of the Welsh Office, within a few miles of Cathays Park, were located the headquarters or major branches of:

a) the four main political parties in Wales;
b) the Welsh headquarters of the major financial institutions which included the Bank of Wales;
c) the headquarters of the main Welsh media and cultural institutions;
d) eighteen of the main twenty-five Welsh quangos (only the former Development Board for Rural Wales, Countryside for Wales, and five of the six Welsh TECs were based outside Cardiff);
e) major industrial, employee, business and commercial representative associations;
f) the main pressure or 'cause groups' groups, trade union and charity headquarters or Welsh bases;
g) the Welsh Local Government Association which acted as the mouthpiece for Wales' 22 unitary authorities;
h) the University of Wales headquarters, four of its federal institutions and Wales' other university – the University of Glamorgan;

i)   the European Commission office and numerous foreign consulates. Because this territorial policy community was linked closely to the location of the main Welsh Office headquarters in Wales at Cathays Park, Cardiff, it is described from hereon as the 'Cathays Park Village'. The importance of the Village in the development of policy has been highlighted in the work of Boyne et al (1991) in relation to local/central government policy making and Wales, and Farrell and Law (1995) concerning Welsh education.

When policy creation or implementation moved on to more specific or definite issues, the Village broke down into even smaller policy issue networks (Rhodes and Marsh, 1992, p. 185). It was within these smaller policy networks that 'modes of resource allocation and transactions occurred neither through discrete exchanges nor by administrative fiat, but through networks of individuals engaged in reciprocal, preferential, mutually supportive actions' (Powell, 1990, p. 12). Entry to these groups could be strictly controlled. Laffin noted the operation of 'stringent entry criteria, varying amongst issue areas, but including such criteria as possessing expert knowledge' (Laffin, 1986, p. 6).

The Cathays Park Village policy issue networks could be further divided into a number of categorical areas, which included (Rhodes and Marsh, 1992, p. 182):

- *The professional network* which involved one class of professionals in the policy making process, of which the most cited example was those of the NHS professionals.
- *The intergovernmental network* which linked the Welsh Office specifically with other areas of the public sector. In Wales this meant the NHS, local government and the Welsh quangos.
- *The producer network* which integrated the public and private sector with policy making interests. Between 1993–1997 the Welsh Office partially formalised this network in the form of the Welsh Economic Council, which brought together Wales' major business and trade union representatives.
- *The issue network* brought together elements of the territorial community and various policy issues, often on an *ad hoc* basis, such as planning for the 1998 Intergovernmental Conference in Cardiff.

The Welsh Office's internal departmental divisions were often structured with the various policy networks in mind. The divisions, for example, established *Contact Officer Lists* which detailed a key contact for every member of the territorial community with whom they dealt with directly (Welsh Office to author). These contacts were then regularly sent information or Welsh Office Circulars by the Welsh Office officials, on matters they believed affected them.

Some departments had extremely close working relationships with members of the territorial policy community. The Industry Department, for example, had a section which interrelated regularly with the Welsh Chambers of Commerce (Welsh Office Industry Department to author). The Agriculture Department (WOAD) ensured that its divisions interacted closely with the National Farmers Union, County Landowners Association and Farmers Union of Wales (WOAD, FUW and CLA to author). Sometimes the Welsh Office even established its own policy network. Farrell and Law (1995, p. 7) identified the development of a Welsh educational 'quangocracy' by the Welsh Office which it used to deviate from educational policy in England over areas such as curriculum development and the establishment of Grant Maintained Schools.

The Village structure meant that civil servants and Village officials often knew each other on first name terms (Welsh Office officials to author). Regular contact ensured that good working relationships developed. These close interpersonal relationships were critical to cementing any policy network (Wilks and Wright, 1987, p. 278). In general, officers came to feel that the Welsh Office was very approachable, in contrast to their experience of other departments in Whitehall. One senior local government official interviewed stated that:

> 'Whitehall consultants were amazed at the ease of access to the Welsh Office and the close relationships that existed between officers and officials . . . we can visit the Welsh Office at virtually any time, just by ringing first (senior local government official to author).'

Village inhabitants described this close knit network as advantageous to all those concerned. It allowed them to both gather information and develop ideas quickly. They could use the arguments provided by the Village in funding battles within Whitehall, and to obtain beneficial amendments for Wales in new legislation (Welsh Office officials to author). For the Village officers it acted as an important addition to their own internal inter-organisational networking system. The Welsh Office provided a format for Village members to link to other parts of the Cathays Park Village network. If Member A had a problem that neither they nor the

Welsh Office knew how to solve, then they could be passed onto Member B or C, who would give the appropriate advice. The need to go outside the Village was therefore rare. This network also enabled many officers to test out the viability of new ideas or to exchange information, which consequently proved useful to the development of their own organisation's objectives.

The development of the territorial policy community was significantly enhanced by the fact that for the majority of the 1980s and 1990s a Conservative government was involved in creating and implementing government policy in a country that was traditionally non- Conservative. If policy making was to take on at least the appearance of a democratic nature then the non-Conservative majority in Wales had to be involved in the policy making process to some extent. The closeness and plurality of the territorial policy community during this period sometimes even surprises those that were at its heart. In the early 1980s, for instance, the relationship between the Wales TUC and the then Welsh Secretary Nicholas Edwards was very good. Outside Wales, the Conservative government and the trade union movement were locked in a bitter battle over the implementation of a series of trade union laws. But at the same time, the leader of the Wales TUC was accompanying the Welsh Secretary on overseas trade missions, both trying to lure inward investment into Wales. Nicholas Edwards even requested advice from the Wales TUC on how the Welsh Office budget should be allocated, but this step was deemed by the Wales TUC to be getting too close to the Conservative governments and they declined the offer (Jenkins to author).

Section 8.2. The occupants of the Cathays Park Village

As already indicated the Cathays Park Village had within it many of the policy influences we have already examined, such as the political parties, the media, think tanks and representatives from Europe. It also encompassed far wider elements. Since the creation of the Welsh Office, most UK-wide organisations, such as the CBI and TUC, had established either a Welsh branch or a separate division in Wales, normally located in Cardiff (Boyne et al, 1991, pp. 9–10). They were attracted by the Welsh Office's wide remit. In the case of the Institute of Directors (IOD), for example, apart from tax raising issues, the Welsh Office coverd the vast majority of their remit within Wales (Lewis to author). This factor was also true for nearly all of the other members of the Cathays Park Village.

This community, over time, developed its own sense of identity and purpose, often far removed from that of England's (Boyne et al, 1991, pp. 9–10). In turn the Welsh Office bolstered the development of this community. Conservative governments encouraged it in order to implement their own policies in a Labour-dominated Wales. The Welsh Office had seen it as a way of developing its own autonomy away from the dominance of Whitehall. All the Welsh Secretaries encouraged the development of this community in Wales, often as part of their own personal agendas (author's interviews with former Welsh Secretaries/ ministers and Welsh Office officials). This section analyses how this Village interacted and formed its own internal policy networking systems.

Within the Village, members operated what was described by them as an 'open door policy' to each other (author interviews). Many of the groups within the Village could also be representatives of further sub-groupings. The Wales TUC, within the Village for example, represented the interests of affiliated trade unions throughout Wales. These representative groupings consequently exerted formal and informal pressure on behalf of their members when dealing with the Welsh Office. The main inhabitants of the Village are illustrated in Figure 8.1.

It was the Cathays Park Village that also played a central part in maintaining distinct Welsh Office policy. The journalist Chris Baur wrote of the Scottish elite in 1978 that 'they all knew each other – a tight circle of politicians, businessmen, civil servants, lawyers, trade unionists, churchmen, academics, and a nostalgic sprinkling of titled gentry. They fix the nation's agenda' (cited in Brown et al, 1996, p. 96). Not all of the Cathays Park Village had the same status or relationship with the Welsh Office, however. The Villagers could be categorised into four distinct groupings, each according to their closeness to the Welsh Office's policy heart. Each of these categories had a differing influence on the shaping of government policy. These grouping are

1. *The outer edge of the policy periphery.* Some extra Parliamentary parties such as the Greens and Socialist Workers, nationalist pressure and cause groups such as *Cymdeithas yr Iaith Cymraeg* deliberately remained on the fringe of the Village. On matters of Welsh culture and democratic issues such as the growth of quangos they clashed frequently with the Welsh Office. Jordan and Richardson (1987, p. 193) described them as 'pressure groups' or policy lobbyist outsiders, those who were regarded as illegitimate to the Welsh Office's policy goal/strategy mix. Through their direct action campaigning on

Figure 8.1
The main inhabitants of the 'Cathays Park Village'

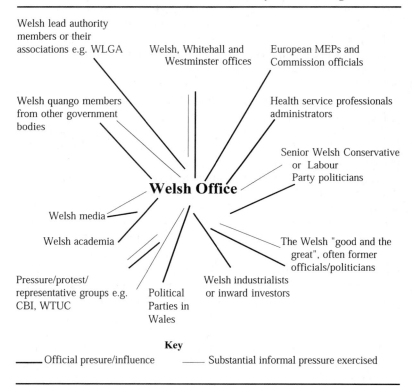

Welsh lead authority members or their associations e.g. WLGA

Welsh, Whitehall and Westminster offices

European MEPs and Commission officials

Welsh quango members from other government bodies

Health service professionals administrators

Welsh Office

Senior Welsh Conservative or Labour Party politicians

Welsh media

Welsh academia

Pressure/protest/ representative groups e.g. CBI, WTUC

Political Parties in Wales

Welsh industrialists or inward investors

The Welsh "good and the great", often former officials/politicians

Key

———— Official presure/influence ——— Substantial informal pressure exercised

language issues, *Cymdeithas yr Iaith Cymraeg* kept both the Conservative run Welsh Office and Welsh Secretary away from the National Eisteddfod for a decade (1987–1997). They also attempted to storm the Welsh Office building itself on several occasions during this period. Their ultimate aim, however, like much of the rest of the community, was to alter or create new Welsh Office policies, in this case concerning the use of the Welsh language.

2. *The inner edge of the policy periphery.* This section of the community had a fair degree of policy autonomy. Its members consisted mainly of the Welsh local authorities, and academic institutions and some pressure groups. All had clashed with the Welsh Office over

policy issues at one time or another, but they had some direct connection with the Welsh Office. Shelter Cymru and Friends of the Earth Cymru, for example, both had some administrative costs paid for directly by the Welsh Office (Shelter Cymru and Friends of the Earth Cymru to author). The Wales TUC and the Institute of Directors had similarly received grants from the Welsh Office (Jenkins and Lewis to author), although it was evident that this in no way compromised their own independence on policy issues.

3. *The outer rim of the Welsh Office policy machine.* These community members received most of their funding from the Welsh Office, which in turn had more control over their direction, aims and targets. The Welsh Development Agency was created in order to implement Welsh Secretaries' economic policies for Wales (Morgan and Henderson, 1997, p. 82). The NHS in Wales and the majority of Welsh quangos were in this outer rim group. They often contributed directly to the Welsh Office policy creation process or took part it fulfilling its policy aims and the Welsh Office was responsible for their existence.

4. *The inner rim of the Welsh Office policy machine.* This section of the community was set up exclusively to fulfil a Welsh Office task. One example was the executive agency Cadw, which dealt with historic monuments. Although they were on the edge of the formal Welsh Office structure, nearly their entire funding and policy interaction was directly with the Welsh Office.

Section 8.3 The failings of the Cathays Park Village

Within a few years of the Welsh Office's establishment the Western Mail was highlighting the extent of the quangocracy in Wales and fact that the 1072 appointments to Welsh quangos came from one man – the Welsh Secretary (Western Mail 19/10/68). There was also much concern the appointments were coming from a very small 'pool of talent'. This caused George Thomas to note that:

'For as long as I was in the department one of our biggest worries, and one about which the Civil Service kept complaining, was that the pool of talent was so limited. I was worried because I thought our goldfish bowl was small and we had the same fat goldfish swimming around all the time. (Western Mail 20/4/72)'

These problems did not go away and the Conservatives used this small pool for developing a Welsh Territorial policy community which it needed to implement policy in a country that was politically dominated by their Labour opponents. Conservative Welsh Secretaries sought to ensure that as far as possible those elements of the Cathays Park Village that could be made to work closely with them were brought further into the fold. The element of the community which they were able to manipulate to the greatest extent was the Non Departmental Public Bodies (NDPBs) or quangos. The Welsh Office did this in a number of ways:

Appointments

Welsh quangos, like those in the rest of the UK, were controlled by boards of unelected appointees, appointed by the Welsh Secretary. In 1974 the *Western Mail* gave details of five men[2] which it said were the ruling clique that ran the Welsh establishment. Twenty years later Morgan and Ellis produced another list which showed that similar *Quango Kings* were still around. Sir Geoffrey Inkin, for example, a former Conservative Party parliamentary candidate, was Chairman of both the Land Authority for Wales and the Cardiff Bay Development Corporation.

Most of the quango boards during the Welsh Office's history consisted mainly of 'white, middle class, businessmen with Conservative leanings' (Morgan and Ellis, 1993, p. 24). There were clear examples of former or future Labour and Conservative politicians running Welsh quangos. The list included the Cardiff Bay Development Corporation, the WDA, the DBRW, South Glamorgan Health Authority, the Welsh Consumer Association and numerous TECs, and Health Trusts (Morgan and Ellis, 1993, p. 24). By appointing their own people, Welsh Secretaries could be sure that these quangos were brought closer to their own policy ideas, they also acted as rewards and refuges for their political friends.

Needless to say, the appointments system, at various time in the Welsh Office's history, received sustained criticism from those who were opposed to it. In the 1990s Russell Goodway, Labour Leader of Cardiff County Council and a quango board member himself, stated that Welsh quangos were '1,400 people whose basic qualification was membership or support of the Conservative Party' (BBC TV, February 1994). Ron Davies, as Shadow Welsh Secretary, described the appointment of quango board members as one in which Conservative *'placemen* were parachuted in to run public affairs' (Morgan and Ellis, 1993, p. 27). From 1995, however, the appointment process became more public. Instead of the Conservative Welsh Secretaries secretly nominating their own preferred board members to these quangos, by 1997 around 1,000 of the 3,000 names on the Welsh Office's Public Appointments Register had now been appointed in response to advertisements for applicants in Welsh newspapers (Welsh Office to author).

Direct control

Over its history the Welsh Office set out various rules and regulations which were meant to keep the Village quangos under control. Kevin Morgan and Ellis Roberts, in their study on Welsh quangos, provided the details of the regulations which the Welsh Office imposed on these bodies (Morgan and Ellis, 1993, p. 28):

- NDPBs were established within a clear policy context, usually following legislation, and which provided their remit;
- NDPBs framed their corporate plans in accordance with Welsh Office policy; these were submitted annually to the Welsh Office in draft form for approval;
- in the majority of cases the Chairman and Boards were appointed by the Secretary of State, who regularly met individual chairmen;
- the Welsh Office had regular meetings with NDPB chief executives and finance officers, and there were said to be frequent opportunities to discuss policy direction;
- every five years each executive NDPB was subject to a Financial Management and Policy Review (FMPR) which, among other things, reviewed the need for the NDPB and examined all areas of its activity.

Despite this monitoring there was a series of critical reports in the 1990s by the Public Accounts Committee, the Welsh Affairs Select Committee and the National Audit Office concerning the Welsh Office's monitoring of its quangos. The majority of criticism was reserved for two quangos: the Welsh Development Agency (WDA) and the Development Board for Rural Wales (DBRW). The reports on both quangos was damning and saw 'heads roll' in both organisations. They brought a number of problems to the public's attention. These included:

- Many millions of pounds spent on unauthorised redundancy payments

(Local Government Chronicle, 22/10/93, p. 6).

- There were irregular payments to members on a car leasing scheme (Western Mail, 13/5/94, p. 5).
- The employment of a convicted fraudster as Marketing Director of the WDA (Morgan and Ellis, 1993, p. 28).
- Several irregular retirement packages, amounting to around £½ million, to quango members (Morgan and Ellis, 1993, p. 28).

When John Redwood was appointed in May 1993, the Welsh media was beginning to uncover more and more stories concerning the lack of probity in Welsh quangos. The *Western Mail* started to run a series of 'quango scandal' stories as its leading stories. The public's attitude, which in the 1960s, 1970s and 1980s had been favourable or indifferent to quangos (as some quangos such as the WDA appeared to bring Wales economic success), changed. Various Commons Committees and the National Audit Office then uncovered more Welsh quango 'horror stories'. Both the media and the Opposition started to demand change, something which John Redwood, a politician in the Thatcherite mould, seemed happy to do. Within two months of his appointment he had summoned the major quango bosses to Whitehall to 'read them the riot act', as the *Western Mail* later described it (Western Mail 30/7/93, p. 1). This was followed up a week later by a letter to the quango bosses that stated (Letter from Redwood to Welsh Quango Chairmen, 9/8/93):

> '. . . government and public bodies owe it to the taxpayer to conduct their affairs in ways which give the very best return for the money which they spend, and were seen to keep good control over costs and use of assets . . . The public had the right to expect all those of us . . . to maintain the highest standards of probity and fairness, and to carry out their activities in an open way. As Secretary of State I am answerable to Parliament for what happens in NDPBs in Wales; your Chief Executive and the Permanent Secretary here also had clear accountability for the proper stewardship of public funds.'

After this a number if changes became apparent:

1. *Resignations over lack of probity.* Five senior officers at the DBRW, WDA, South Glamorgan Health Authority and Health Promotion Wales resigned after Mr Redwood's appointment, over matters relating to breach of probity (Western Mail, 4/2/94 p. 2, and Western Mail, 13/5/94, p. 5).

2. *Shake-ups.* The WDA and DBRW, underwent significant 'shake-ups', which resulted in some of the latter's functions being transferred to local government. The DBRW only escaped total merger with the WDA because time could not be found for the necessary legislation to go through Parliament. Ron Davies, however, did ensure that it was merged together with the LAW and WDA to form one super economic quango in Wales.

3. *Deceleration in expansion.* The increase in quango administrators, such as those in the Welsh NHS, and the Welsh Office and local government sponsored quangos, was halted (Deacon and Deacon, 1994, p. 5). Linked to this was a cut in the quangos' budgets. In the 1995/96 Welsh Office budget allocation, Redwood halved fiscal support for the WDA and DBRW, cut Tai Cymru's budget by 20 per cent, and required administrative cuts across a number of Welsh quangos (Western Mail, 15/12/94, p. 6).

4. *Production by Redwood of a public list of all Welsh quango members.* This measure was undertaken despite the fact that no similar lists were made available in Scotland or England (BBC TV, 5/6/95).

5. *Tightening the rules on patronage.* The political affiliations of quango appointees were revealed, if the Welsh Secretary deemed it to be relevant to the appointment. The Welsh Office also publicly advertised quango board positions.

6. *The allowance of greater democratic accountability than in England.* The government planned to turn the local authority controlled National Parks into semi-quangos, with half of the members of these Park Authorities being from unelected bodies. Redwood made sure that this figure was limited to a third of the Boards, in Wales' three National Parks (Western Mail 30/6/95, p. 9).

Redwood was the first Conservative in Wales to attempt to cull the growth of quangos, a record that he used in his unsuccessful leadership bid in 1995, although he still made use of them in the implementation of his own party's policy agenda. The Nolan Commission on 'Standards in Public Life' in 1996 did much to tighten up the running of Welsh quangos by setting minimum standards (HMSO, 1995A). To those outside of the Conservative Party, however, the scandals in Welsh quangos proved a useful drum to beat in their campaign for a Yes Vote in the Welsh referendum. Labour, Liberal Democrats and Plaid Cymru had made it clear that a Welsh Assembly/Senedd/Parliament would help solve the quango problem for good (Wales Labour Party, 1995A, 1996A, Liberal

Democrats Wales, 1996, and Plaid Cymru, 1995). Although Labour did scrap some quangos such as Tai Cymru and Health Promotion Wales and merge others together such as the WDA, LAW and DBRW many others still remained, under the control of the new Assembly.

The influence of the inner edge of the policy periphery on the policy creation process

When Welsh Secretaries wanted to make policy in a pluralistic setting, they would ensure that the Welsh Office consulted those Village members on the inner and outer edge of the Village on forthcoming legislative and policy initiatives. These members in the Village had, in theory, the chance to give their views on new policy or policy reviews, and to state how they should be shaped to reflect their own interests. Welsh Secretaries such as Nicholas Edwards, Peter Walker and David Hunt consulted widely in order to achieve, or at least appear to achieve, a degree of consensus amongst those elements of the Village where this was required.

Tewdwr Jones (1997) noted that the "Welsh Office was juxtaposed between operating within an institutional framework widely recognised as 'British', while protecting territorial and cultural concerns that were acutely 'Welsh' " (pp. 59–60). This meant that groups who possessed a defined political viewpoint against a British policy were sometimes alienated from the Welsh Office policy process. As the Conservative government reached its second decade of power in Wales, it frequently went over the heads of the Village community on the inner and outer edge of the policy making periphery, and against the vast majority of Welsh public opinion. For instance, on the policy of the opting out of schools from local authority control a number of ballots were held in which parents soundly defeated opting out proposals. On the pretext of irregularities the Welsh Office ordered reruns of the voting which still resulted in a 'no' vote. Similarly the Welsh Office planned the introduction of the nursery voucher scheme, something that was opposed by all 22 unitary authorities. In addition to trying to enforce unpopular policies, increased fiscal restraint caused what Rhodes and Marsh describe as 'economic catalysts for change' in the relationship between the Welsh Office and local government in Wales (Rhodes and Marsh, 1992, p. 194). As the Welsh Office's settlement grant became less generous, so Welsh local government relations with the Welsh Office worsened. In 1996 Welsh local authorities withdrew from the process of consultation with the Welsh

Office on the financing of local government, there were frequent public rows in public between local government and the Welsh Office over issues of policy (Welsh Local Government Association, 1996, p. 5). These events signalled the worst period in central/local government relations in Wales since the Welsh Office's foundation in 1964.

Those on the inner edge of the policy periphery had become increasingly disillusioned with its relationship with the Welsh Office. Paul Griffith of the Welsh Local Government Association described the way the Welsh Office operated as 'highly ritualistic, (where) the decisions that were first thought of were always carried through' (Griffiths, 16/6/95). Mari James referred to the consultation process as 'being merely a legitimisation of control' (James, 16/6/95). It was the policy consultation process which appeared to emphasise the extent of the 'partnership imbalance' that existed between the Welsh Office and some Village members. It was seen by some as a one way traffic of ideas flowing down from the Welsh Office (Davies, J to author).

Rhodes (1997, p. 149) noted that in the distribution of European structural funds the Welsh Office tended to act in a more confrontational fashion when dealing with local government than did the Scottish Office. In May 1996 the Welsh Local Government Association produced a damning report concerning its relationship with the Welsh Office. In it they stated that:

'More often Welsh local government finds that Welsh Office ministers have their own political objectives and instead of being a conduit for the expression of Welsh interests they become a filter for or a barrier to such expression. The expression of interests which benefit Wales is undertaken selectively and unenthusiastically' (Welsh Local Government Association, 1996).

Similarly Morgan and Handerson noted that:

'Many of the partners see partnership in a horizontal sense in which equal partners work towards common ends. Central government has tended to view partnership in vertical terms in which the Welsh Office plays the decisive role with any alternative model viewed as unacceptable' (Morgan and Henderson, 1997, p. 95).

Even when the Welsh Office did open up the policy process to new ideas, it was felt by some Village members that there was a tendency to ignore issues relating to policy principles, and instead attention was paid only to issues concerning the actual practicalities of implementing any proposals. It was thought by some Village members that the reason behind this may have been political, or merely the civil service concept of political neutrality.

Village members adapting to an autocratic Welsh Office

Prior to the arrival of the Welsh Assembly there was only one full-time professional lobbyist in Wales (Ingham, 30/1/95). Consequently the Cathays Park Village members became adept at undertaking their own lobbying. As the Welsh Secretary and Welsh Office officials normally had an 'open door policy', there was little problem with direct access for lobbying purposes. The majority of lobbying that was undertaken was around the area of increased fiscal resourcing or additional powers for Village members.

As the Conservative Welsh Office and Welsh Secretary became adept at avoiding commitment, Village members learnt to tailor their requests to suit the ideological position of the Conservatives (Stone and Griffith, P to author). Thus if *Shelter Cymru* (pressure group for the homeless) required an increase in social housing it would lobby for an increase in the grant aid to be given to housing trusts, rather than given to local authority housing departments. They were aware that the Welsh Office wished to reduce the amount of local authority housing. Thus their aims had to be achieved through Welsh Office approved housing associations.

All Conservative Welsh Secretaries had fostered a particularly close relationship with Wales' business community. As a result many prominent businessmen had found their way onto the boards of Welsh quangos, helping to implement Welsh Office policy. The Welsh Secretary also supported the Welsh business community directly. He had frequent meetings and made appearances in support of the Welsh region of the Confederation of British Industry (CBI), Institute of Directors (IOD), and Cardiff Business Club. This did not mean that businessmen were always listened to. For example, the Wales CBI's desire for eight unitary authorities at local government level was ignored (Haywood to author). Nevertheless their advice was still keenly sought. One of the main economic proposals in David Hunt's 1992 Conservative Party Manifesto for Wales concerned putting this relationship on a more formal setting, by the construction of the Welsh Economic Council (WEC). The WEC's aim was 'to establish and further sound economic foundations for the future of Wales' (Conservative Manifesto, 1992, p. 5). The WEC eventually saw light under John Redwood who chaired it at regular intervals. It incorporated members from the WTUC, Welsh CBI, WDA and TECs with various other Welsh public bodies attending. Described as being a little Neddy[3], there was seldom a formal agenda and meetings therefore tended to be very informal, with a report issued of what had been discussed but with no views attributed (Jenkins to author). This gave it the reputation of a powerless talking shop, and indeed there was little heard of it after establishment, but it remained a key ideological pointer.

Conclusion

Part of the main reason that Welsh Office policy sometimes evolved differently to that in England was that it developed its own policy community to support it, the 'Cathays Park Village'. Though the extent to which this Village was a true policy community may be questionable, it nevertheless played an important role in the Welsh Office policy process. It was this Village that the Welsh Office consulted, was lobbied by, was served by and sought to serve, when creating its policy for Wales.

Two models of the policy process highlight the relevance of the policy community that surrounded the Welsh Office. The pluralist model of society assumes that policy was dispersed in society to various interest groups which comprise it – business, labour, agriculture and so on. These bodies 'make themselves heard at some critical stage in the policy process of decision' (Jordon and Richardson, 1987, p. 16). The corporatist model of policy making assumes there to be an alliance between ministers, civil servants and the leaders of pressure groups in which the latter were given a central role in the policy making process (Jones, 1997, p. 450). Neither of these models easily defined the Welsh Office's relationship with the territorial policy community. The fact that the Welsh Office could readily ignore some key aspects of the policy community such as local government or the Wales TUC and CBI seems to indicate that both the pluralist and corporatist models did not readily apply.

The territorial policy community developed partially because Conservative governments had lacked the necessary democratic mandates at a Welsh Parliamentary and local government level to implement their policies directly. Therefore a territorial policy community had developed to supplement their failings and enhance the legitimacy of the policy-making process. Within the Welsh quangos Labour and then

Conservative governments made sure that their key supporters often chaired these bodies to ensure that their policies would receive a sympathetic hearing and be readily implemented.

The Welsh Office, through the power of primary and secondary legislation, had the ability to mould policy to the desires of the territorial policy community in Wales. Towards the end of the Major government some aspects of this community, such as local government, spent more time fighting the elements of policy they did not desire than combining with the Welsh Office in order to shape the policy that they did want. This consultation process, was sometimes little more than an exercise in legitimising Welsh Office domination. The overall history of the Welsh Office, however, was one in which there were numerous of examples of policies shaped to suit the Welsh territorial policy community.

Notes

1. This section makes great use of those interviews conducted with members of the Cathays Park Village. This includes organisations such as the: Institute of Directors, Wales CBI, Wales TUC, Welsh local government, the four main political parties in Wales, farming and industry trade unions, University of Wales and the Welsh academic and media community. Where there is no direct reference for a particular point it comes from this interview pool.
2. The men were Sir Ben Bowen Thomas, Lord Heycock, T. Mervyn Jones, Dr Alun Oldfield-Davies and Col. W.R. Crawshay
3. 'Neddy' comes from the acronym for the Labour government's National Economic Development Council (NEDC) now disbanded.

Chapter IX

The Welsh Office and the Policy Process in Action:– The Establishment and Development of a National Curriculum for Wales

Introduction

The previous chapters have illustrated the role played by different policy actors and groups in the Welsh policy process, a process that developed over time. This chapter sets out to provide a clear example of how these different parties interacted in order to produce a set of policy outcomes. Chapter I indicated that some of the clearest examples of the Welsh Office and the surrounding policy community determining policies different from those in the rest of the UK were in the field of education policy. It is therefore fitting that this chapter examines the part the Welsh policy community played in establishing and developing a National Curriculum for Wales.

The first section draws on previous chapters of the book and summarises how policy was made at the Welsh Office. It examines the role played by both those inside and outside of the Welsh Office. In particular, it examines the role of the educational policy community within the Cathays Park Village. The literature written on policy communities is also reviewed to see whether it can provide any indication as to how policy was made in a Welsh context.

Although elements of Welsh educational policy were always unique, it was only in the 1990s that this emerged to a significant degree (Jones, G.E., 1997). The period prior to the introduction of the National Curriculum in Wales is explained in the second section. This period was important in that it was during this time that the Welsh Office and the surrounding educational policy community began to develop to the extent that it could specifically anticipate distinctive Welsh policy outcomes.

The opportunity to determine a specifically Welsh policy agenda in primary and secondary education, however, began with the Education Reform Bill (Act) of 1988. This is examined in the third section, along with the interactions within the Welsh Office policy community during the initial construction of the National Curriculum in Wales.

Once the consultation process on the National Curriculum in Wales was started, great emphasis was laid on co-operation between the Welsh Office and interested parties. The fourth section assesses the input to the policy process. It explores the impact of the education working groups, which were established by the Welsh Office, and contained key members of the educational policy networks. The section goes on to examine the factors behind the determination of Welsh language education policy and the overall strength of the consultation process.

The fifth section details the educational policy output which evolved from the consultation process and the operation of the working groups. In particular, the section examines the consultation output in Welsh language policies in education and also details the determination of the so-called 'Curriculum Cymreig'.

The final section assesses the National Curriculum in Wales as an example of the broader engagement of the wider policy community. It examines how this specific policy area provides a clear example of the Welsh Office and the policy process in action. The section also details how the National Curriculum in Wales still had repercussions in popular party politics some ten years after it first arrived on the scene in Wales.

Section 9.1. The major influences on Welsh Office policy creation

In Chapter I it was noted that Jones (1996) was the model used to ascertain the closeness of policy groupings to the policy centre. The following chapters examined the influence of each of these groupings on the policy process within the Welsh Office. This section therefore summarises the influence of each of Jones's adapted groupings on the Welsh Office and the policy process.

Those actors or groups who were connected to the policy process at the Welsh Office were:

1. At the policy core the Prime Minister, Cabinet (Welsh Secretary), Cabinet Office and Policy Unit.
2. Policy actors of secondary importance – ministers, civil servants, inquiries, key economic groupings and think tanks.

3. Next in importance in determining Welsh Office policy output were those policy actors associated with legislatures.
4. The final major link was the territorial policy community.

The remainder of this section examines these groupings in greater detail.

At the policy core – Chapters II to IV illustrated that at the policy core were the Prime Minister, Cabinet, Cabinet Office and Policy Unit. Chapter II indicated that the Prime Minister was the key determinant of policy, although theoretically he also needed the consent of the Cabinet in order to determine policy fully. The Prime Minister determined who the Welsh Secretary was, what Cabinet committees he sat on, the government's political agenda and the parliamentary timetable. The Prime Minister and the Cabinet also determined the exact remit of the Welsh Secretary's policy arena.

Sometimes the European Union tied the Prime Minister and the Cabinet's hands on issues of policy such as agriculture or environment, which were then passed on to the Welsh Office. The Cabinet also determined Welsh Office spending through the Treasury 'block grant' and the Barnett formula. This, and the fact that Welsh Office spending plans had a three to four year advance timetable, were perhaps the greatest influence on the Welsh Secretary's own policy determination. He could only plan new policies which had spending commitments, when money was not already allocated or if he had won additional resources from the Treasury.

Chapter III noted that the Welsh Secretary was regarded by academics and those in Whitehall as probably the least influential member of the Cabinet. His more senior colleagues, therefore, tended to have a greater influence on policy, even if this affected Wales directly. There was also evidence to indicate that sometimes Welsh Secretaries' views were ignored in Cabinet, and at times they were not even consulted on Welsh matters. Despite this, the Welsh Secretary remained the most important senior policy actor in regular contact with the Welsh Office and the conduit through which all internal Welsh Office policy creation had to flow. The Welsh Secretary could either accept or reject policy initiatives from all other actors in the Welsh Office policy process. As for his own policy creation activities, a strong Welsh Secretary could continually test the boundaries of Welsh Office policy making. A weak Welsh Secretary merely caused the Welsh Office policy machine to slip into second or third gear and to produce mirror images of Whitehall policy output.

Policy actors of secondary importance – Chapters III and V indicated that next in importance for policy determinations were ministers, civil servants, inquiries, key economic groupings and thinktanks. These chapters pointed to the limited impact of inquiries and think tanks on the Welsh Office policy process, although it did not dismiss them entirely and noted the particular importance of bodies such as the Institute for Welsh Affairs. Ministers and civil servants, however, had a greater influence on the Welsh Office policy process. Ministers stated that their influence was normally only curtailed by the Welsh Secretary or by advice from their civil servants. The policy influence of the special advisors and Parliamentary Private Secretaries was less well documented, but was likely to vary depending upon that post holder's relationship with the Welsh Office minister they served. The civil servants' influence on the Welsh Office policy process was substantial, because they were the main source of policy advice that the minister received. In a nation such as Wales, the relatively small pool of policy expertise in most areas enhanced their power. It was the Welsh Office officials who advised whether a policy was feasible or if the government should accept amendments to its proposed policy. If this expertise was lacking then the officials had to go to another source such as their sister department in Whitehall or the surrounding policy community.

Next in importance in determining Welsh Office policy output were those policy actors associated with legislatures. Chapters VI and VII indicated that Parliament, political party sources, select committees and the Opposition had a degree of influence over Welsh Office policy output. Parliament acted as a legitimisation mechanism for Welsh Office policy through primary or secondary legislation. The Opposition had little impact on Welsh Office policy, although on occasions there were concessions to them on primary legislation. Some Parliamentary bodies, such as the Welsh Affairs Select Committee and the Parliamentary Affairs Committee, were also able to influence policy within the Welsh Office policy process. Other Parliamentary mechanisms, such as the Welsh Grand Committee and Welsh Question Time, had virtually no impact in either altering Welsh Office policy or holding it to account. There was little indication that party sources influenced Welsh Office day to day policy issues which were determined by the ministers.

The final major link in the policy process was *the territorial policy community*, the so-called 'Cathays Park Village'. Chapter VIII noted that this was used by the Welsh Office to bolster its own policy output. This Village was consulted constantly on issues of policy making in the past, but in the last years of the Major government there was substantial evidence to indicate that the Welsh Office ignored the advice of the Village and that its influence on the policy process diminished.

The concept and influence of policy communities has become increasingly evident in much of the literature on policy making in the UK (Rhodes 1992, 1996, Rhodes and Marsh 1992, and Marsh 1998). While many of these studies are concerned with dynamic and changing phenomena, they do not offer many reflections on this process, such as how these policy actors achieve central positions in the community?

In addition there is little academic literature on the operation of territorial policy communities such as the Cathays Park Village. The main sources of information concerning the operations of the former territorial policy communities, are case studies such as Connolly and Knox's (1991) study of Housing Policy in Northern Ireland, or Keating and Carter's (1987) study of the Scottish Office's development of Cumbernald Newtown. These, however, are more useful as historical records of how policy developed, rather than political science models of their operation. There are no extensive studies of how the Cathays Park Village operated in the policy determination process: therefore the extent to which the educational policy community in Wales could have been categorised as a true policy community is unknown. In the absence of more concise data, however, the Cathays Park Village is referred to as a (territorial) policy community throughout this chapter.

Thus the study so far has indicated that the Welsh Office could create and provide its own policy agenda. The book has illustrated that the whole policy process depended upon the status and nature of the Welsh Secretary. Although Welsh Secretaries were often tied to their predecessors' policies or to those determined by the Cabinet, they did have tremendous scope to facilitate and determine the Welsh Office's policy agenda. Once they determined a particular policy path to follow, it was often up to the Welsh policy community to flesh out the bones. The rest of this chapter tests this theory in the context of the development of a Welsh version of the National Curriculum.

Section 9.2. The background to the changes

In 1988 the Welsh Office detailed plans to develop the National Curriculum in Wales. Over the next few years the Welsh Office, and the education policy community surrounding it, developed a 'Curriculum

Cymreig'. This provided substantial elements of a unique Welsh curriculum, differing in many aspects to the National Curriculum in England. This section examines the background to the introduction of the National Curriculum in Wales, and the development of the educational policy community that aided the Welsh Office in establishing it.

Variations in educational policy in Wales were first evident after the introduction of the 1889 Welsh Intermediate Education Act (Wales). This introduced a system of secondary schooling that was unique to Wales (Jones, G.E., 1990, p. 192). This system, however, was repealed by the 1944 Education Act. From this date onwards the secondary and primary system in Wales was closely modelled on what occurred in England.

There was no distinct Welsh educational policy community in the post-war years. The pattern of educational policy making in this period was defined by Bogdanor:

'The process of elite accommodation reached its apogee during the post-war period when, so it was believed, many policy decisions in education were taken over lunch at the National Liberal Club by a troika consisting of Sir William Alexander, Secretary of the Association of Education Committees, Sir Ronald Gould, General Secretary of the National Union of Teachers, and the Permanent Secretary at the Department of Education. If these three agreed on some item of educational policy, it would more often than not be implemented' (Bogdanor, 1979, p. 161).

From the start of the 1960s, however, power began to shift from the centre to the Local Education Authorities (LEAs) [Rhodes, 1992, p. 257]. The educational system in Wales, like that in England, was firmly under the control of the LEAs (Jones, G.E., 1990). As local government was mainly Labour controlled in Wales, policies that occurred in England were followed in Wales with some socialist zeal (Jones, G.E., 1990, p. 193). Thus the introduction of the comprehensive system was implemented with particular enthusiasm in Wales. The year 1979, for instance, saw the removal of all but three grammar schools – and even these disappeared shortly afterwards – whereas even today in England some areas still retain grammar schools (Jones, G.E., 1990, p. 193). In practice, however, there were few significant policy differences between England and Wales. Those differences that did occur were in the way that policy was implemented. In Wales these concerned the position of the Welsh language and cultural tradition in the local curricula. The general curricula, however, was hardly any different from that taught in schools throughout England (Phillips, 1996).

Although the Welsh Office political actors had the right to deviate on educational policy from 1970, they did not do so (Jones, G.E., 1990). As was seen in Chapter IV, the Welsh Secretary and his junior Ministers sat on the Cabinet Subcommittees that dealt with Education. They acted more as a barrier to English educational reform totally encompassing Wales, than as a mechanism for determining distinctly Welsh educational policy (Farrell and Law, 1995, p. 6). But even attempts to filter English educational policy were heavily muted. The Welsh Office and the Welsh educational establishments were, in essence, a mere shadow of the Department of Education and Science (DES) during the 1970s and most of the 1980s. It was the DES that was 'the most important single force' at the centre of the educational policy community for England and Wales (Rhodes, 1992, p. 258).

Besides the DES, the other important actors in the policy process were the local education authorities (LEAs), through the associations (in Wales this meant the WJEC), and the teachers' unions. Lodge and Blackstone (1982, p. 40) saw these other actors as being pre-eminent 'amongst' the small fraction of the formally defined constituency of educational government who are consulted'. As most of the power over educational change remained within the DES, the Welsh educational policy community of the 1970s and 1980s was still very limited in its influence.

The development of a Welsh Education Policy Community

Although the Welsh Office was subservient to the DES for much of its history, it did however help develop an educational policy community of its own. Chapter VII cited the work of Rhodes and Marsh (1992) who noted that when Welsh Office policy creation or implementation moved onto more specific or definite issues, the Cathays Park Village broke down into even smaller policy issue networks. As seen in previous chapters, the policy process was structured into a number of groupings. By the end of the 1980s the educational policy community (or territorial community) could be clearly defined as encompassing:

Political actors: The key political actors were the Welsh Secretary Peter Walker and his junior minister, Sir Wyn Roberts, who held the education portfolio. As seen in Section I, it was these political actors who often determined the 'seeds of policy', which the other actors in the policy community helped grow into fully fledged ideas. Peter Walker advocated a 'Toryism of partnership, political consensus and public spending and tended to cultivate public opinion' (Snicker, 1998, p. 142). Walker, unusually for Welsh Secretaries, also held high status within the Cabinet, being ranked as number eight (Walker, 1990). The other key political actor, Sir Wyn Roberts, had, like Walker, gained considerable stature in Wales as a politician, both inside and outside of his party.

The Welsh Office officials: in 1970 the Welsh Office was given direct responsibility for primary and secondary education in Wales. By the late 1980s it had only built up a staff of around 70 covering all aspects of educational policy in Wales (Jones, Barry, 1988), whilst the DES had some 2,500 staff (Hennessy, 1989, p. 426). The low level of specialised staff within the Welsh Office clearly indicated that any widespread autonomous policy changes in Wales would need to engage specialised support from outside of the Welsh Office.

The Cathays Park Village. A number of professional bodies or trade unions had established themselves around the Welsh Office, which had the side effect of enhancing the size of the Welsh educational policy community. Boyne et al (1991, p. 9) described the 'Welshification' of educational policy groups in Wales, with branches of the National Union of Teachers and National Schoolmasters and the Union of Women Teachers strengthening their operations in Wales. There were also two important committees connecting local government education authorities to Cathays Park Village. These were:

1. The *Welsh Joint Education Committee* (WJEC). This committee, established by Statutory Order, was constituted by representatives of the LEA Education Committees in Wales. It provided a forum for educational debate within Wales, and was entrusted with the devising of subject syllabuses and the conducting of public examinations based upon them (Jones, P.E., 1988, p. 99).
2. The *Pwyllgor Datblygu Addysg Gymraeg* (PDAG) [The Welsh Language Educational Development Committee]. This brought together local government and the Welsh Office in order to formulate Welsh language educational policy. Its work is defined in greater detail later in this chapter.

This 'Welshification' of educational policy groups in Wales, together with the establishment of joint bodies for these policy groups to produce output provided a classic example of a developing policy community (Rhodes, 1997, p. 38).

Shaping of events in Wales

Authors such as Jones (1988) and Reynolds (1989) note that, although the Welsh Educational Policy Community during the 1970s and 1980s tended to be reactive rather than proactive to changes in education, it was nevertheless growing in power. The issues in which the community was able to develop and expand itself revolved around 'Welsh language education' and the issue of 'standards of education'. The education policy community was developed in response to the need for policy action. This section explores the events prior to the 1988 Education Act, which enabled an expansion of the policy community to occur in Wales.

Welsh language education

The Welsh language had, for some decades, been an extremely volatile political issue for those Welsh politicians who served at the Welsh Office (Roberts, W., 1995, pp. 4–8). It was this issue that concerned the Welsh Office almost from its formation, and around which a substantial Welsh policy issue network had already been established. The Welsh language was the first issue upon which the Welsh Office was to get Parliament to legislate in the 1960s. As seen earlier, the new Conservative Welsh Office (apart from the establishment of S4C) was quick to endorse the notion of supporting the Welsh language. Less than a year after coming to power in April 1980, the key political actor, Welsh Secretary (see Chapter IV), Nicholas Edwards, made a speech to Gwynedd County Council. It was entitled: 'The Welsh Language: A Commitment and Challenge', and committed both himself and his government to supporting the use of the Welsh language in schools. He said:

> 'While there are people who want to speak it, Governments will respond with the means of supporting it and giving it strength.' (Griffiths, 1986, p. 111)

As a result of Welsh Office input to the 1980 Education Act Section 21, the Welsh Secretary was able to make direct grants to Welsh LEAs for schemes designed to promote the Welsh language in education. The following year, in July 1981, the Welsh Office's discussion paper, 'Welsh in Schools', made it clear that 'every local education authority, board of governors and all of those concerned with education in schools were expected, while taking account of local needs, to implement policies which support and encourage the language' (Griffiths, 1986, p. 112). All of these developments enhanced the power and the status of the Welsh language policy community.

Despite the gradual improvement in the position of Welsh in the education system in the mid-1980s, there were some problems with the provision of Welsh medium education. The major issues which concerned the Welsh language policy community were (Williams, 1989, p. 57):

1. Even though there was a growth in Welsh language teaching, few inroads were made into reducing the number of secondary school pupils who were not taught Welsh at all. In Gwynedd virtually every secondary school pupil was taught Welsh, whereas in Gwent less than 10 per cent were.
2. The defence of a flexible programme of bilingual education at the national level was needed.
3. Gwynedd's new language policy needed to be articulated and emulated across Wales (they had adopted six models of bilingual competence for their high schools).
4. The necessary debate on the relation of providing bilingual education and other priorities, such as resources, training or curriculum development, was lacking.

It also became a concern of those in the policy community that, despite the Welsh Office putting large sums of money into the teaching of subjects through the medium of Welsh, the number taking exams in this area decreased substantially throughout the 1980s (Jones, P.E., 1988). These issues caused concern for all members of the policy community that supported maintaining the strength of the Welsh language in Wales. Particularly in the area of primary and secondary education, continued pressure was, therefore, exerted by members of the Welsh policy network, notably the LEAs, to ensure that education played its full part in the battle to save the language.

The first major step the Welsh Office and the educational policy community took to address the concern of Williams and others occurred in 1987. After consultation with LEAs and other bodies, the Welsh Office set up the Pwyllgor Datblygu Addysg Gymraeg (PDAG) [The Welsh Language Educational Development Committee]. Its remit was to examine the growing need to institute a national forum for Welsh medium education. The Welsh Office appointed a Director and two Development Officers to initiate and oversee the deliberations of several temporary working parties. They reported their initial findings which were referred on for full development by a permanent committee, comprising of 36 members drawn from representative sections of education and local government in Wales. Each working party devoted itself to one of the following sectors: nursery/primary/secondary/ tertiary, adult education, publicity and research sectors. The PDAG brought all elements of the language policy community closer together.

But the role of the PDAG was thought by some outside the mainstream of the language and education policy communities, such as Cymdeithas yr Iaith Gymreig (CIG) [the Welsh language protest group], to be too limited and too slow in its actions. CIG sought, through a campaign of direct action, to increase the role of PDAG and the promotion of Welsh-medium education (Western Mail, 2/12/87). These protests involved:

- a raid on the Conservative Party headquarters in Cardiff,
- painting slogans on the Prime Minister's (Margaret Thatcher) Finchley constituency office, and
- a sit down protest at the Conservatives London Central Office.

The campaign to increase the power of the PDAG failed, as Peter Walker refused to meet CIG whilst they engaged in direct action against him (Western Mail, 27/1/98). All parties then awaited the reporting back of the PDAG.

Improving Welsh education and developing a 'Curriculum Cymreig'

Outside of the issue of the language, political actors in Wales also regularly expressed concern about standards of education. There had been a long tradition of Welsh pupils being educationally behind their English counterparts. This became more prominent from the 1960s onwards (Jones, G.E., 1988, pp. 84–85). In 1978, stimulated by Welsh Office statistics and

HMI reports which made it clear that Welsh education was in a poorer state than that of England, the Welsh Office held the 'Mold Conference' (Reynolds, 1995a, p. 9). Here it published a series of documents highlighting the extent of educational under-achievement in Wales (Reynolds, 1995a, p. 5). In 1981 the Loosemore Report revealed that in 1977/8, 27.6 per cent of pupils left school in Wales without any qualifications. The comparative figure for England was 14.2 per cent (Jones, G.E. 1990, p. 197). Over the next decade the high levels of failure within Welsh schools continued, with standards significantly below those in England (Reynolds, 1989).

In 1987 the National Curriculum was launched in Wales, in the same year the HMI report indicated that Welsh education continued to vary between 'very poor quality and generally satisfactory'. This report saw the advent of the National Curriculum as already beginning to stimulate 'a review of all subject areas' (HMI, Wales, 1988, p. 11). It was perhaps no wonder that Professor David Reynolds dubbed the period between 1979–1989 as the 'wasted years' in Welsh education (Reynolds, 1989). Therefore, the only distinctive feature of the education system in Wales during the period 1944–88, apart from linguistic differences, was the apparent mediocrity of its educational standards (Phillips, 1996, p. 32).

While the debate concerning Welsh educational standards continued, there was little progress on the need to make the curriculum much more relevant to the history and culture of Wales. Jones noted that, from the establishment of the Welsh Department of the Board of Education in 1907 to the appointment of O.M. Edwards as its chief inspector, the government was generally indulgent in its feelings towards the Welsh language in education. Edwards saw the central subjects in Wales as being Welsh language and literature, Welsh history and the geography of Wales (Jones, G.E, 1988, p. 93). Although these subjects were taught through the medium of Welsh there was very little notion of a 'Welsh curriculum' or 'Curriculum Cymreig', between the establishment of the Board of Education and the arrival of the National Curriculum in 1988 (Phillips, 1996, p. 32). Although all Welsh LEAs and the WJEC had curriculum policy statements in respect of the Welsh language and religious education by 1988, few had curriculum policy statements on other areas of the curriculum (HMI, Wales, 1988, p. 2).

Jones noted in 1988 that:

> 'No area of the curriculum is in more need of imaginative initiatives than the Welsh dimension, involving the co-ordination of the study of its language, history and culture' (Jones, G.E., 1988, p. 94).

Reynolds also noted that the power and strength of the Welsh language policy community, and the concentration upon language policy, had led to the neglect of distinctive Welsh policies in virtually every other Welsh educational policy area (Reynolds, 1989, p. 45). The result of this was that the curriculum in Wales was still linked very closely to that of England.

Section 9.3. The opportunity for change

As seen in the previous section, although the Welsh educational policy community became more developed, its distinctive policy output were still mainly limited to issues concerning Welsh language medium education. When the Conservatives began to 'pilot' their ideas on educational reform in the general election campaign of 1987, Reynolds (1995b, p. 7) noted that, to all intents and purposes, 'Wales was yoked to England' in the proposed policies. Despite this close link there were still some concessions to the distinctive nature of Welsh issues in the Conservative manifesto. The presence of the Welsh language policy community ensured that there was a specific reference to the need to include the Welsh language as a core subject in Welsh medium areas and schools, and as a foundation subject in all others (unless there were endorsed exemptions by the Secretary of State for Wales) [Reynolds, 1995b, p. 7].

The first formal assertion of the difference between England and Wales on the National Curriculum, by Sir Wyn's Welsh Office Education Division, was the production of 'The National Curriculum in Wales' shortly after the Conservative's 1987 general election victory. Although in many ways the Welsh Office document paralleled the Department of Education and Science's 'The National Curriculum 5–16', an important deviation occurred as the Welsh Office accepted that Welsh language and literature should be a compulsory part of the curriculum (Jones, G.E., 1997, p. 185). The strength of the Welsh language policy community was acknowledged by the fact that a 'Working Group' comprising of members from this community was established immediately.

Aside from the language issue, the Education Reform Bill 1988 provided the opportunity for the educational policy community to start to act on their policy concerns. At the heart of the Bill was the concept of the National Curriculum. This was to be introduced in order to 'guarantee that everywhere a broad and balanced education is provided, and by setting standards to be reached and monitoring progress, to raise standards' (Smith

· et al, 1992, p. 72). As we have seen, these 'standards' were worse in Wales than in England. Kenneth Baker, the then Secretary of State for Education in England, had devised the National Curriculum as a reassertion of subject based education, rather than one based on areas of experience or interdisciplinary combinations that had become more common throughout education teaching (Jones, G.E., 1997, p. 184). The concept of this new National Curriculum raised in Wales the issue of 'which nation is to be served by the curriculum, Wales or England?', but in the absence of an 'autonomous institutional educational framework or theoretical base' in Wales the solutions were, at the start *ad hoc* (Jones, G.E., 1997, p. 184).

On the surface therefore, the 1988 Education Reform Act presented the educational policy community in Wales with the opportunity 'to create, for the first time ever, a state school curriculum which is unique to Wales in content and context' (Jones, G.E., 1997). The policy community was given a significant boost by the arrival of Sir Wyn Roberts at the portfolio of Education in the Welsh Office. As seen in Chapter IV, Sir Wyn was regarded highly by both the Welsh Secretaries and Prime Ministers he served, so his views normally held some considerable sway on issues of policy. Egan noted that the educational establishment saw:

'Sir Wyn Roberts as a breath of fresh air because he brought Welsh language issues forward. Also he was a long serving Welsh speaking Minister whose continuity in post enabled the education establishment to get closer to the Welsh Office. Finally he was amenable to responses from outside bodies when they pushed for change to the Welsh education agenda' (Egan to author).

The educational policy community (external to the language issue) was also brought into the policy process. Reynolds noted that the process of consultation in Wales was much friendlier than in England, and cites a statement by Sir Wyn Roberts to this affect:

'We have always tried in Wales to listen to what teachers have to say. Teachers are the people who know the curriculum because they know the pupils they have to reach'. (Welsh Office Press release, 27 April 1993 cited in Reynolds, 1995, p. 11).

The ethos behind the development of the National Curriculum in Wales was to ensure an increased involvement of those within the policy community in comparison with what was occurring in England (Davies et al,

1997, p. 256–7). Davies et al (1997, p. 256) indicated that the Welsh Office made it clear from the beginning that, unlike in England, the texts of the National Curriculum were to be 'explicitly mediated, recontextulized and re-orientated in recognition of the distinctive practices and aspirations of local communities and the wider interest of Wales'.

Section 9.4. The input

The Welsh Office's consultation document on the National Curriculum in Wales laid immense emphasis on co-operation between the Welsh Office and the rest of the policy community. Therefore, it was not surprising that there was a large amount of input from the Welsh educational policy community and beyond. The extensiveness of Welsh Office consultation over the National Curriculum process is detailed in Figure 9.1.

The Welsh Office produced its first consultation document in July 1987. In December 1987 the Welsh Office reported back on the state of this consultation process. They also gave details on the key actors in the Welsh educational policy community. The report stated that:

'In Wales written responses were received from more than 150 organisations, including the Welsh Joint Education Committee (WJEC), all local education authorities (LEAs) and teachers unions, and from many individuals. Meetings were held at the Welsh Office with the WJEC, the Welsh Consultative Committee for Local Government Finance, Directors of Education, all the teacher unions in Wales, the Parent/Teacher Associations of Wales, parents for Welsh Medium Education, and the Welsh Language Education Development Committee' (Welsh Office, 1987, p. 1).

The response from those within the policy community indicated that there was a strong desire and will to differentiate aspects of the National Curriculum in Wales from that of England (Welsh Office, 1987, p. 1). What was to be the defining factor in differentiating the curriculum in Wales from that in England, however, was the fact that the Welsh Office handed over the specification of the details of the curriculum to elements of the policy community who were formed into working groups. These working groups used their delegated powers in order to help determine curriculum development with the wider policy community.

Figure 9.1
The Welsh Office and the consultation process over the
setting up of the national curriculum subjects

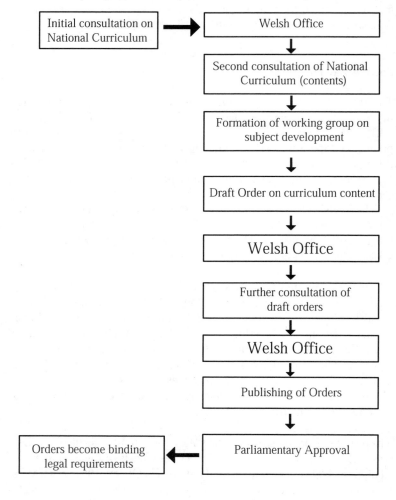

Welsh Office, 1987, pp. 3–4, Welsh Office, 1988, p. 22.

Consultation on the Welsh language

The Welsh language and literature working group was the first to be formed. This action provided an indication of the strength of the Welsh language policy community within the Welsh Office policy process. The formation of the Welsh language working group, to work towards improving the status of the language issue, was at the heart of the key political actors' policy desires. Sir Wyn Roberts's, and by implication the Welsh Office's, major concern was the future of the language in Welsh schools (Roberts, W., 1995, p. 8). The Welsh Office's National Curriculum document stated that:

> 'The Welsh language is part of the curriculum of most children in Wales. The Government's policy, set out in Welsh in Schools (July 1981), is that the experience of the language is an important component of a broadly balanced curriculum for pupils in Wales; that in English speaking areas all pupils should be given the opportunity of acquiring a sufficient command of Welsh to allow for communication in Welsh while bilingual education should be available to pupils whose parents desire it for them' (cited in Roberts, W., 1995, p. 9).

The Welsh Office had 173 submissions from various parties when it consulted the policy community on the issue of the inclusion of Welsh in the curriculum they had. Some 126 were in favour of its inclusion (Roberts, W., 1995). Originally the White Paper suggested that Welsh be only designated as a foundation subject, but pressure from Sir Wyn Roberts and bodies within the policy community, such as the PDAG and Gwynedd County Council, ensured that it became a core subject. This was only in schools, however, where more than half of the foundation subjects were taught partly or wholly through the medium of Welsh. They maintained that not having Welsh as a core subject would undermine existing local authority language provision, even endanger it being taught as a second language (Thomas, 1994, pp. 310–311).

When PDAG reported back in 1988 it recommended a comprehensive programme for the extension of Welsh language teaching, costing £18 million over three years (Williams, 1989, p. 60). This would have allowed the government to teach every facet of the National Curriculum through the medium of Welsh (Thomas, 1994, p. 309). In reality the Welsh Office was not so generous, in 1989 it provided some £500,000 towards implementing the most pressing parts of PDAG's recommendations. This caused a split in the community with one PDAG committee member resigning and calls by CIG for Sir Wyn Robert's resignation (Western Mail, 20/3/89). But the Welsh Office did give further financial commitment to sponsor research into the effects of the Education Reform Act 1988 and its link to the 'new' national curriculum. PDAG was thus able, along with other bodies and organisations, to press for a central place for Welsh in the National Curriculum in Wales (Thomas, 1994, p. 309).

Mike Joseph, a member of the National Curriculum Welsh Working Group, identified three reasons why the idea of compulsory Welsh came to be accepted onto the new curriculum (Joseph, 1989):

1. The strength of the Welsh language lobby (policy community) who made their views strongly known during the period of consultation.
2. The nature of the Education Reform Act which had styled itself on 'reforming standards'. Thus, if Welsh was to be part of the National Curriculum, then the same criteria had to be adhered to (Thomas, 1994, p. 314).
3. The advent of Peter Walker as Secretary of State for Wales and his claim that the middle ground now belonged to the pro-Welsh lobby. The fact that Walker came from outside Wales helped the cause of giving Welsh a proper status in the new curriculum, because the language issue was being supported by an English Secretary of State who held high status in Whitehall and Westminster. Walker could be objective in the Welsh speaker versus English speaker debate. The fact that a politician who spoke no Welsh, and was not frightened of that fact (Walker, 1990), was prepared to endorse the enhancement of the Welsh language helped reassure the non-Welsh speaking elements of the educational policy communities.

Despite the occasional periods of conflict, the Welsh Office – under Nicholas Edwards and then Peter Walker – was far more responsive to the demands of CIG and the wider Welsh language policy community in general than were previous Labour governments (Williams, 1989, p. 61). That the teaching of Welsh should now permeate the schools was accepted with some enthusiasm and a remarkable degree of acrimony. For many it was a touchstone of national identity (Jones, G.E., 1997, p. 186). As the government was seen to be very responsive to the Welsh language in education, the appeal of CIG, which was a constant thorn in the Welsh Office's side, lessened. In the late 1980s CIG, for example took part in a series of break-ins to Welsh Office buildings to back up its demands on the national curriculum in Wales. These demands included the introduction of 'Welsh community studies' in all Welsh primary schools (Western Mail, 8/5/89).

The formation of the non-Welsh language working groups

As seen earlier, the Welsh educational policy community was involved in the National Curriculum policy process at two levels, the English-Welsh level (DES policy territory) and at the Wales only level (Welsh Office policy domain). This section deals with both the English-Welsh working groups and Welsh non-language curriculum working groups. Welsh language groups aside, the formation of solely Welsh working groups was hampered by internal and external factors. This was due to the fact that, as Jones, G.E. (1997) noted, Welsh curriculum planning lacked an overview, due to the fact that there was little consensus within the policy community on what should constitute a Welsh National Curriculum. Thus, initially, policy making was *ad hoc*. David Egan, a member of the Welsh History working group noted that:

> 'The changes in Wales were really a reaction to the English education agenda. It wasn't a case of saying let's have a different curriculum for Wales but let's add a bit of Welsh distinctiveness into the curriculum as well' (Egan to author).

The degree to which a subject group became separate depended upon the strength of the professional group surrounding that subject in Wales. As seen earlier, a working group for Welsh language and literature could be established very early on in the consultation process. This was relatively uncontroversial because it did not impinge on any area of the English-Welsh curriculum, it was supported by much of the educational policy community and enjoyed a consensus across the political parties. Beyond these Welsh language working groups, however, it was different matter. There was clearly a desire for a 'Curriculum Cymreig'. The NUT in Wales from the outset, for instance, stressed the need for the 'Welsh dimension' to be recognised, not just in the language, but in subjects like English, History, Geography and Music (Lloyd, 1990, p. 38). Putting this policy desire into reality proved more problematic.

Few subject areas were strong enough indigenously to set up autonomous groups immediately. One working group did quickly emerge, however, based around history, because the history group was the strongest non-Welsh language element of the Welsh educational policy community. The Association of History Teachers in Wales was founded in 1982, and soon built up a sound academic reputation which was sufficient for it to be invited by the Welsh Office to put its case for special arrangements to be made for history (Jones, G.E. 1997). A delegation led by the Association's president Sir Glanmor Williams, FBA, argued that the subject was central to pupils' understanding of their national heritage. Ideally they wanted a separate group for Wales, or at the minimum at least double its representation on the 'England and Wales' group. The strength of feeling on the difference of history in Wales was summed up by Barbara Lloyd from the NUT in Wales:

'Welsh history is the history of 'y werin' – the people. It is the history of the Chartists, the Rebecca Riots, the political union of Wales with England, the dark side of the industrial revolution' (Lloyd, 1990, p. 38).

The History Committee for Wales was therefore set up as a result of pressure from concerned groups in Wales, the NUT among them (Lloyd, 1990, p. 38). Jones noted that 'there was considerable satisfaction (within the policy community) when the Welsh Office granted Wales its equivalent of a history working group to operate in tandem with England' (1997, p. 187). There were some initial restrictions placed on the autonomy of this group, however, by key political actors. Peter Walker stated that 'I expect the committee to give weight to the essential core of British history which should be common to all children in England and Wales, as well as covering the history of Wales' (Hansard, 13/1/89, cl. 745). Within this guideline, the Committee – under Professor Robert Rees Davies – was at liberty to pursue an entirely independent line over content; thus the final report and subsequent Statutory Orders gave substantial weight to Welsh history in a British and European context (Jones, G.E., 1997, p. 187). Their conclusions proved to be uncontroversial. There was a limited response to the History Committee's report, with only some 10 individual history teachers and no others replying to the final report (Hansard, 12/3/91, cl. 447).

The Association of Geography Teachers in Wales was established after the history group. They had seen how the history group had developed and wished to have an equal impact on the thinking of the curriculum. Their final report recommended, unsurprisingly, that Welsh pupils should study Wales as a separate entity to England. The arts and music working groups in Wales were also able to exert their own influence. But this time it was not solely a matter of the differences in traditions/culture between England and Wales. The groups preferred the emphasis to be more on pupils' creativity than the historical aspects of art and music, which was regarded as part of a right wing educational agenda. These working groups were supported in their views by the newly established Curriculum Council for Wales, and also by the Welsh Office Ministers who had a political desire to emphasise the divergence between the 'English' and 'Welsh' National Curricula (Jones, G.E., 1997, p. 188). Thus music and art, like history and geography in Wales, was determined mainly in Wales, and so presented a different curriculum base to that of England.

For every one of the remaining National Curriculum subject areas in England and Wales, an English-Welsh working group was established. These working groups formed a type of 'producer network' of English and Welsh educational policy networks. This meant that they 'served the producer (education policy community) interests' in arriving at fulfilling their desired outcomes (Marsh and Rhodes, 1992). The working groups also helped support the wider educational policy community by bringing together many of the key actors to negotiate curriculum policy outcomes, thus resulting in 'increasing the acceptability of that policy and improving the likelihood of compliance' (Rhodes, 1999, p. 31).

These English-Welsh working groups contained nominees from the Secretary of State for Education, and one member, working in Wales, nominated by the Welsh Secretary. The extent of the influence of these members varied. The National Curriculum for English did not reflect Welsh literature, which caused some disappointment in elements of the Welsh educational policy community. Where possible, therefore, the Welsh educational policy community pushed for all-Welsh working groups (Jones, G.E., 1997, p. 186).

The inclusiveness of the educational policy process

The key political actor in constructing a National Curriculum for Wales, Sir Wyn Roberts, laid great emphasis on 'supporting teachers and a co-operative approach to working with local education authorities' (Hansard, 27/2/90, cl. 101). The establishment of the various working groups was proof of this policy in action, as was the actual length of the consultation process, see Figure 9.1. This also provided the Welsh educational policy community with a wealth of Welsh Office produced documentation to respond to. By July 1989 the Welsh Office had issued some 19 Circulars, Draft Circulars and Guidance notes on the National Curriculum (Hansard, 27/7/89, cl. 801). Towards the end of the consultation period the Welsh Office was proud of what it saw as a successful exercise in defining the curriculum in Wales. In December 1990, David Hunt told the Welsh Grand Committee that the:

> "National Curriculum is not something that has been imposed on teachers. Teachers have been closely involved in every stage of its development. We are fortunate in Wales that our communication lines with the profession are short. We have been able to consult teachers at every stage, and we have made a point of doing so. We have listened to what we have been told and we have responded. We have been fortunate that many busy and able teachers have given generously of their time to help us with work" (Welsh Grand Committee, 5/12/90, cl. 13).

It is not unusual for politicians to make claims that they were consulting widely, as David Hunt had done. It is unusual, however, for the other political parties either to refrain from criticising or condemning such a major educational measure as the National Curriculum. The four main political parties in Wales both accepted and encouraged the concept of a National Curriculum in Wales and, in particular, the setting up of a Curriculum Cymreig.

As seen in Section 9.3, it was the Conservatives who had introduced the notion of a national curriculum in Wales, and they had suggested this in their 1987 Welsh manifesto (Conservative Party, 1987). The only real dissent within the Conservatives in Wales was over the issue of compulsory teaching of Welsh in the first three years of secondary education. Nicholas Bennet, the MP for Pembrokeshire, raised the issue of some Pembrokeshire schools opting out from this process nine times in the House of Commons between June 1988 and December 1990 (Hansard, various 1988–90). There was also some dissent from individual teachers who argued that curriculum differences would adversely affect pupils who moved between England and Wales (Egan to author).

The Labour Party's response to the National Curriculum was crucial if it was to enjoy successful implementation in Wales. It was the Labour Party who controlled the majority of the LEAs, and whose members were represented in the educational policy community, from the WJEC to the trade unions, in some force. The Labour Party, coincidentally, had long been a supporter of the concept of a National Curriculum. In October 1976 the Labour Prime Minister, James Callaghan, in a speech at Ruskin College declared that there was 'a strong case for the so-called core curriculum of basic knowledge' (Jones, G.E., 1997, p. 149). This set the scene within the Wales Labour Party for the following decade and a half (Egan to author).

The Labour Party supported the idea of a National Curriculum, and the various deviations from the English curriculum that occurred in Wales. Indeed, no Labour politician in the House of Commons voted against the principle of a National Curriculum during its Committee stages (Welsh Grand Committee, 1990, p. 58). The only area where there was conflict with the Welsh Office was over the resources given to implement the National Curriculum in Wales. Throughout 1989 and 1990 Shadow Welsh Secretary, Barry Jones pressed the Welsh Office Ministers on the levels of support they would be providing for the implementation of the National Curriculum (Hansard, various). In June 1989, and again in July 1990, Barry Jones called, unsuccessfully, for 'a conference of local education authorities in Wales to discuss the impact of the national curriculum upon educational practice in Wales' (Hansard, 22/6/89, cl. 244 and 12/7/90, cl. 286). At no time did the Wales Labour Party at Westminster criticise the Welsh Secretary or his Ministers in Parliament about the curriculum content in Wales (Hansard 1988–92).

Plaid Cymru was also very supportive of the concept of a National Curriculum, and in particular the enhancement of the Welsh elements within it. The party's leader, Dafydd Elis Thomas, openly supported the expansion of the 'Curriculum Cymreig' at Westminster. He said:

> 'I do not want the idea to get around that the only essential difference in the curriculum in Wales has to do with the Welsh language. We have our own national curriculum . . . We need to ensure that the input is across the curriculum, and not merely a subject group to deal with language (Welsh Grand Committee, 1988, cl. 40).'

In addition, Cynog Dafis, the future Plaid Cymru MP for Ceredigion, saw the need to have a curriculum with origins in Wales which worked its way outwards and influenced the curriculum in England, rather than the other way round (Egan to author).

The Welsh Liberal Democrats were also in favour of the national curriculum, but initially argued that it was not broad enough in its provisions to deal with a Welsh curriculum. They also backed full Welsh language provision across Wales (Welsh Grand Committee, 1990, cl. 30, Hansard, 1/3/90 cl. 282).

Thus the major players in the policy process, from Welsh Secretary to Cathays Park Village, were all in agreement of the need for a National Curriculum in Wales and for it to be shaped to suit Welsh circumstances.

Section 9.5. The output

The Welsh Office had worked together with the DES in order to help achieve its own wider educational policy objectives. This interdepartmental networking involved Kenneth Baker and Sir Wyn Roberts (Roberts, W., 1995). They had to fight hard to keep the core and foundation subjects fixed as their respective ministries desired. Roberts noted that the Prime Minister was far from happy about extending the National Curriculum beyond English, mathematics and science. Both Ministers stood their ground and got what they – and their departments – desired. For Sir Wyn, despite an hour long probing by the Prime Minister on the Curriculum in Wales, 'there was only a minor cosmetic change in the definition of a Welsh speaking school' (Roberts, W., 1995, p. 10).

The eventual output of the Roberts-Baker partnership in Cabinet was that in England there were three 'core' subjects (English, mathematics and science) and seven 'foundation' subjects (history, geography, technology, a modern foreign language, art, music and physical education). In Wales, the Welsh Office and the policy community were able to obtain Welsh as either an additional core or foundation subject, depending on the type of school. It was not just the presence of Welsh on the curriculum that made Wales different from England, however, there was also a whole host of differences in the curriculum content and the way in which the subjects were delivered and assessed (Jones, G.E., 1990).

The arrival of the National Curriculum in Wales also saw an increase in the involvement of the policy community (Cathays Park Village) in developing education to an unprecedented degree. The Welsh educational policy community through the working groups became the main determinant of curriculum content in subject areas such as history, geography and art for the first time. This meant that the Welsh Office followed the demands of the policy community and started to shape the curriculum so that it had a significant element of 'Curriculum Cymreig' within it.

This determination of distinctly Welsh educational policy output also meant that educational resource providers (schools) had to be expanded if this new 'Curriculum Cymreig' was going to be operated successfully. One of the first Welsh institutions developed to serve the 'Curriculum Cymreig' was the Curriculum Council for Wales (CCW) in 1989. This met the aims of the policy community by being inclusive. In one of CCW's earliest publications, 'A Framework for the Whole Curriculum 5–16 in Wales' (1989), it was stated that any curriculum in Wales:

> "must aim to develop pupils' understanding of the distinctive and varied nature of the Welsh experience. All pupils have the entitlement to learn about Welsh culture and history as well as the language; the curriculum and ethos of schools in Wales will need to reflect this Welsh identity" (CCW, 1989, p. 3).

The Welsh Office and policy community, via the CCW, went on to fully develop a 'Curriculum Cymreig'. This meant Welsh as a first or second language, music, art and history all becoming distinctive to Wales, reflecting Welsh cultural, social, geographical and historical traditions (Farrell and Law, 1995, p. 8). By 1991 the CCW was ready to declare that the 'Curriculum Cymreig' was here, and that there were the following differences between the National Curriculums of England and Wales (CCW, 1991, p. 4):

1. Provision for the Welsh language as a subject (as well as a medium of teaching and learning in Welsh-medium schools).
2. Some statutory requirements ensuring that aspects of the curriculum were distinctive to schools in Wales (for example, in history and geography).
3. The general Welshness pervading pupils' learning experiences. As the CCW stated: 'the social, cultural, economic and environmental contexts to which knowledge, skills and concepts are related in teaching and learning programmes can, and should be concerned with Wales as well as with the wider world . . . all subjects should be taught in such a way that the content is meaningful to the pupils' own experience within his/her community'.

It was evident that the educational policy community of the Cathays Park Village had interacted with the political and administrative actors at the Welsh Office to produce some unique curriculum outcomes. These were designed in Wales to be implemented in Wales. An output was making Welsh a core subject in all 'Welsh speaking' schools (schools in which more than half the basic curriculum subjects, other than English and Welsh, were taught wholly or partly in Welsh), and a foundation subject in all other schools. The National Curriculum elevated the status of the Welsh language in schools. The strength of the Welsh language policy community could be gauged by the fact that the Welsh Office now insisted, for the first time, that Welsh be taught in all schools in Wales (Baker, 1993). For the inclusion of Welsh in the curriculum there was much praise from one of the key political actors most involved with the policy process, Peter Walker, who stated:

'The Welsh Language now has, for the first time, a firm statutory place in the school curriculum for pupils from five to 16 in Wales within the national curriculum. I believe that the decision to include Welsh as part of the national curriculum will have a significant impact on the language for many years to come' (Hansard, 1/5/90, cl. 497).

His successor David Hunt remarked:

'In the past year there have been a number of developments in education, most notably the decision that Welsh should be included as a foundation subject in the national curriculum. I am strongly and firmly committed to policies which secure and strengthen the position of the Welsh language' (Hansard, 28/2/91, cl. 1146).

The imposition of a National Curriculum realised the dreams of the more 'cultural autonomist' elements of the educational policy community led by Sir Wyn Roberts (Snicker, 1998). The National Curriculum provided an opportunity to consolidate Welsh features in the system by guaranteeing some study of the language, history and culture in every school syllabus.

The extent to which the Welsh Office had followed a truly radical Welsh policy agenda could be confirmed by comparing Welsh Office educational output with the aims of Cymdeithas yr Iaith Gymreig (CIG). CIG normally remained outside of the mainstream of the policy community by virtue of its campaigning techniques. In their first manifesto, published in 1971, CIG stated that Welsh could only be saved by a complete transformation of the status of the language in Wales. They went on to suggest how this could be achieved in public life, in courts of law, in education and the media. By 1992, the education reforms demanded by CIG had, or were being undertaken (Davies, 1993, p. 115). Others also noted that the extent of the change in Welsh education was indeed significant. Farrell and Law (1995, p. 25) saw the 1988 Education Reform Act as having the greatest impact on Welsh education since the founding of the Welsh Office. Reynolds saw this Act as greatly increasing the divergence of the educational policies between England and Wales from 1988 onwards (Reynolds, 1995a, p. 11).

Section 9.6. The ongoing process

As seen earlier, the Curriculum Cymreig and the policy community have continued to expand, with the encouragement of the Welsh Office. In the spring of 1993, the English language curriculum was revised in both Wales and England. Building on the differences it has already established in the four foundation subjects of geography, history, art and music, the Curriculum Council for Wales (CCW) sought to establish different curricular orders for Wales. Despite Cabinet pressure to closely follow the line being carried out in England, David Hunt followed a Welsh one (Roberts, W., 1995). This exercise once again involved a wide-spread consultation process. Sir Wyn Roberts told the press that 'his department thought highly of the views of the CCW', and said 'the views of teachers would be heeded'. Referring to the possibility of developing an English curriculum different from that in England Sir Wyn noted 'if we need to be different we shall not hesitate to be different' (Jones, 1993, p. 114). The 1993 English language and literature curriculum in Wales did indeed see some contrasts to England. Welsh authors, writing in English and those who had a special relevance to Wales, were included. Teachers in Wales were also allowed greater scope on the type of teaching, with no one teaching type being prescribed. Also there was a strong emphasis on assessment results in schools not being linked to the money going into individual schools, the so called 'payment by results'.

The contents of the National Curriculum did not stop developing in Wales. In 1993 the CCW published a further paper, *Developing a Curriculum Cymreig*, which reinforced the presence of the Curriculum Cymreig, stating that as many elements of the curriculum in Wales as possible should emphasise the Welsh dimension. This should include appreciation of the part played by Welsh people in the past in industry, technology, commerce, design, literature, sports and science (CCW, 1993, p. 3). In May 1994 John Redwood announced a slimmed down National Curriculum in Wales. This time it was a direct consultation and policy development exercise between the Curriculum Council for Wales and the wider educational policy community, with limited direct Welsh Office input (Welsh Office, 9/5/94). The Curriculum Council for Wales received some 8,000 responses to their request for comments on this revised curriculum (Welsh Office, 9/11/94). The slimming down of the Curriculum was not seen, however, to damage Welsh elements. Rod Richards noted that 'We have also made sure that there will be ample opportunities for pupils to learn about our distinctive linguistic, economic and cultural heritage in Wales' (Welsh Office, 9/11/94).

By 1994, Reynolds was able to indicate that every sector of education in Wales was either now coming into direct daily contact with the Welsh Office, or one of its sponsored bodies, and that the potential for policies coming directly from Wales and not London had dramatically increased (Reynolds, 1994).

The National Curriculum as a contemporary political issue

Apart from the scaling down of the content and size of the national curriculum, which was common to both England and Wales, the major curriculum issue in Wales concerned the rebellion against the compulsory teaching of Welsh in schools.

Despite the enthusiasm for the teaching of Welsh in every school by various Conservative Welsh Secretaries, this was not always universally supported by the party they represented. The requirement was particularly controversial in schools which were in predominantly English-speaking areas, especially those represented by Conservative MPs. When the national curriculum was introduced, Welsh was also not originally taught in any of Gwent's 232 primary schools (except for six special units). From the outset doubts were raised about the feasibility of achieving the national curriculum's targets for the teaching of Welsh in Gwent (Jones and Carlin, 1990). The Parent Teachers Association of Wales argued that some parents would resort to sending their children to school in England. In Gwent, east Clwyd and south Pembrokeshire there was a degree of hostility to the introduction of Welsh into schools. The Welsh Office retained the power to allow some schools to opt out from compulsory teaching in Welsh. The then Chairman of Gwent

County Council Education Committee, Graham Powell, predicted that three quarters of schools in his county would request this opt out (Thomas, 1994, p. 311). For a while there was a break from the compulsory learning of Welsh in schools, as resources failed to meet demand. The statutory requirement for schools to teach Welsh as a second language in the 14 to 16 years curriculum was temporaly withdrawn (September 1995) due to a shortage in the supply of teachers (Farrell and Law, 1997, p. 174). Welsh was not finally implemented in all schools until September 1999 (Welsh Office to author). This was exactly as the PDAG had predicted in their report some ten years earlier, i.e. if the supply of Welsh language teachers was not significantly increased, then Welsh could not become universally available.

As the Welsh Language Board was reconstituted on a statutory basis in 1993, the Welsh Office disbanded the Welsh Language Education Development Committee (PDAG). The PDAG had done much to promote teaching through the medium of Welsh. Its disbanding displeased the LEAs who stated that 'the removal of the PDAG will destroy any coherent overview of Welsh Language Education by dispersing such responsibility amongst non-elected bodies' (WJEC, 1993, p. 1). It also had the effect of removing a powerful Welsh language pressure group.

But the issue of the Welsh language being taught in anglicised areas remained controversial, with some schools continuing to press for exemption from the teaching of Welsh. Having introduced the Welsh Language Act in 1993 and supported the Welsh language to an unprecedented degree, Rod Richards, a former Conservative Welsh Office Minister and later on an Assembly Member, stated that it should be removed from the core curriculum in some parts of Wales, he said:

'In certain areas of Wales such as Monmouthshire and Newport, there is strong opposition. It is causing a lot of controversy and is creating a lot of resentment against the language, but in other areas there would be no call for it to be scrapped' (Western Mail, 3/2/99).

Ten years after a Conservative Welsh Secretary announced that Welsh would be introduced as either a core or foundation subject in all schools for the first time, (distinguishing the Curriculum from the National Curriculum in England), the Conservatives were supporting its limited removal. They brought forward plans in their Assembly manifesto to end the teaching of Welsh to pupils aged 14 to 16 where their parents did not desire it. The same party that, whilst in residence at the Welsh Office, had seen the introduction of Welsh into every school in Wales as a vote winner, now saw its withdrawal in some areas as a vote winner.

Summary – The developing policy community

When examining the development of the Welsh Office and the educational policy community, our thinking is influenced by a number of approaches. Firstly, it is clear that institutions matter. Institutions create – or help to create – policy spaces. Processes have to take account of an institution: they divert the path of the policy flow. The Welsh Office had constructed a consultation process and established its own educational bodies and committees which aided the creation of this policy space. They diverted the policy flow in the desired direction of the Welsh Office and the surrounding policy community. Secondly, policy issues such as the National Curriculum provide opportunities for a range of educational groups to influences the development of an educational policy community and policy outcomes. These groups could define their educational agenda in such a way that it influenced policy developments and assisted in creating an extensive educational network where only an embryo had existed beforehand. Thirdly, the state was important in creating new networks, partly because they could legitimise various groups, such as the Welsh history and geography groupings, and partly because they could assist in the creation of these groups, namely the Welsh arts and music groupings.

The construction of the National Curriculum in Wales proved to be a clear example of the interaction between the Welsh Office and the surrounding educational policy community (or perhaps two, one based on Welsh medium education and the other on non-Welsh medium education). The participants in the construction of a Welsh Curriculum had open access to the policy process that made up the National Curriculum, and on the whole enjoyed consensus on what objectives should be achieved (Marsh, 1998, p. 14). Although there was some discontent about the compulsory teaching of Welsh in all schools, there was very little concern about introducing a 'Curriculum Cymreig' in other subject areas. The conflicts that did occur with the National Curriculum did not so much concern the content of the curriculum, designed in Wales, but the amount, and testing of this curriculum. The size and nature of the educational policy community is seen in Figure 9.2.

Figure 9.2 indicates that the educational policy community did not stand alone. It interacted both with neighbouring communities such as local government and the Welsh language policy communities, although we should note that members of one were often members of another. It also interacted to a significant degree with Whitehall and Westminster and English partners of elements of the policy community. It was also clear that some elements of the community had greater influence on policy output than others. Figure 9.2 indicates that although the Welsh Secretary and his Welsh Office team were at the core, MPs may have had more or less influence than the Cathays Park Village depending upon their closeness to the government. Government MPs clearly had more influence than Opposition MPs.

The education system in Wales, since the days of state schooling, had never been allowed to stray too far from what was occurring in England. The existence of the Welsh Office, and its education department, however, legitimised the Welsh educational policy community's claims for some differences (Jones, G.E, 1988, p. 91). Wales then developed core elements of a 'distinctive' education policy (Phillips, 1996, p. 32). This chapter has indicated that that the Welsh Office, together with elements of the policy community, created a Curriculum Cymreig to the extent that education in Wales, in some areas, went on to differ considerably in content from that of England. This result came about for a number of reasons:

It was the desire of the key political actors

Chapters I to III stated that political actors in the Cabinet and at the Welsh Office were the most important in defining Welsh Office policy output. This was clearly the case with the National Curriculum. Once Kenneth Baker and Sir Wyn Roberts had succeeded in getting the Prime Minister and the Cabinet to accept the format of the National Curriculum, it was left to their respective departments to continue shaping the output. It was also crucial that the Welsh Secretaries Walker and Hunt were consensus politicians who desired to consult widely on new policy initiatives and involve the Welsh policy communities. They also trusted Sir Wyn Roberts to pursue the Welsh Office agenda.

Sir Wyn Roberts played a key role in the process of defining a 'Curriculum Cymreig'. It is hard to say whether there would have been a 'Curriculum Cymreig' without his presence', Sir Wyn was at the Welsh

Figure 9.2. The Welsh Educational Policy Community*

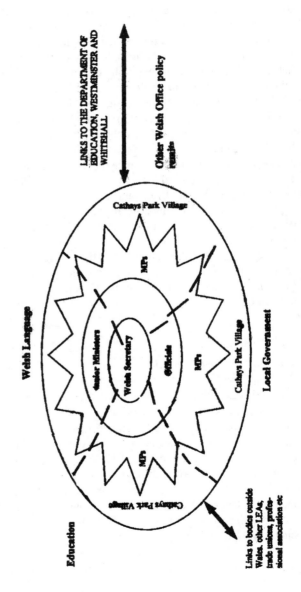

* The diagram only displays those elements of the neighbouring policy communities
that were closely linked to the establishment of the national curriculum.

Office for nearly two decades, during which his power and stature grew both within government and the surrounding policy community. His personal drive, however, certainly pushed the agenda forward. In Chapter III he was quoted describing the junior Ministers at the Welsh Office as the 'policy dynamos'. They formulate, push through, and shape policies at the Welsh Office. He undertook this role as the Welsh Office Education Minister. It was the continuity in office of the Welsh speaking Sir Wyn which enabled both the Welsh Secretaries he served, and the policy community that surrounded the Welsh Office, to benefit from his enthusiasm for and knowledge of things Welsh. Sir Wyn was regarded as a 'cultural autonomist' (Snicker, 1998, p. 143). This became evident in his desire to ensure that the Welsh Office played the role of an enabler for a distinctive Welsh National Curriculum, or 'Curriculum Cymreig' (Roberts, W., 1995). It was Roberts who became actively involved in the policy process surrounding the National Curriculum. He was also instrumental in setting up a 'producer network' in the form of the Working Groups on Welsh curriculum subject areas (Rhodes and Marsh, 1992).

The educational policy community expanded to support Welsh Office policy.

The working groups proved to be an example of the almost 'symbiotic interaction' of the Welsh educational policy community (Marsh, 1998, p. 5). Here each actor within the community needed the others to succeed and therefore the style that developed was symbiotic. The political actors desired a strong Curriculum Cymreig, as did most of the educational policy community of the Cathays Park Village. The Welsh Office did not have the resources to develop this on its own, it therefore provided the opportunity to establish different Welsh curriculum areas; the policy community was able to provide the professional resourcing to meet both their own and the Welsh Office's policy desires in the form of the working groups. The working groups had the professional expertise and status to construct a 'Curriculum Cymreig' in some areas, independent of the DES. The Welsh Office Education Division, restricted by numbers and internal professional resourcing, could not have done this without the aid of the wider Welsh policy community.

The Welsh Office Ministers were aided by a Welsh educational policy community that became evermore self confident in deciding Welsh educational policy issues, without too much help from across the border. Thomas noted that: 'In Wales the presence of central government has allowed a sophisticated body of voluntary organisations and interest groups to grow up, which had helped to obtain funding from the government and had instigated various teaching methods and the most successful way of encouraging the use of Welsh in an oral context' (Thomas, 1994, p. 327). The development of this Welsh educational policy community can be seen in Table 9.1. below.

Table 9.1
The Development of the Welsh Educational Policy Community

Time period	Key Central Government Actors	Secondary Central Government Actors	Key Local Government Actors	Others
1964–70	Department of Education	None	LEAs, WJEC	Trade Unions
1970–80	Department of Education	Welsh Office	LEAs, WJEC Association of Welsh Counties (AWC)	Trade Unions (Welsh branches) or uniquely Welsh Union, CIG
1980–88	Department of Education	Welsh Office	LEAs, WJEC AWC	Trade Unions, PDAG, Professional Associations
1988–99	Welsh Office	Department of Education	LEAs, WJEC AWC	Trade Unions, PDAG, Curriculum working groups, CCW

The Welsh educational policy community expanded around the need for action. It expanded because of:

1. The new opportunities provided by the Education Reform Act 1988.
2. The broad policy of inclusiveness instigated by Walker and Roberts.
3. The greater sense of Welshness in educational policy making.
4. The fact that the Conservatives, as a minority political force in Wales, could not sustain this policy agenda through its own party in Wales, or through the Welsh Office machine, and needed to seek additional help.

As stated before, the most visible collaboration between the Welsh Office and the wider policy community was the establishment of the all-Welsh curriculum working groups. With the growing sense of a greater educational difference to England, enhanced by these groups, the Welsh Office established new Welsh educational institutions such as PDAG and the Curriculum Council for Wales. This became the Qualifications, Curriculum and Assessment Authority in 1997 (known by its Welsh acronym of ACCAC).

ACCAC remains as a lasting legacy of the difference in the National Curriculum between Wales and England. It is the tangible evidence of the Welsh Office and the educational policy communities' interaction to develop the National Curriculum in Wales. It was well resourced in 1998/99; ACCAC had a budget of almost ten million pounds and a staff of 69 (Wales Yearbook, 1999, p. 279). It had only 13 less staff than the entire Welsh Office Education Division (Welsh Office, 1998, p. 4). The Welsh Office and policy community had successfully brought control of significant elements of the National Curriculum to Wales without increasing its own staffing.

The desire for consensus was widespread

The Welsh Office showed that, on the issue of the National Curriculum, it was its desire to have a broad consensus of inclusiveness. The government in Wales was prepared for more compromise than in England. Farrell and Law (1995, p. 6) noted that:

> 'The historical dominance of the non-Conservative political forces has impacted on the nature of the education network. Although the LEAs and the Labour party do not solely control the network, they were, nevertheless, very influential. As a consequence, it was unlikely that the education reforms in Wales, initiated by a Conservative government, would have been embraced with as much enthusiasm as they might have been under a Labour government'.

The consensus politicians Walker and Hunt were, therefore, much more open to persuasion and compromise by those from the Cathays Park Village. Walker was also a powerful enough politician not to be afraid to deviate from government policy in Wales and to fight his own corner. It may have also been true that the Welsh Office was simply not powerful enough in itself to shape events and, therefore, in order to achieve effective policy output it had to encourage the development of a more autonomous policy network (Rhodes, 1996, p. 659).

The links between administrative actors and the policy community allowed for consensus policy output

The links between the administrative actors and the education policy community in Wales, as seen already in this chapter, were very good. Osmond noted that: 'It is possible for the Welsh Office civil servants to establish personal relationships and acquire detailed knowledge of just eight LEAs in a way that is much more difficult for Department of Environment officials who have to deal with hundreds of local authorities in England' (Osmond, 1995, p. 235). Welsh LEAs saw their roles positively, following on from the Education Reform Act, and saw themselves as part of a network (Boyne et al, 1991, p. 46). The Welsh Office perceived their relations with LEAs to be good and indicated the strength of their co-operation by submitting their LMS schemes on time (Boyne et al, 1991, p. 45). In the Spring of 1990, Barbara Lloyd from the NUT in Wales, a union that cannot be accused of being close to any Conservative government, stated:

> "I would maintain however that because of the unique nature of certain Welsh educational institutions, and the close liaisons that were possible within a small nation, between teachers and administrators, between the established institutions and the schools, and even between the Welsh Office mandarins and the local authorities, we have in Wales a greater cause for optimism for the future of education." (Lloyd, 1990, p. 37).

Thus the Welsh Office establishment of a 'Curriculum Cymreig' was not really part of a purely rational policy process, although there were elements of rationality within the changes, for example the desire to improve standards. It was not known or even planned at the start which subject areas would be fashioned in Wales and which would be fashioned outside of it. The policy process owes perhaps more to what has been described as the 'Garbage Can Model' in which policy is determined by four streams: problems, solutions, participants and choice opportunities (Stoker, 1993, p. 4). Under the 'Garbage Can Model' policy was determined more by chance or through *ad hoc* solutions than through a process of rational planning.

In Wales the policy problem arose when the concept of the national curriculum arrived. The Welsh Office were unsure as to what they should do at the start of the process. Should they totally accept the same curriculum as England (the Welsh language apart), adapt some or the entire curriculum to Wales? The Welsh Office went on to develop a solution to this problem with the surrounding educational policy community. Therefore decisions were only made when a 'window of opportunity emerged' or was perhaps widened by Sir Wyn Roberts. The National Curriculum was this window and it was the educational policy community, and in particular the working groups, which came in with their pet solutions. The Welsh Office accepted these solutions and thus policy was made in response to the emerging window of opportunity which allowed a distinct 'Curriculum Cymreig' to be shaped.

Conclusion

It was noted in Chapter VII that the Welsh Office did not always interact closely with the Cathays Park Village. It did not always wish, or have the ability, to be interactive with the surrounding policy communities. This chapter, however, has provided extensive evidence of interaction between the Welsh Office and the policy community to produce policy outcomes that were unique to Wales. The Welsh Office integrated itself with the surrounding policy community. As a consequence of this, Jones noted that: 'sufficient battles have been won for us to be able to talk of a curriculum for Wales, not just a curriculum in Welsh (Jones, G.E., 1997, p. 159). The Welsh Office was able to act in the role of a 'Voice for Wales' in Whitehall in ensuring that its own educational policies became truly distinctive. The formulation and introduction of the National Curriculum provides us with a clear example of the broader engagement of the wider policy community. The existence of the Welsh Office and its education department have provided channels for Welsh policy communities' aspirations for curricular distinctiveness. But this in turn has only been possible because of the expansion of the wider Welsh educational policy community. The community did not stand still when given the opportunity to expand its influence; for example it helped form working groups. The result was that the last decade has seen a growing distinctiveness in Welsh educational policies. Ten years after the introduction of the National

Curriculum some aspects were still being played out in popular party politics. This could be seen most clearly in the compulsory introduction of Welsh as a core or foundation subject in all schools, which the Conservative Party rejected.

The inclusion of Welsh as a national curriculum subject, and the difference in knowledge content within some subjects, was followed by policies distinct from those in England such as:

- The absence of any publication of primary school performance tables.
- A decision not to adopt highly prescriptive English literacy and numeracy strategies.
- The absence of the harsh rhetoric about school performance that has emanated from Ministers at the Department for Education and Employment and from the Office of Standards in Education.
- The continued emphasis within Wales on the need for schools to be in the 'driving seat' of change, through processes such as school review, contrast with the use of market pressure as the 'driver' of change in England (Jones and Reynolds, 1998, p. 231).

The distinctiveness of the Welsh educational system, started by the National Curriculum, allowed an evolutionary process to occur in Wales. This approach owed perhaps more to the 'Garbage' School of Policy Making rather than any rational policy model. In the first two decades of the Welsh Office's existence, the education system in Wales too often 'schooled for failure'. Since the advent of the National Curriculum in Wales, however, outcomes such as the proportion of pupils gaining five GCSEs or more at grades A-C have improved rapidly over the last five or six years (Jones and Reynolds, 1998, p. 232). The Welsh educational policy community was given the opportunity to shape its own educational development from within for the first time. The existence of the Welsh Office had made this possible. The success of the development of the National Curriculum meant that the Welsh education system was now probably self-confident enough to determine change in its own right.

Was the educational policy community a true policy community? In section 9.1 and in Chapter VII it was seen that there was little academic literature that can provide a political science view of the territorial policy community. The works of Rhodes and Marsh (1992, 1999, 1997 and 1998) define the classic policy communities, but these tend to be more restrictive in their membership, interaction resource and power base than the Welsh educational policy establishment. The educational policy community was also more powerful than the policy model described as an Issue Network (Marsh and Rhodes, 1992). It did not, from the evidence of the output from the Curriculum Cymreig, suffer from the 'limited consensus' or 'ever-present conflict' of an issue network. This book has indicated that, from evidence of the establishment of a Welsh national curriculum, the territorial policy community in Wales was more of a proto-policy community, developing its own unique Welsh characteristics than the classic models would indicate.

Chapter X

Welsh Office to the Welsh Assembly:–
The Policy Process

The aim of this book was to explore the history of the Welsh Office and the policy process. From the previous chapters it has become clear that the Welsh Office helped to give Wales a presence in the policy process of the UK far greater than its population merited. No region of England was able to adapt government policy to its own advantage in the way that Wales could. Neither did these regions have a seat in the Cabinet, nor a powerful input into a wide variety of government policies in the way that the Welsh Office provided.

Although the Welsh Office was classified by some as one of the most junior government departments, and had its views ignored at times by both Whitehall and Westminster, its very presence became of paramount importance to the Welsh nation in developing a distinct identity. Over the thirty five years it existed, the Welsh Office expanded from a government department with a purely supervisory role to the premier civil service department in Wales. Adaptability proved to be perhaps the Welsh Office's greatest virtue. It constantly readjusted itself, and the territorial policy community that surrounded it altered it in order to deal with new situations and the policy whims of the government of the day.

Section 10.1. The end of the Conservative era

The Conservatives were instrumental in setting up the first minister for Wales. Yet they balked at the idea of establishing a Welsh Office and Welsh Secretary. Despite this initial reluctance, they developed the Welsh Office to a stage where it became almost on an equal footing with the much longer established Scottish Office. Every Welsh Secretary had been an empire builder. The Conservatives, however, found it very difficult to fill the Welsh Office ministerial portfolios. The last Conservative Welsh Secretaries, unlike their Scottish counterparts, did not hold a personal mandate in the country they governed. They were English based politicians in Wales. The calibre of Welsh Tories was not deemed suitable for the high ranks of Cabinet Office, and appropriate Secretaries therefore had to be brought in from outside. This meant that they always had to be trained in the Welsh Office policy process. It also meant that they had no interest in a future within Wales and therefore the Welsh Office was used as a mechanism to promote their own political ambitions onto the UK stage. Because the Welsh Office gave them access to the myriad of Cabinet Committees ranging from Health to Agriculture, they had the background and excuse to promote their own policy agenda on virtually any domestic policy issue. John Redwood and later William Hague became the prime examples of Conservative politicians using the Welsh Office as a stepping stone for the leadership of their own party.

The Conservative Party that had shaped the Welsh Office and government policy in Wales for almost two decades ceased to exist at a parliamentary level in Wales after 1977. Even the practice of appointing English MPs to serve the Conservatives in their top Welsh portfolio was abandoned. This meant that William Hague became not only the Conservatives' last Welsh Secretary but also their last Shadow Welsh Secretary. The post of Shadow Welsh Secretary disappeared soon after its last incumbent, William Hague, won the Conservative Party leadership contest in the Summer of 1997.

The defeat of the Conservatives in Wales had some mixed blessings for the former Conservatives at the Welsh Office. William Hague's victory as Conservative Party leader, for a while, made him the most successful former Conservative Welsh Secretary ever. The fact that Hague went on to lead the Conservative Party, and also married a Welsh Office civil servant, had an important influence on the development of the Conservative Party in Wales. For the first time, somebody at the top of the Conservative Party had a first hand knowledge of the political situation in Wales. This factor proved vital to the rapid evolution of the Conservative Party in Wales. Within the space of a year, the Welsh Conservative party has developed its own elected leadership, internal organisation structure and devolved policy making process (Deacon, 1999).

If the Conservatives had won the 1997 general election it is likely that the Welsh Office would have evolved to become the centre of a more Welsh civil service machine but still dominated by English politicians. Traditions and culture in the Welsh Office were changing. It had become a ministry that was increasingly separated from its counterparts in Whitehall, caused partly by its Conservative overlords having no link with Wales and ambitions elsewhere. It had for instance, developed its own pay and management structures. This distancing had not occurred just because the Welsh Office lay on the periphery of the UK civil service. It occurred because the Welsh Office was developing or moulding more government policies to have an increasingly Welsh angle to them. There was an increase in the need for staff to become ever more specialised (professional) in dealing with Welsh Policy. The *Welsh Language Acts* also provided the Welsh Office with another reason to distinguish it from the rest of Whitehall. It was the only truly bilingual ministry in the United Kingdom. Few civil servants from the rest of the UK could therefore easily come in and replace Welsh speaking civil servants.

The end of the Welsh Office

The Conservatives did not win the 1997 general election. Instead the Labour Party set about the task of ensuring the Welsh Office's demise. Before May 1997 it had been a long time since a Labour politician has been referred to as 'minister' by a Welsh Office official. A whole generation of civil servants had passed through the Welsh Office since John Morris, the last Labour Welsh Secretary, stood at the Despatch Box to answer Welsh Questions until Ron Davies arrival there. Yet one of the factors that led to the Labour Party's failure at the 1979 General Election, devolution, had once again become the central plank of the Labour Party's policies concerning the future of the Welsh Office. The Labour Party made it clear that they would introduce the legislation for an elected Assembly for Wales in their first year in power if the referendum was successful. The Welsh Office would then be required to transfer its accountability and its operational remit to this new Assembly. Its main purpose would be to act as a secretariat to the new Assembly with a small Welsh Office also remaining to serve the Welsh Secretary. In 1983 the constitutional expert Jim Bulpitt defined the concept of a Welsh Assembly as it applied to 1979:

> 'The devolution package obviously did not represent a general change in the United Kingdom's territorial constitution: England and Northern Ireland were omitted. Moreover, even though an elected Assembly was to be established in Wales, its powers were limited to those subsumed under the concept of executive devolution: it would merely execute the laws laid down by Westminster. In constitutional terms at least, the Welsh Assembly was meant to be little more than an enlarged county council. In addition Welsh representation at Westminster remained the same and this was combined with continued existence of

the Secretary of State, who was granted considerable power over the new Assembly. The actual institutional loser in the game was the Welsh Office, the Centre (Whitehall) in general lost few important functions. The potential losers were local authorities and ad hoc nominated agencies whose function, indeed existence, were subject to the authority of the new Assembly' (Bulpitt, 1983, pp. 189–190).

Bulpitt's comments on the 1979 Assembly proposals could be said to apply equally to its 1990s counterpart which differed very little from that proposed in the 1970s (Deacon, 1996). Political devolution therefore much talked about and discussed during the previous three decades of the Welsh Office's existence, was finally becoming a political reality.

The very impetus behind this devolution was to alter the 'Welsh Office and the Policy Process'. It was to go from being in the hands of one man (the Welsh Secretary), a few Ministers, and what was seen to be an unaccountable policy community, into the hands of an Assembly of some 60 elected members. The period since the end of this study has seen some interesting changes, the foremost of which are explored in this short section, which brings the book to a close.

Changing characters and policy directions

It was not just those Conservatives associated with the Welsh Office who suffered mixed political fortunes, see later. The three Shadow Ministers at the time of the 1997 general election suffered different fates, which took them away from the Welsh Office. The first to go, or not even arrive, was Rhodri Morgan. Tony Blair left him on the backbenches. Something that was regretted by Ron Davies and Alun Michael not least because he challenged them both for the leadership of the Wales Labour Party and remained there as the heir apparent. Morgan eventually became First Minster after Michael's departure. The second of the three Shadows to depart was Win Griffiths. He got to the Welsh Office but was replaced within a year by Jon Owen Jones[1], the Labour Welsh Whip. Ron Davies felt the sacking of Win Griffiths was unjustified. Davies felt that Blair did this because he wanted to change the personnel in all Ministries with the Welsh Office being no exception (Davies to author). Alun Michael, then at the Home Office, couldn't understand why Win Griffiths was sacked either. He felt, however, that Davies should have protected him and fought his corner with Blair over keeping Griffiths (Michael to author).

The political devolution process seemed to become something of a paradox at the Welsh Office. It seemed as though London, in the shape of Number 10, was allowing political devolution but at the same time keeping a tight reign on things in Wales. Huw Roberts, Ron Davies's former Political Adviser, noted this factor and criticised the exclusion of Rhodri Morgan and removal of Win Griffiths at a time when the devolutionary process at the Welsh Office required their additional input. The Scottish Office created an extra Minister, providing Scotland with seven to Wales's three. Ron Davies had pushed for an extra minister but the request was ignored by Blair (Davies to author). Roberts saw the New Labour Government as having a 'worrying lack of sensitivity to Wales and Welsh issues' (Roberts, 1999, p. 19).

When Tony Blair openly campaigned for Alun Michael to become the new First Secretary, against the wishes of the majority of the Welsh grass roots membership, Labour MPs such as Paul Flynn and John Marek began to express the same point as Huw Roberts (Western Mail, 11/11/98).

Ron Davies, the acknowledged mastermind behind political devolution in Wales, seemed to be riding the crest of a political wave until he was brought down by a 'sexual scandal' in December 1998. He went from being Welsh Secretary and potentially the first 'First Secretary' of the New Assembly to Westminster backbencher within the space of a week. In his short term in office, Davies had ensured that a permanent all Wales democratic mandate would be brought to the policy process in Wales. At the same time he ensured that the Welsh Office continued to mould Westminster policies to Welsh circumstances, whether they were concerned with economic planning or local government reform. The last Shadow Welsh Secretary to take office, Nicholas Edwards, had been in post as Welsh Secretary for eight years. Davies was in post for barely a year and a half, but he had enabled a greater revolution to occur in Welsh politics than any Welsh Secretary before him. His tenure in the Welsh Office was missed by many within the Cathays Park Village who saw him, as the main policy actor behind devolution in Wales.

Thus within a year and a half, all three Shadow Welsh Front bench spokesmen had gone and Tony Blair had chosen a new team. Alun Michael was summoned to Number 10 during the middle of a meal with a *Financial Times* journalist to be told he would be the next Welsh Secretary (Michael to author). The fact that Michael had served on the Shadow Welsh Front bench team and had fought the devolutionary corner formerly editing the *Wales Radical Cymru*, since the 1970s was ignored by most politicians and the media. It was the fact that he had been Blair's number two while both were shadowing the Home Office and the close relationship he had enjoyed with him since then that came to the forefront. Opponents both inside and outside of his party labelled him as Blair's man in Wales. Something he was unable to shake off.

It was not just the Welsh Office Ministers whose time had come to move on. Rachel Lomax, the first female Permanent Secretary at the Welsh Office, announced she was to head the Department of Social Security. She had enjoyed a close working relationship with Ron Davies over devolutionary issues (Davies to author). Her predecessor at the Welsh Office, Michael Scholar, had left some three years before to head the Department of Trade and Industry. It was not now the position of Secretary of State that was to be the spring board for the up and coming, instead it was the Permanent Secretary's position. Lomax had taken the position of Permanent Secretary out of the dark shadows. She had made frequent public talks and written widely on her role and the Welsh Office in general. Her departure meant that the Welsh Office would lack any continuity in its most senior positions, between those who steered the Welsh Office along the road to devolution and those who would steer Welsh Office and Welsh Assembly together, namely Davies and Lomax.

At the start of this chapter we saw what a potential Conservative Welsh Office may have evolved into. This, however, was not to be, the Conservatives lost all six of their Welsh MPs in the May 1997 General Election. For the first time since the Welsh Office's formation there were no Conservative MPs in Wales. Despite their constant resistance to devolution, the Conservatives made a dramatic about turn and accepted devolution after losing the September 1997 referendum. Many of the Welsh Conservative politicians who had to failed to win seats in the 1997 general election or campaigned against the very existence of the Assembly, went on to become candidates and then Members of the new Assembly (including former Welsh Office Minister Rod Richards). The new Labour controlled Welsh Office wholeheartedly encouraged them to come in and support the Assembly. Professor Nick Bourne, leader of the No Campaign and formerly Chief Spokesman for his party in Wales, was even brought onto the National Assembly Advisory Group in order to shape the very institution he once tried so hard to stop.

History appeared to be repeating itself. As was seen in Chapter II, when the Welsh Office was established some three decades before, the Conservative Party had opposed it, but within six years they were increasing its size and power. Would the same thing now happen to its views about the Assembly? We wait for history to judge.

The devolutionary policy shake-up

With the Conservative's electoral defeat, the scene was set for a massive evolutionary shake-up in the way that policy making was undertaken. The then Shadow Welsh Secretary Ron Davies was appointed the first Labour Welsh Secretary for 18 years. The major defining policy difference between the Conservative and Labour Parties during the 1997 general election had been on Welsh political devolution. The Labour Party had been publicly in favour and the Conservatives against. With a massive Labour election victory in May 1997, even by Welsh standards, the stage was set to change the way policy making was undertaken in Wales forever. Wales was to have an elected Assembly created to take over the policy making role of the Welsh Office.

The process, however, of even getting political devolution to the stage of a referendum in Wales had been the result of a difficult and tortuous internal policy process within the Wales Labour Party. In February 1999, in a speech to the Institute of Welsh Affairs, Davies stated that:

> 'I was guided by the need to be pragmatic. It was all very well for academics and arm-chair critics to devise grandiose schemes which satisfied constitutional theories but unless there was support for proposals within the Labour Party and in particular in the Policy Commission and the Welsh Executive Committee then such schemes were pretty futile. The policy making process in the Party was less than ideal. There was insufficient open and informed debate. As a result the formation of policy was left to manoeuvring and compromise within the innermost circle' (Davies, 1999, p. 6).

The exclusiveness of the Labour Party decision making process had, ironically, started a process of political evolution that, in time, could ensure inclusiveness within the policy making process for more people and interest groups than the Welsh Office ever had.

Now that the Wales Labour Party was officially behind political devolution, the next hurdle was to get the Welsh people to back it in a referendum. Davies, with the help of the politicians from his own and many other political parties, and people from no party, worked hard for a 'Yes' vote in the referendum. On 18 September 1997 they achieved their narrow majority for the 'Yes' vote. The operation to introduce a political Assembly to Wales went into operation. After over three decades of administrative devolution, Wales was now set to receive political devolution. The *raison d' être* of the Welsh Office's founding father, Jim

Griffiths, and subsequent Welsh Secretaries, Cledwyn Hughes and John Morris, was finally achieved by Ron Davies.

The very basis of much of the Yes Campaign and the concept of the new Assembly was to open up the policy process in Wales. The previous eighteen years of Conservative rule at the Welsh Office were widely condemned by the Yes Campaign. It was argued that the Welsh Office policy process was being determined by 'unelected Quangos' which meant that 'we've had no choice and no voice' (Yes for Wales, 1). The campaign slogan adopted by the Wales Labour Party was 'Wales Deserves a Voice' (Yes for Wales, 3). Therefore, Yes Campaign literature emphasised that 'a' Welsh Assembly will be able to speak up for Wales in Britain and Europe. It will mean that our voices are heard and we can set out our own priorities on the services that matter most' (Yes for Wales, 1). The new Assembly would be inclusive in determining policy outcomes: 'An Assembly will be a forum for all who live in Wales – young and old, North and South, urban and rural . . .' (Yes for Wales, 2). Indeed much of the run up to the Assembly referendum was filled with the Yes Campaign emphasising how the policy process would be opened up to business, the voluntary sector and, in fact, virtually anybody that wished to have a say on policy creation. Alun Michael was eventually to put this in concrete in the form of Partnership Councils between business, local government and the voluntary sector.

The changing policy scene

As seen earlier, the introduction of the Assembly was designed to open up the policy process in Wales. The new Assembly took over two of the key policy areas of the Welsh Office. These were deemed by the National Assembly Advisory Group (NAAG) as being:

- *Policy development within Wales.* Identifying problem areas, consulting outside bodies, looking at best practice, deciding on priorities for action, setting objectives and targets.
- *Implementing policies.* Once the Assembly decides on its priorities it will need to put them into effect through new legislation for example, or new targets for public bodies funded by the Assembly. The Assembly will often need to work in partnership with other organisations, such as local government and voluntary organisations, to achieve objectives (NAAG, 1998A, p. 6).

NAAG consulted widely on the issue of the Assembly and its policy making process. In its recommendations, it required the Assembly to formalise relationships with much of the Cathays Park Village. As mentioned earlier Welsh local government, for instance, has joined with the Assembly to form a Partnership Council, whereas the voluntary sector has formed a Voluntary Sector Forum (NAAG, 1998B, p. 54).

The power to determine much of the Welsh policy distinctiveness has passed from the Welsh Secretary and his Ministers to the First Minister and the 8 Assembly Secretaries, in a Cabinet structure known as the Executive Committee. NAAG saw that this system would 'facilitate the development of a new approach to government – characterised by a more consensual approach to policy making together with clear decision making' (NAAG, 1998B, pp. 35–36). The Secretaries are obliged to consult widely within the Assembly and beyond when constructing policy (NAAG, 1998B). Only the extent to which they listen and act on the policy desires they receive from outside of their own elite will truly differentiate the Assembly and policy making from that undertaken by the Welsh Office.

The Wales Secretary (the new, although widely un-used, name for the Welsh Secretary) still plays a minor role in aiding policy development. He will be needed to aid the Assembly in its desire for both further funding from the Treasury and in getting primary legislation through Westminster (Bradbury, 1998, p. 13). In the initial stages of the Assembly's existence, the First Minister also held the post of Welsh Secretary, in the shape of Alun Michael. Michael found the combination of both posts together with the elections for leadership, followed by the Assembly elections to be very difficult (Michael to author). Most of the time he was troubled by 'events' ranging from the rapid decline in agricultural fortunes in Wales to saving the Ford plant at Bridgend from closure (he flew directly to Detroit in the USA to address Ford bosses). He also pursued some of his own pet projects on NHS management, and his particular favourite youth education and training (Michael to author). It is therefore not surprising with so many distractions that civil servants were soon complaining that an ever-increasing backlog of decision making was permanently in the Welsh Secretary's in tray awaiting his approval (Welsh Office officials to author).

When Michael resigned after becoming First Minister he was replaced by Paul Murphy. The new Welsh Secretary is not privy to the policy processes of the Assembly in the way that Michael had been, but Michael and Murphy maintained a very close relationship politically (both are strongly anti-nationalist politicians). This is not the case with Paul Murphy and Rhodri Morgan, however. The extent to which Murphy is still in the Welsh political 'loop' remains unknown.

The Cathays Park Village

It is not just the faces that govern Wales that are changing. The surrounding Cathays Park Village is also altering. The centre of power has moved from the Welsh Office in Cathays Park to the new Assembly buildings in Cardiff Bay. Thus there is now a Cardiff Bay Village as opposed to a Cathays Park one. As seen earlier, much of the policy interaction between the Village and the Welsh Office has been formalised in various committees termed Partnership, Forum or Advisory Group (NAAG, 1998B). This makes the links between the Welsh Assembly and the Village much more clear and accountable than with the Welsh Office. Thus, when the Welsh Assembly decides its yearly budget it consults widely with the policy community outside (Bradbury, 1998, pp. 10–11).

It is not just the policy community that desires to see its own policy demands fulfilled in the new Assembly. There is the input on matters of policy from the 50 or so Assembly members who do not serve in either the Assembly's Cabinet or as Presiding or Deputy Presiding Officer. They make consistent political and informational demands of the Assembly. The former Welsh Office now serves 57 more politicians than under the old system. It helps determine Welsh policies that do not just differ from Whitehall ones around the margins, but are either totally unique or radically different from those in London. The Assembly can now introduce Private Bills in Westminster creating its own raft of legislation which could develop a separate legal structure in Wales. This means that the traditional reliance on Whitehall departments and other expertise in England has become more limited as the Assembly's policy becomes more detached from government policy in England. The policy community may well find itself filling this gap, but also becoming more isolated from its counterparts in England.

At the same time the Assembly must also ensure that these policies are implemented. Over coming decades the Welsh Assembly and the policy process will be shaped in Wales in ways which were unthinkable at the Welsh Office's foundation in 1964. The thirty five year period before the Welsh Assembly, however, allowed the Welsh Office to build up the mechanisms and expertise. The very nature of the policy community is also altering to take account of the new Assembly. Prominent Welsh quangos such as Health Promotion Wales and Tai Cymru have been merged into the Assembly. Whilst others, such as the WDA, the DBRW and the Land Authority for Wales (LAW), were merged together to form a new economic super quango. This was aimed to ensure that the new Assembly is able to determine its own policy agenda in the way that the old Welsh Office was never able, or perhaps even allowed, to do, at least publicly.

Concluding comment: was the Welsh Office really a conduit for distinctive Welsh policy?

The Welsh Office was part of the Home civil service and was closely integrated within its overall structure. The Welsh Office was in the group of ministries referred to as the territorial ministries. Of this group it was similar to the Scottish and Northern Ireland Offices, but was weaker than them in the following areas:

1. policy coverage;
2. civil servants employed;
3. budget;
4. number and status of its ministers;
5. career prospects of its ministers but not its civil servants.

These differences made it politically weaker than its territorial sister departments and less able to influence the policy process to its own advantage. Earlier studies indicate that the role and function of the Welsh Office was as a junior ministry designed in some way to be both the policy voice of the Cabinet in Wales, and that of Wales in the Cabinet. Thus the Welsh Office could be seen to a degree as an exponent of Welsh political consciousness. Over its last decade this role was seen by many to have been thwarted by a number of factors, the foremost of which were that the Welsh Office:

1. suffered from the transfer of the running of the Welsh Office from Welsh-based to English based Welsh Secretaries, which resulted in the imposition of 'alien policies' (Griffiths, D. 1996; Osmond, 1996);
2. was a ministry which suffered from a low ministerial status and a low public profile outside Wales and was run by Welsh Secretaries who had more interest in their own policy desires than the policy needs and aspirations of Wales (Thomas, 1987, Rose, 1987 and King, 1994);
3. was little more than a rubber stamping mechanism for Whitehall policy (Goldsmith, 1986, Thomas, 1987, Boyne et al, 1991 and Griffiths, D., 1995) although some have also indicated the benefits of being somewhat distanced from Whitehall (Jones, 1990; Lightman, 1995).

This book has examined each of these factors in turn. For *point one* it indicated that the original Welsh Secretaries and Permanent Secretaries were men of Wales who returned from England in order to help run Wales. Their policy aspirations were often pro-political and administrative devolution. This all changed in 1987 with the appointment of Peter Walker as Welsh Secretary. In the ten years that followed, Welsh aspirations and hostility to government policies such as the poll tax and the opting out of schools were mainly ignored. Although some of these policies were cushioned to a far greater extent than in England, they nevertheless remained alien to the vast majority of Welsh politicians. The Parliamentary mechanisms used to represent Welsh opinion proved insignificant in opposing ideology that the vast majority of the Welsh electorate had never endorsed. It was clear that on a number of important issues the voice of Wales was not being heard in the Cabinet but the voice of the Cabinet was being heard loud and clear in Wales. Welsh Secretaries such as Redwood and Hague became more interested in using Wales to determine their own status in UK-wide politics. The Welsh Office was not being effective as an exponent of Welsh policy distinctiveness as its original creator James Griffiths had anticipated. It was under these same secretaries, however, that the Welsh National Curriculum bloomed.

Point two, the Welsh Office for virtually the whole of its existence 'suffered from a low ministerial status and a low public profile outside of Wales'. The study indicates that this was enhanced by:

- the difficulty the Conservative government had in finding either Welsh based or other Cabinet ministers to take on the Welsh Office portfolio. After Peter Walker left the post in 1990 there were indications that Conservative Cabinet ministers refused to take the post and consequently it was always offered to 'up and coming' junior ministers. This gave the Welsh Office the reputation of a training ground for Cabinet, although in fact no Welsh Secretary, Labour or Conservative, ever progressed into one of the top posts in the Cabinet. It also had the effect of concentrating power in London, as Welsh Secretaries ceased to reside in Wales on a constituency basis. This was only reversed in the Welsh Office's last two years.
- the poor coverage of the Welsh Office by the London-based media which reduced the Welsh Secretary's profile to the small Welsh-based media. Such small media coverage may have enhanced the Welsh Secretary's own policy autonomy in Wales but it did nothing to improve his status in the political arena of Whitehall and Westminster. In a

political system in which status was shown by the departments importance to the London based media the Welsh Office remained an ob-
scure and 'low-key ministry'.

The fact that the Welsh Office remained a low key ministry therefore
detracted from its ability to effectively represent Welsh policy concerns
at the Cabinet table.

Point three, despite the fact that this book supports the view that English Welsh Secretaries have introduced 'alien policies' and caused the
Welsh Office to continue to suffer from a low-key status it does not support the view that the Welsh Office was merely a 'rubber stamping mechanism' for Whitehall. The first, sixth and ninth chapters provide clear
empirical evidence of distinctive Welsh policies being followed by the
Welsh Office. As part of this process the Welsh Office was able to manipulate primary and secondary legislation to its own advantage. However, the Welsh Office's small size and relative lack of expertise compared to the much larger Whitehall ministries meant that it often relied on
them to take the lead on policy initiatives. Occasionally the secondary
legislation did merely have 'Made in England' replaced with 'Made in
Wales' on it without any changing of the contents.

One of the moves of the last Labour Welsh Secretaries was to bring the
Welsh Office back to Wales, from Gwydyr House in London back to Cathays
Park in Cardiff. Pressure groups and other groups had become adept at
going up to London to address their issues. This was to change, politics had
once again become more local the focus was to change from London to
Cardiff on many important Welsh issues, (Davies and Michael to author).

We can therefore conclude this book by stating that the Welsh Office
did have the ability to act as the voice of Wales in the Cabinet. It could
create or adapt legislation, or establish new public bodies in order to fulfil Welsh needs and desires. This voice however, was muted both by the
junior position of the Welsh Secretary within the Cabinet and by his lack
of durable interest in maintaining a high political profile in Wales. Under
the Welsh Office, policy had to bear in mind collective responsibility.
This meant it couldn't deviate too far and too publically from the national agenda. Any policy idea could be blocked by Whitehall at any
stage. Both the Welsh Secretary and the Welsh Office were therefore not
fulfilling the role and function anticipated by their creator James Griffiths
by fully developing a Welsh policy agenda.

Final words

In the period leading up to the referendum and afterwards, few kind words were said about the Welsh Office and the Policy Process. It was seen as being 'elitist, out of touch and a mechanism for Whitehall and Westminster domination of Wales'. Yet for 35 years it had been the prime beneficiary of devolved administrative power to Wales. It had enabled a joined up approach to government to operate in Wales decades before it was attempted in England. In some policy areas, such as education, it had shaped a Welsh agenda, which would probably not have been possible without its existence. Perhaps most importantly it had developed a civil service and public sector that could be quickly tuned to serving a democratically elected Assembly.

The ceremony that marked the Welsh Assembly's opening did not follow one marking the Welsh Office's closing. Nevertheless the Welsh Office led the way to making the Welsh Assembly possible. It had some Welsh policy successes which both officials and politicians who served there can be rightly proud of. Much of the Assembly's 'new policy openness' will be built upon the previous work of the Welsh Office. The Welsh Assembly, however, is able to examine and construct policy in far more detail and analysis than any Welsh Office Minister could have done. Although the Welsh Office and the Policy Process are now nothing more than a memory, its legacy is to be found in the policy processes and ideals of the new Assembly.

Notes

1. Owen Jones was himself dropped from the junior minister's post in the new Office of Welsh Secretary in June 2000.

Appendix 1

Table A.1
The Minister for Welsh Affairs

From 1951–1957 this post was held by the Home Secretary, and from 1957–1964 by the Minister of Housing and Local Government.

1951	Sir David Maxwell Fyfe
1954	Gwilym Lloyd-George
1957	Henry Brooks
1961	Charles Hill
1962	Sir Keith Joseph

Table A.2
Welsh Office Ministers

Secretary of State	Party	Junior Ministers
James Griffiths 1964–66	Labour	Goronwy Roberts 1964–66 Harold Finch 1964–66
Cledwyn Hughes 1966–68	Labour	George Thomas 1966–67 Ifor Davies 1967 Eirene White 1967
George Thomas 1968–70	Labour	Ifor Davies 1968–70 Eirene White 1968–70 Ted Rowlands 1969–70
Peter Thomas 1970–74	Conservative	David Gibson-Watt 1970–74
John Morris 1974–79	Labour	Ted Rowlands 1974–75 Barry Jones 1974–79 Alec Jones 1975–79
Nicholas Edwards 1979–87	Conservative	Michael Roberts 1979–82 Wyn Roberts 1979–87 Sir John Stradling Thomas 1983–85 Mark Robinson 1985–87
Peter Walker 1987–90	Conservative	Sir Wyn Roberts 1987–1990 Ian Grist 1987–90

(Table A.2 *contd.*)

Secretary of State	Party	Junior Ministers
David Hunt 1990–93	Conservative	Ian Grist 1990 Sir Wyn Roberts 1990–93 Nicholas Bennett 1990–92 Gwilym Jones 1992–93
John Redwood 1993–95	Conservative	Sir Wyn Roberts 1993–1994 Gwilym Jones 1993– Rod Richards 1994–
David Hunt 1995 (Caretaker)	Conservative	Gwilym Jones 1995– Rod Richards 1995–
William Hague 1995–97	Conservative	Gwilym Jones 1995–1997 Rod Richards 1995–1996 Jonathan Evans 1995–1997
Ron Davies 1997–98	Labour	Win Griffiths 1997–1998 Peter Hain 1997–1998 John Owen Jones 1998
Alun Michael 1998–1999	Labour	Peter Hain 1998–1999 John Owen Jones 1998–1999

Table A.3
Welsh Office Permanent Secretaries*

Date	Name
1964–69	Goronwy Daniel
1969–71	Idwal Pugh
1971–80	Hywel Evans
1980–85	Trevor Hughes
1985–93	Richard Lloyd Jones
1993–96	Michael Scholar
1996–98	Rachel Lomax
1998–	John Shortridge

* Until 1974 the most senior position was that of Permanent Deputy Secretary

Appendix 2

Table A.4

Important steps on the road to establishing the Welsh Office

Year	Event
1536–1542	Acts of Union between Wales and England were carried out by Henry VIII.
1540s–1860s	Anglicisation of Welsh life, especially among middle and ruling classes.
1830	Abolition of the Court of Great Sessions, the last major Welsh institution left over from the Acts of Union.
1868	Start of '50 years of Welsh political nationalism as a major force in British public life' mainly under the Welsh Liberals.
1886	*Cymru Fydd* (Young Wales) movement started, which sought to promote Welsh devolution.
1889	Welsh Intermediate Education Act – acknowledged Wales as a separate administrative region for the first time.
1892	The National Institutions (Wales) Bill 1892 which proposed the creation of a Secretary of State for Wales was defeated.
1892	Foundation of the University of Wales, whose graduates later went on to campaign for, then create and run the Welsh Office.
1896	Central Welsh Education Board (CEB) was set up to administer the 1889 Education Act. The first all-Wales public administration body.
1897	Foundation of Welsh Liberal Council, the first Welsh focus within a political party.
1906–1921	Golden Era of Welsh Liberal administrative devolution. The period marked devolution of the administration of Education, Health, Agriculture and Fisheries to Wales.
1920	Disestablishement of the Church in Wales.
1921	Private Members Bill seeking to introduce a Welsh Secretary failed.
1925	Foundation of *Plaid Genedlaethol Cymru* (later known as Plaid Cymru), whose initial aims were to promote increased Welsh devolution.
1938	Pro-Welsh Secretary delegation led by Morgan Jones, Labour MP for Caerphilly was informed by Neville Chamberlain that he would not allow a Welsh Secretary/Office to be established. He gave the grounds of 'expense, the existing devolved administrative structure being adequate and the lack of a *significant distinction* existing between Welsh and English public administration'.
1939	Ministry of Health in Wales, headquarters, was built in Cathays Park, Cardiff (by E. Turner & Sons). The building was later to become the Welsh Office headquarters.
1943	Churchill rejected further calls for a Welsh Secretary.
1944	Welsh Question time established in the House of Commons.

(Table A.4 *contd.*)

Year	Event
1945	Devolutionist Welsh Labour Party candidates called for an economic planning authority and a Welsh Secretary via political pamphlet *Llais* (Voice of Labour) *Llabur*.
1945–51	Labour Party remained split on the issue of a Welsh Secretary/Office with Aneurin Bevan leading the anti and James Griffiths the pro-groups.
1949	An 'independent' Advisory Council for Wales and Monmouthshire (Welsh Council) established to advise the government on Welsh Affairs.
1951	The Conservatives added the remit of Minister for Welsh Affairs to the Home Secretary's portfolio (David Maxwell Fyfe at the time.
1956	S.O. Davies, MP for Merthyr Tydfil, put forward a Private Members Bill for a Welsh parliament. The Welsh Labour Party opposed it and the Bill failed.
1956 April	A petition of some 250,000 signatures, supporting a Welsh Parliament, was presented to Parliament by Goronwy Roberts, Labour MP for Caernarfon.
1957	Labour Party members who supported a Welsh Parliament turned their attention to the campaign for a Welsh Secretary.
1957	The Welsh Council resigned *en bloc* after Harold Macmillan (Prime Minister) refused to support their motion calling for the establishment of a Welsh Office.
1957 December	Responsibility for Welsh Affairs was transferred to the Minister of Housing and Local government, Henry Brooks. Harold MacMillan recommended that he held the title Secretary of State for Wales in addition to his existing title. The idea was rejected by Rab Butler (Deputy Prime Minister) who feared that it would lead to greater demands for Welsh devolution.
1959	Dr Huw T. Morgan, Chairman of the Welsh Council, resigned from the Labour Party over their failure to support the policy of a Welsh Office/Secretary.
1959	Pro-Welsh Office Parliamentary Group led by Cledwyn Hughes helped persuaded Hugh Gaitskell of the need for a Welsh/Office Welsh Secretary.
1959	Aneurin Bevan ended his, effective, veto over the establishment of a Welsh Office.
1959 autumn	Labour published *Forward with Labour: Labour's Policy for Wales* which gave a firm commitment to a Welsh Secretary/Office.
1959	Pro-Welsh Office Labour lost the general election. The Conservatives who were strongly against a Welsh Office won it.
1961	The Conservatives established a Welsh Grand Committee (consisting of all Welsh MPs) in order to placate the growing demands for a Welsh Secretary/Office.
1964	The Labour Party repeated the promise of a Welsh Secretary/Office in their general election manifesto: *Signposts for a New Wales*.

(Table A.4 *contd.*)

Year	Event
1964 October	Labour won the general election. James Griffiths was appointed Secretary of State for Wales, Goronwy Roberts and Harold Finch were appointed his junior Ministers. Goronwy Daniel was appointed as the first Permanent Under Secretary.
1965 April	The Welsh Office was officially opened for business.

Table A.5

Important events influencing policy direction during the Welsh Office's first 32 years

Date	Event
1964 October	James Griffiths became Welsh Secretary at the age of 74. Goronwy Daniel joined the Welsh Office from Fuel and Power to become the Welsh Office's first Permanent Under Secretary.
1964	Housing, Local Government, Town and Country Planning, New Towns, Water & Sewerage, Forestry, National Parks, Ancient Monuments & Historic Buildings and the Welsh Language, Regional Economic Planning, National Parks, National Museum and National Library and Highways were all transferred to the new Welsh Office.
1965 April	Welsh Office started operations with 225 staff.
1965	Welsh Development Act was introduced to help cope with the fall of King Coal.
1965	Sir Myrddin Evans Commission on Welsh Local Government Reform suggested a reduction in the role of the Welsh Council, but was rejected by Griffiths. A new internal Welsh Office Commission was set up under Goronwy Daniel.
1966	Plans for a new Welsh capital in the Caersws, Llanidloes, Newtown area were rejected after protests from Cardiff County Borough and Mid Wales land owners.
1966	The Hughes Parry Report, that stated that the Welsh language should have equal status with English within Wales, was accepted.
1966 April	Labour won the general election, Cledwyn Hughes was appointed Welsh Secretary.
1966–68	Cledwyn Hughes failed to get Agricultural responsibility given to the Welsh Office, Agricultural Secretary Fred Peart resisted the measure 'at every stage'.
1966 October	116 young children and 28 adults died in the Aberfan Disaster . Welsh Office helped co-ordinate relief efforts. Cledwyn Hughes went to London to inform the House of Commons.
1967	First Welsh Office derived Act: The Welsh Language Act. This started

(Table A.5 *contd.*)

Date	Event
	the administrative policy of equalisation between the English and Welsh languages. South Wales Valleys designated Special Development Areas.
1967	Daniels Internal Panel, on Welsh local government change, delivered its recommendations, in secret, to Cledwyn Hughes. First option was on rationalisation of Welsh local government; the second was on 8 unitary authorities and a Welsh Senate. The latter was roundly defeated both in cabinet and in Whitehall, the former was lost in years of delay.
1967	Welsh Arts Council established, Welsh Office's first quango.
1968	Tourism and Health transferred to the Welsh Office.
1968 April	Cledwyn Hughes became Secretary of State at Agriculture; George Thomas was then appointed Welsh Secretary. Eirene White became the first and only female minister to be appointed to the Welsh Office.
1968	Militant nationalists exploded a bomb opposite the Welsh Office. It caused £4 – 5000 worth of damage to the Welsh Office.
1968	Royal Mint was relocated to Wales; partially as an economic measure to counteract the rise in Welsh political nationalism but the move also emphasised the growing power of the Welsh Office.
1969 April	Welsh Office gained joint control over Welsh agriculture with MAFF. This was mainly due to the influnce of Cledwyn Hughes, who had become Secretary of State at Agriculture.
1969	Investiture of Prince of Wales, the Welsh Office helped organise the event and George Thomas presided over events.
1969	Goronwy Daniel left the Welsh Office to become Principal of Aberystwyth University. Idwal Pugh was appointed as the new Permanent Under Secretary from Ministry of Housing and Local Government.
1969	Welsh Tourist Board established.
1970 June	Conservatives won the general election. First Conservative Welsh Secretary Peter Thomas was appointed; he was also Party Chairman. Both he and his junior minister David Gibson-Watt held English constituencies.
1970	Primary and Secondary Education transferred to the Welsh Office.
1971	Child Care relinquished by the Home Office and given to the Welsh Office, Sports Council for Wales established.
1971	Welsh Office created Welsh Water Authority in response to recommendation in the Welsh Councils Report : *The Water Problem*
1972	Sir Idwal Pugh returned to the Ministry of Housing and Local government to become Second Permanent Secretary. Sir Hywel Wyn Evans became the next Permanent Under Secretary, he came from within the Welsh Office.
1972–74	Reorganisation of Welsh local government. Initial Welsh Office proposals failed and the changes became a duplicate of the Department of

(Table A.5 *contd.*)

Date	Event
	Environment's changes occurring under Peter Walker in England.
1974	Reorganisation of Health Care in Wales; the Welsh Office now acted as a Regional Health Authority for Wales.
1974	Post of Permanent Under Secretary regraded to full Permanent Secretary.
1974	The two general elections of 1974 both brought a Labour Welsh Secretary. Pro-devolutionist John Morris was appointed Welsh Secretary to implement Labour's devolution proposals. This was instead of George Thomas, who was opposed to devolution. The next four years saw a steady increase in the powers arriving at the Welsh Office, intended for the proposed new assembly.
1974	Plans to reverse the Conservatives' 1974 local government changes were dropped after many councils expressed a lack of will.
1975	Industry and Export Promotion arrived at the Welsh Office, transferred from the Department of Trade and Industry.
1975	Civil Service Commission review established a Welsh Office Permanent Secretary's Division.
1976	Welsh Development Agency and Development Board for Rural Wales established.
1978	Full responsibility for Agriculture (most functions) was transferred from MAFF.
1978	Higher & Further Education (excl. Universities) Teachers and Manpower Planning given to the Welsh Office.
1978	White Paper *Our Changing Democracy* was adapted to form the Wales Act 1978. The Welsh Office was set to lose 98 per cent of its public expenditure responsibilities to the new Assembly, envisaged by this Act.
1978–1979	'Winter of Discontent'. John Morris went on TV to announce that troops had been called in to drive the ambulances within Wales.
1979	St David's Day Referendum on a Welsh Assembly was defeated by a majority of four to one. John Morris the Welsh Secretary considered resignation but the government fell shortly afterwards.
1979 May	Thatcher government elected, Nicholas Edwards appointed Welsh Secretary. He became the only Conservative Welsh Secretary to hold a Welsh constituency. The coming decade saw the establishment of numerous Welsh quangos including: a Schools Curriculum Council for Wales; the Welsh Language Education Development Committee; Tai Cymru/Housing for Wales; a Welsh Language Board; a Welsh Health Promotion Authority; CADW, established inside the Welsh Office to administer and promote sites of historic interest; and the Cardiff Bay Development Corporation.
1979	Welsh Affairs Select Committee established.
1979 Sept	William Whitelaw, Home Secretary, stated that the pledge to establish the Welsh language fourth channel would not be honoured. The new Welsh

(Table A.5 *contd.*)

Date	Event
	Secretary and his junior ministers felt unable to stand up to such a senior politician despite their unaninous desire for fourth channel for Wales.
1980	Trevor Hughes replaced Hywel Evans as Permanent Secretary. His previous post was as a Deputy Secretary at the Department of Transport.
1980	Nicholas Edwards was given almost total discretion over how the 'Welsh Block' (Treasury allocated money to Wales) was spent.
1980	Welsh Office moved into their own purpose built accommodation in Cathays Park. Majority of Welsh Office staff were in the same location for the first time.
1980 Sept	William Whitelaw reversed his decision on Welsh Channel Four after pressure from the Welsh 'Good and the Great' and also a campaign of civil disobedience by *Cymdeithas yr Iaith Gymraeg* and a pledge by Gwynfor Evans, Plaid Cymru's elder statesman, that he would fast to death unless the decision was reversed.
1981 April	Transfer of power over the Welsh Rate Support Grant to the Welsh Office, increasing fiscal autonomy.
1984–85	Coal Strike. Nicholas Edwards maintained a close relationship with Police. Llanwern Steel Works saw one of the strikes' most bitter battles. After the strike the Welsh Office sought to cope with the implications of the job losses.
1984/85	Pro-Welsh language Welsh Secretary and Ministers were now supporting the Welsh language at £2,600,000 a year. Four times that spent in 1979.
1985	Financial Management Initiative introduced delegated budgeting to Welsh Office line managers.
1987	Richard Lloyd Jones replaced Trevor Hughes as permanent secretary. He had been promoted from within the Welsh Office but had served right across Whitehall.
1987	Nicholas Edwards retired from politics. The Conservatives were re-elected and Peter Walker (Worcester) was the surprise appointment for Wales. He was a Cabinet moderate. Welsh Opposition and media treated the appointment as 'an Englishman come to conquer Wales'. Welsh Office's status moved up in Whitehall ratings, from 22nd to 7th, due to Walker's senior rating.
1988	The Valleys Initiative was launched. Its aim was to restore the economic fortunes of the South Wales Coalfield Communities. Much of Welsh Office economic policy was now devoted to this and its equivalent in North Wales: *The Road to Opportunity* based around the A55.
1988 onwards	Peter Walker toured the world seeking to increase inward investment from overseas. Companies from Japan, Korea, Germany and the United States came to Wales in increasing numbers. The 'Rents to mortgages' scheme was piloted, there was a dramatic increase in private housing projects and work by housing associations.
1989	The age of those appointed to quangos was deliberately lowered in an

(Table A.5 *contd.*)

Date	Event
	effort to increase new blood. Walker succeeded in having another army regiment stationed in Wales, and plans for a new Severn Bridge to be built were agreed.
1990 May	Peter Walker retired but helped choose his successor, Welsh-born David Hunt.
1990	Sir Anthony Meyer, the North Wales Conservative MP challenged Margaret Thatcher for the Conservative leadership. Welsh born Michael Heseltine then entered the ring. After Thatcher departed, all three Welsh Office Ministers backed Heseltine against Major and Hurd. After Major won pro-Heseltine minister Ian Grist was replaced by pro-Major Nicholas Bennet. Welsh Conservative backbenchers sent a letter of protest to the Prime Minister.
1990–92	Continuation of Valleys Initiative, Ebbw Vale Garden Festival, Cardiff Bay Development Corporation.
1991 April	Cadw became the Welsh Office's first Executive Agency.
1991 November	The concept of Market Testing was introduced to the Welsh Office as part of the *Competing for Quality* initiative.
1992	Employment training transferred to the Welsh Office. Welsh TECs came under Welsh Office control.
1992	St David's Day White Paper *Local Government in Wales: A Charter for the Future* was published. It stated that Welsh district and county councils would be merged into a system of unitary authorities. Unlike the 1972 reforms, the Welsh Office this time had a far greater say on what happened.
1992	Conservatives celebrated 13 years of policy implementation at the Welsh Office by publishing *The Dragon Awakes: A Decade of Development*.
1992 June	Conservatives won the general election. Nicholas Bennet and Ian Grist, minister and former minister, lost their seats; Bennet was replaced by Gwilym Jones. Conservatives now held only six seats in Wales, its lowest figure since 1966. Lack of Welsh backbenchers became a problem for the government in the Welsh Select Committee.
1992	Welsh Office assumed direct funding for the University of Wales.
1993 May	Chancellor Norman Lamont was sacked from the Cabinet, this brought about a reshuffle in which John Redwood (Wokingham) was appointed Welsh Secretary. *Western Mail* noted the 'only link with Wales is the M4'. Redwood replied 'judge me on my record'. He was the youngest Welsh Secretary to date, having been an MP for just 6 years before arriving there.
1993	Welsh Funding Councils established for further and higher education in Wales.
1993	Michael Scholar replaced Richard Lloyd Jones as Permanent Secretary. Scholar came directly from the Treasury.
1993	Second Welsh Language Act established the Welsh Language Board and introduced other measures to help promote the language.

(Table A.5 *contd.*)

Date	Event
1993	'Men in grey suits' speech by Redwood 'declares war' on public administrators in Wales. Over the next two years he reduced the budgets for Welsh quangos, stopped further administrative recruitment in NHS and cut 400 jobs from the Welsh Office.
1994	Local Government (Wales) Act received Royal Assent; Wales' 8 counties and 37 districts were subsequently turned into 22 unitary authorities from 1996 onwards.
1994	Welsh Office internal health divisions underwent a major restructuring. John Redwood announced that all existing DHAs and FHSAs were to be merged into five new authorities.
1994	Longest serving Welsh Office minister, Sir Wyn Roberts, left. Rod Richards, the only other Conservative MP in Wales fluent in Welsh, replaced him.
1995	Results of civil service 'Continuity and Change' review announced. The senior management structure was to be slimmed down.
1995	John Redwood resigned from the Welsh Office to contest the Conservative Party leadership. David Hunt took over in a caretaker role.
1995 July	William Hague (Richmond) took over from Hunt as 10th Welsh Secretary. Even younger than Redwood, he was the youngest Cabinet minister since 1945. One of his first measures was to announce a further 500 job cuts from the Welsh Office.
1996 June	Rod Richards resigned from the Welsh Office in the wake of a 'sex scandal'. Non-Welsh speaking Jonathan Evans took over. For the first time since its creation there was no longer a Welsh speaking minister at the Welsh Office.
1996 June	The Constitution Unit published its study into Welsh devolution it indicated that an Assembly could lead to the post of Welsh Secretary being abolished.
1996 July	Rachel Lomax became the first female to become a Permanent Secretary at the Welsh Office.
July 96–May 97	The Welsh Office maintained an anti-devolutionary stance under the Conservatives.
1997 June	General election resulted in the end of Conservative rule in Wales and the start of a new devolutionary era. A Labour Party was elected which was committed to replacing the Welsh Office with an elected Assembly. Shadow Welsh Secretary Ron Davies becomes Welsh Secretary.
July 1997	The Welsh Office published: *A Voice for Wales*, which outlined the future of the Welsh Office under the Welsh Assembly.
1997 Sept 18th	The Welsh Assembly Referendum was held. Just over half of the Welsh population voted. The result was a narrow majority for the Yes campaign. 50.3% yes, 49.7% No.
1997 October	The Welsh Office established a National Assembly Advisory Group (NAAG) to plan the shape of the new Assembly.

(Table A.5 *contd.*)

Date	Event
1998 July	The Government of Wales Act gained Royal Assent.
1998 August	The Welsh Office set up a Standing Orders Commission to draw up the rules for the running of the new Assembly.
1998 October 27th	Ron Davies resigned from the Welsh Office after a 'moment of madness' on Clapham Common'. Alun Michael was appointed as the new Welsh Secretary.
1999 May	Assembly elections held. Alun Michael formed a minority Labour government.
1999 July	The Welsh Office became the Welsh Assembly.

Bibliography

AARONOVITCH, D. (1996). 'Taking shelter in Wales as political storms gather', *The Independent*, p. 2.

ABERACH, J.D., PUTMAN, R.D. and ROCKMAN, B.A. (1981). *Bureaucrats and Politicians in Western Democracies*, Cambridge, Mass, Harvard University Press.

ALDER, J. (1994) 2nd edition. *Constitutional and Administrative Law*, London, Macmillan.

ALLEN, M. and THOMPSON, B. (1996) 4th edition. *Cases and Materials on Constitutional and Administrative Law*, London, Blackstone Press Limited.

BAGGOTT, R. (1989). 'The Policy Making Process in British Central Government', *Politics*, Winter 1990/91, Vol. 3, No. 2, Manchester, The Politics Association, pp. 50–56.

BAGGOTT, R. (1990). *Pressure Groups Today*, Manchester, Manchester University Press.

BAKER, C. (1993). 'Bilingual Education in Wales' in H.B. Beardsmore (ed.) *European Models of Bilingual Education*, Clivedon, Multilingual Matters Ltd.

BALSOM, D.F. (1979). 'The Nature and Distribution of Support for Plaid Cymru', *Studies in Public Policy*, 36, Glasgow, University of Strathclyde.

BALSOM, D.F. (1985). 'The Three-Wales Model' in John Osmond's (1985) *The National Question Again: Welsh Political Identity in the 1980s*, Llandysul, Gower.

BALSOM, D.F. and BURCH, M. (1980). *A Political and Electoral Handbook for Wales*, Farnbrough, Gower.

BALSOM, D.F., MADGWICK, P.J. and VAN MECHELEN, D. (1983). 'The Red and the Green: Patterns of Partisan Choice in Wales', *British Journal of Political Science*, Vol. 13, Part 3, July 1983, pp. 299–325.

BBC TV (Wales). *Week in Week Out*: The Game of Government, February 1994.

BENN, T. (1980). 'The Mandarins in Modern Britain', *Guardian*, 4 February 1980.

BIRCH, A.H. (1993) 9th edition. *The British System of Government*, London, Routledge.

BOGDANOR, V. (1979). 'Power and participation', *Oxford Review of Education*, Oxford, Oxford University Press, Vol. 5, No. 2, pp. 157–168.

BORRAS, S. (1993). "The 'Four Motors for Europe' and its Promotion of R & D Linkages: Beyond Geographical Contiguity in Interregional Agreements", *Regional Politics & Policy*, Vol. 3, No. 3, Autumn 1993, London, Frank Cass, pp. 163–176.

BOYNE, G.A., GRIFFITHS, P., LAWTON, A. and LAW, J. (1991). *Local Government in Wales: Its Role and Functions*, York, Joseph Rowntree Foundation.

BOYNE, G.A., JORDON, G. and MCVICAR, M. (1995). *Local Government Reform: A Review of the Process in Scotland and Wales*, London, LGC Communications.

BOYNE, G.A. and LAW, J. (1993). 'Bidding For Unitary Status: A Review of the Contest in Wales', *Local Government Studies*, London, Frank Cass, Vol. 19, pp. 537–57.

BRADBURY, J. (1997). 'Territory and Power revisited: Interpreting British Government and Territorial Politics', Paper presented at the annual conference of the *Political Studies Association*, Belfast, April 1997.

BRADBURY, J. (1998). 'Towards a new Welsh politics? Procedural preparation for the National Assembly', *PSA British Territorial Politics Seminar*, University of Newcastle.

BRENNAN, K., EDWARDS, H. and SOUTHCOTT, M. (31/10/96). Pamphlet entitled: 'Voting the Visions: A fair electoral system for the Welsh Assembly', Cardiff.

BRENNAN, K. (1997). 'Electing The Welsh Assembly', Cardiff, *Wales Review*, Issue No. 5, January 1997.

BROWN, A. MCCRONE, D. and PATERSON, L. (1996). *Politics and Society in Scotland*, London, MacMillan Press Ltd.

BROWN, R. and STEEL, D. (1979). *The Administrative Process in Britain*, 2nd Edition, London, Meuthuen & Co Ltd.

BULPITT, J. (1983). *Territory and Power in the United Kingdom*, Manchester, Manchester University Press.

BULPITT, J. (1995). 'Historical politics: macro, in time, governing regime analysis' in J. Lovenduski and J. Stanyer (eds) *Contemporary Political Studies 1995*, York, Vol. 2, pp. 510–520.

BULPITT, J. (1996). 'Historical politics: leaders, statecraft and regime in Britain at the accession of Elizabeth II', in I. Hampsher-Monk and J. Stanyer (eds) *Contemporary Political Studies 1996*, Glasgow, Vol. 2, pp. 1093–1106.

BURCH, M. and WOOD, B. (1990) 2nd edition. *Public Policy in Britain*, Blackwell, Oxford.

BUTLER, C. (1985). 'The Conservative Party in Wales: Remoulding a Radical Tradition' in John Osmond's (1985) *The National Question Again: Welsh Political Identity in the 1980s*, Llandysul, Gower, pp. 155–164.

BUTLER, C. (1986). 'Special Advisers – A Semi- Secret Circle', Planet Aberytywth, Planet, Vol. 55, pp. 13–20.

BUTLER, D. and BUTLER, G. (1994). *British Political Facts 1900–1994*, Basingstoke, Macmillan.

CALLAGHAN, J. (1987). *Time and Change*, London, Collins.

CALVERT, H. (1985). *An introduction to: British Constitutional Law*, London, Financial Training Publications Limited.

CARMICHAEL, P. (1996). 'Devolution – The Northern Ireland Experience', *Public Money and Management*, Vol. 16, No. 4, October–December 1996, Oxford, Blackwells, pp. 5–12.

CAMPBELL, C. and PETERS, B.G. (1988). 'The Politics/Administration Dichotomy: Death or Merely Change', *Governance*, Vol. 1, No. 1, pp. 79–99.

CLARK, A. (1993). *Alan Clark Diaries*, St Ives, Phoenix.

CONNOLLY, M. and KNOX, C. (1991). 'Policy Differences within the United Kingdom: the Case of Housing Policy in Northern Ireland 1979–89', *Public Administration*, Vol. 69, No. 3, Autumn 1991, Oxford, Blackwells, pp. 303–324.

CONNELLY, P. (1992). *Dealing with Whitehall: A Practical guide to understanding and influencing government decisions*, Century Press.

The Constitution Unit (1996A). *An Assembly for Wales: Senedd i Gymru*, London, Colorworks Ltd.

The Constitution Unit (1996B). *Scotland's Parliament: Fundamental for a New Scotland Act*, London, Colorworks Ltd.

The Constitution Unit (1996C). *Regional Government in England*, London, Colorworks Ltd.

CORNOCK, M. (1995). 'The Welsh Bland', *Western Mail*, 2/2/95.

CRICKHOWELL, N. (1999). *Westminster, Wales and Water*, Cardiff, University of Wales Press.

Curriculum Council for Wales (1989). *A Framework for the Whole Cur-*

riculum 5–16 Wales–A Discussion Paper, Cardiff, Curriculum Council for Wales.

Curriculum Council for Wales (1991). *The Whole Curriculum – Principles and Issues for Consideration by Schools in Curriculum Planning and Implementation*, Cardiff, Curriculum Council for Wales.

Curriculum Council for Wales (1993). *Developing a Curriculum Cymreig*, Cardiff, Curriculum Council for Wales.

DANIEL, G. (1969). The Government in Wales, Lecture given in Cardiff on 5 December 1969.

DAFIS, C. (1994). 'A Welsh Government That Evolves' in J. Osmond (Editor) *A Parliament For Wales*, Llandysul, Gomer.

DAVID, R. (1968). 'Future of the Welsh Office', Aberystwyth, *Planet*, Vol. 1, pp. 85–87.

DAVIES, A.J. (1995). *We, The Nation: The Conservative Party and the Pursuit of Power*, London, Little Brown and Company.

DAVIES, B., EVANS, J., PENNY, D. and BASS, D. (1997). Physical education and Nationalism in Wales, The Curriculum Journal, Vol. 8, No. 2, Summer 1997, London, Routledge, pp. 247–270.

DAVIES, J. (1995). 'Plaid Cymru in Transition', in John Osmond's (1985) *The National Question Again: Welsh Political Identity in the 1980s*, Llandysul, Gower, pp. 124–149.

DAVIES, J. (1993). 'The 1992 Manifesto of Cymdeithas yr Iaith Gymraeg', *Planet, The Welsh Internationalist*, No. 97, February/March 1993, pp. 113–115.

DAVIES, R. (1996). 'The tools for the job', *Welsh Agenda*, Winter 1996/7, Cardiff, The Institute of Welsh Affairs, pp. 18–20.

DAVIES, R. (1999). *Devolution: A process Not An Event*, The Gregynog papers, Volume Two, Number Two, Cardiff, Institute for Welsh Affairs.

DEACON, R. (1996A). 'Labour Day': Wales' First Unitary Authority Elections, *Representation*, Winter 1995/96, Vol. 33, No. 3, London, Arthur McDougall Fund, pp. 80–85.

DEACON, R. (1996B). "New Labour and the Welsh Assembly: 'Preparing for a New Wales' or updating the Wales Act 1978?", *Regional Studies*, Vol. 30:7, Regional Studies Association, pp. 689–693.

DEACON, R. (1997A). 'How the Additional Member System was Buried and then Resurrected in Wales', *Representation*, Autumn/Winter 1997/98, Vol. 34, No. 3 and 4, London, Arthur McDougall Fund, pp. 219–225.

DEACON, R. (1997B). 'Identifying the Origins of Welsh Local Government

Reform', *The Journal of Legislative Studies*, Vol. 3, No. 3, Autumn 1997, pp. 104–112, London, Frank Cass.

DEACON, R. (1999). *The Road to the Manifesto: The Political parties in Wales and the Policy Process: A Discussion Paper*, Cardiff, Institute of Welsh Affairs.

DEACON, R. and DEACON, T. (1994). 'Reform of the Health Service in Wales', Vol. 14, No. 3, *Public Money & Management* July-September 1994, Oxford, Blackwells, pp. 5–9.

DEAKIN, N. [ed] (1986). *Policy Change in Government: Three Case Studies*, London, Royal Institute of Public Administration.

Dod's Parliamentary Companion 1994 (1994) 157th edition. London, Dod's Parliamentary Companion Ltd.

Dod's Parliamentary Companion 1996 (1996) 159th edition. London, Dod's Parliamentary Companion Ltd.

DOREY, P. (1991). 'The Cabinet Committee System in British Government', *Talking Politics*, Autumn 1991, Vol. 4, No. 1, Manchester, The Politics Association, pp. 11–15.

DOREY, P. (1994). Widened, Yet Weakened; The Changing Character of 'Collective Responsibility', *Talking Politics*, Winter 1994/95, Vol. 7, No. 2, Manchester, The Politics Association.

DOREY, P. (1995). *British Politics since 1945*, Oxford, Blackwells.

DOWDING, K. (1995A). *The Civil Service*, London, Routledge.

DOWDING, K. (1995B). 'Model or Metaphor? A Critical Review of the Policy Network Approach', *Political Studies*, Vol. 43, No. 1, Oxford, Blackwell Publishers, pp. 136–158.

DRUCKER, H.M. and BROWN, G. (1980). *The Politics of Nationalism and Devolution*, London, Longman.

DU CANN, E. (1984). *Commons Select Committees: Catalysts for Progress?* Edited by Dermot Englefield, Bath, Longman.

DUBS, A. (1989). *Lobbying: An Insider's Guide to the Parliamentary Process*, London, Pluto Press.

DUNLEAVY, P. (1995). 'Estimating the Distribution of Positional Influence in Cabinet Committees under Major' in R.A.W. Rhodes and Patrick Dunleavy (ed) Prime Minister, *Cabinet and Core Executive* (1995) London, MacMillan.

DUNLEAVY, P. and O'LEARY, B. (1993). 'The evolution of Marxist approaches to state organization' in Hill, M's [ed] *The Policy Process: A Reader*, London, Harvester Wheatsheaf, pp. 69–85.

DUNLEAVY, P. and RHODES, R.A.W. (1990). 'Core Executive Studies in Britain', *Public Administration*, Vol. 68, Spring 1990, pp. 3–28.

ELSON, J. and MACDONALD, R. (1997). 'Urban Growth Management: Distinctive Solutions in the Celtic Countries?' in MacDonald, R. and Thomas, H's (eds) *Nationality and Planning in Scotland and Wales*, Cardiff, University of Wales Press, pp. 113–132.

The Economist 13/8/88. 'A small place but their own' p. 23.

EVANS, G. (1996). *For the Sake of Wales*, translated by Meic Stephens, Cardiff, Welsh Academic Press.

FARRELL, C.M. and LAW, J. (1995). Educational Accountability in Wales, York, Joseph Rowntree Foundation.

FARRELL, C.M. and LAW, J. (1997). 'A more separate education system for Wales', *Contemporary Wales*, Volume 10, Cardiff, University of Wales Press.

FLYNN, N. and STREHL, F. [Ed] (1996). *Public Sector Management in Europe*, Hemel Hampsted, Prentice Hall/Harvester Wheatsheaf.

FOULKES, D., JONES, BARRY and WILFORD R.A. [Ed] (1983). *The Welsh Veto: The Wales Act 1978 & The Referendum*, University of Wales Press.

GAMBLE, A. (1990). Theories of British Politics, *Political Studies*, Vol. 38, No. 4, Blackwells, Oxford, pp. 404–420.

GEORGE, K.D. and MAINWARING, L. (1988). *The Welsh Economy*, University of Wales Press.

GOLDSMITH, M. (1986). *Urban Political Theory and the Management of Fiscal Stress*, Aldershot, Gower Press.

GRAHAM JONES, J. (1988). 'Early Campaigns to Secure a Secretary of State for Wales, 1890–1939', *Transactions of the Honourable Society of Cymmrodrion*, pp. 133–175.

GRAHAM JONES, J. (1992). 'The Parliament For Wales Campaign, 1950–1956', *The Welsh History Review*, Vol. 16, No. 2, 1992, pp. 207–236.

GRAHAM JONES, J. (1993). 'The Liberal Party and Wales, 1945–79', *The Welsh History Review*, Vol. 16, No. 3, 1993, pp. 326–355.

GRAY, C. (1994). *Government Beyond The Centre: Sub National Politics in Britain*, Basingstoke, MacMillan.

GRIFFITHS, D. (1996). *Thatcherism and Territorial Politics: A Welsh Case Study*, Aldershot, Avebury.

GRIFFITHS, J. (1968). *Pages from Memory*, London, Dent.

GRIFFITHS, P. (1996). 'Legislating for Wales – Local Government (Wales) Act 1994', *The Journal of Legislative Studies*, Vol. 2, Summer 1996, London, Frank Cass, pp. 63–79.

GRIFFITHS, M. (1986). *The Welsh Language in Education*, Cardiff, WJEC.

HAINSWORTH, P. (1985). Northern Ireland in the European Community, in Keating, M. and Jones, Barry. [eds] (1985) *Regions in the European Community*, Oxford, Clarendon Press, pp. 109–133.

HALL, K. (1993). *Essential Central Government*, London, Local Government Communications.

HAM, C. (1992) 3rd edition. *Health Policy in Britain*, Basingstoke, Macmillan.

HAM, C. and HILL, M. (1993) 2nd edition. *The Policy Process in the Modern Capitalist State*, London, Harvester Wheatsheaf.

HAMBLETON, R. and MILLS, L. (1993). 'Local Government Reform in Wales' *Local Government Policy Making*, Vol. 19, No. 4, March 1993, pp. 45–53.

HARVIE, C. (1982). *Against Metropolis*, London, Fabian Tract 484.

HARVIE, C. (1995) 2nd edition. *Scotland and Nationalism: Scottish Society and Politics 1707–1994*, London, Routledge.

HASELL, N. (1994). Testing Market Testing, *Management Today*, May 1994, pp. 39–42.

HAWES, D. (1993). *Power on the Back Benches: the growth of select committee influence*, Bristol, SAUS.

HEADEY, B. (1974). *British Cabinet Ministers: The Roles of Politicians in Executive Office*, London, George Allen and Unwin Ltd.

HEALD, D. (1994). 'Territorial Public Expenditure in the United Kingdom' *Public Administration*, Vol. 72, Summer 1994, pp. 147–175.

HEATH, E. (1998). *The Course of My Life*, London, Hodder and Stoughton.

HELCO, H. and WILDAVSKY, A. (1981) 2nd edition. *The private government of public money*, London, Macmillan.

HELCO, H. and WILDAVSKY, A. (1996). 'The Whitehall Village' in Peter Barberis's (ed), *The Whitehall Reader*, Buckingham, Open University Press.

HENNESSY, P. (1989). *Whitehall*, London, Fontana Press.

HOGWOOD, B.W. (1992). *Trends In British Public Policy: do governments make any difference?*, Buckingham, Open University Press.

HOGWOOD, B.W. (1995). 'Regional Administration in Britain Since 1979: Trends and Explanations', *Regional & Federal Studies*, Vol. 5, No. 3, Autumn 1995, London, Frank Cass, pp. 267–91.

HOGWOOD, B.W. (1996A). 'Devolution: The English Dimension', *Public Money and Management*, October–December 1996, pp. 29–34.

HOGWOOD, B.W. (1996B). *Mapping the regions: boundaries, co-ordination and government*, Bristol, The Policy Press.

HOGWOOD, B.W. and GUNN, L.A. (1981). *The Policy Orientation*, Centre for the Study of Public Policy, University of Strathclyde.

HMI, Wales (1988). *A Report by HM Inspectorate (Wales), Review of Educational Provision in Wales*, 1987–88, Cardiff, Welsh Office.

HUME, I. (1983). 'The mass media in Wales: some preliminary explorations', in I. Hume and W.T.R. Pryce (eds.), *The Welsh and Their Country*, Llandysul, Gomer Press.

INGLE, S. (1996). 'Party Organisation', in *The Liberal Democrats* edited by Don MacIver, Hamel Hempstead, Prentice Hall/Harvester Wheatsheaf.

Institute of Welsh Affairs (1996). *The Road to the Referendum: requirements for an informed and fair debate*, Cardiff.

JAMES, M. (1994). 'Defending the High Ground of Democracy: Local Government in a Welsh Parliament', in *A Parliament for Wales*, Osmond, J. (ed), Llandysul, Gomer.

JAMES, S. (1992). *The British Cabinet*, London, Routledge.

JAMES, C. and WILLIAMS, C. (1997). 'Language and Planning in Scotland and Wales' in MacDonald, R. and Thomas, H. (ed) *Nationality and Planning in Scotland and Wales*, Cardiff, University of Wales Press.

JOHN, P. (1990). *Recent Trends in Central-Local Government Relations*, York, Joseph Rowntree Foundation.

JONES, BARRY, and WILFORD, W. (1986). *Parliament and Territoriality: The Select Committee on Welsh Affairs 1979–83*, Cardiff, University of Wales Press.

JONES, BARRY. (1985). 'Wales in the European Community', in Keating, M. and Jones, B. [eds] (1985) *Regions in the European Community*, Oxford, Clarendon Press, Oxford, Clarendon Press, pp. 89–109.

JONES, BARRY. (1988). 'The Development of Welsh Territorial Institutions: Modernisation Theory revisited', *Contemporary Wales*: An Annual Review of Economic & Social Research, Vol. 2, 1988, Cardiff, University of Wales Press.

JONES, BARRY. (1990). *The Welsh Office: A Political Expedient or an Administrative Innovation?* Lecture given to the Society at the British Academy, 13 November 1990.

JONES, BARRY (1994). 'The transformation of Wales since 1979', in Osmond, J's (ed) *A Parliament for Wales*, Llandysul, Gomer.

JONES, BILL. (1998). 'The Policy-Making Process', in Bill Jones et al, *Politics UK*, 3rd Edition, London, Prentice Hall, pp. 449–462.

JONES, BILL and KAVANAGH, D. (1994). *British Politics Today*, 5th Edition, Manchester, Manchester University Press.

JONES, E.P. and REYNOLDS, D. (1998). 'Education' in Osmond, J's (ed) *The National Assembly Agenda*, Cardiff, Institute of Welsh Affairs.

JONES, E.H.G. and CARLIN, P. (1990). 'Welsh in Gwent Schools: the Basque Example', *Planet, The Welsh Internationalist, 82*, Aberystwyth, Berw Cyf, pp. 107–108.

JONES, G.E. (1988). 'What are Schools in Wales for? Wales and the Education Reform Act', in *Contemporary Wales*, Vol. 2, Day, G. and Rees, G. (eds), Cardiff, University of Wales.

JONES, G.E. (1990). *Which Nation's Schools? Direction and Devolution in Welsh Education in the Twentieth Century*, Cardiff, University of Wales Press.

JONES, G.E. (1994) 2nd edition. *Modern Wales: A Concise History*, Cambridge, Cambridge University Press.

JONES, G.E. (1997). *The Education of a Nation*, Cardiff, University of Wales Press.

JONES, P.E. (1988). 'Some Trends in Welsh Secondary Education, 1967–1987', in *Contemporary Wales*, Vol. 2, Day, G. and Rees, G. (eds), Cardiff, University of Wales.

JONES, T.H. (1993). 'The English Curriculum, *Planet, The Welsh Internationalist*, No. 99, June/July 1993, pp. 112–115.

JORDAN, A.G. and RICHARDSON, J.J. (1987). *British Politics and the Policy Process: An Arena Approach*, London Allen and Unwin.

JORDAN, G. and SCHUBERT, K. (1992). 'A preliminary ordering of policy network labels', *European Journal of Political Research*, Vol. 21. 1992, Netherlands, Kluwer Academic Publishers, pp. 7–27.

JOSEPH, M. (1989). 'The New School Bible', *Planet, The Welsh Internationalist*, No. 77, October/November 1989, pp. 35–37.

KAUFMAN, G. (1980). *How to be a Minister*, London, Sidgwick and Jackson.

KAVANAGH, D. (1990) 2nd edition. *British Politics: Continuities and Change*, Oxford, Oxford University Press.

KEATING, M. and WALTERS, N. (1985). 'Scotland in the European Community' in Keating, M. and Jones, B. [eds] (1985) *Regions in the European Community*, Oxford, Clarendon Press, Oxford, Clarendon Press, pp. 60–89.

KEATING, M. and CARTER, C. (1987). 'Policy-Making and the Scottish Office: The Designation of Cumbernauld New Town', *Public Administration*, Vol. 65, Winter 1987, pp. 391–405.

KELLAS, J. (1989A). 'The Scottish and Welsh Office's as Territorial Managers', *Regional Politics and Policy*: An International Journal.

KELLAS, J. (1989B). *The Scottish Political System*, Fourth Edition, Cambridge Cambridge, University Press.

KELLAS, J. and MADGEWICK, P. (1982). 'Territorial Ministries: the Scottish and Welsh Offices' in P.J. Madgwick and R. Rose's, *The Territorial Dimension in United Kingdom Politics*, London, Macmillan.

KEMP, P. (1994). 'The Civil Service White Paper: A Job Half Finished', *Public Administration*, Vol. 72, Winter 1994, pp. 591–598.

KENDLE, J. (1997). *Federal Britain: A History*, London, Routledge.

KING, R. (1990). 'Policy and process in the modern state' in Simmies, J. and King, R's *State in Action: Public Policy and Politics*, London, Pinter Publishers.

KING, A. (1994). Ministerial autonomy in Britain in Laver, M. and Shepsle, K.A's, *Cabinet Ministers and Parliamentary Government*, Cambridge Cambridge, University Press.

LAFFIN, M. (1986). *Professionalism and policy: the role of professions in the central-local government relationship*, Aldershot, Gower.

LAWTON, A. and ROSE, A. (1994) 2nd edition. *Organisation and Management in the Public Sector*, London, Pitman Publishing.

LIGHTMAN, I. (1988). The Welsh Office: Wales' Little Whitehall, *Public Money & Management*, Vol. 8, No. 3, Winter 1988.

LIGHTMAN, I. (1995). 'Yes Minister – Myth or Reality', *Welsh Agenda*, Vol. 2, Iss. 2, April 1995, Cardiff, Institute of Welsh Affairs, pp. 17–19.

LINDBLOM, C.E. and WOODHOUSE, E.J. (1993) 3rd edition. *The Policy-Making Process*, New Jersey, Prentice Hall.

LLOYD, B. (1990). 'Education in Wales in the 1990s', *NUT Education Review*, Spring 1990, London, NUT Education.

LODGE, P. and BLACKSTONE, T. (1982). *Educational Policy and Educational Inequality*, Oxford, Martin Robertson.

LOMAX, R. (1999). 'Now the Agenda is political', *Agenda*, Spring 1999, Cardiff, Institute for Welsh Affairs.

LYNN, J. and JAY, A. (1984). *The Complete Yes Minister: The Diaries of a Cabinet Minister by the Right Hon. James Hacker MP*, Vol. One, Bath, Chivers Press.

LYNCH, P. (1995). 'From Red to Green: The Political Strategy of Plaid Cymru in the 1980s and 1990s, *Regional and Federal Studies*, Vol. 5, Summer 1995, No. 2, London, Frank Cass, pp. 197–210.

LYNCH, P. (1996). *Minority Nationalism and European Integration*, Cardiff, University of Wales Press.

LYNCH, P. (1997). 'Regional Party Organisations and Territorial Politics in Britain', Paper presented to the *Political Studies Conference*, Belfast 1997.

MACKAY, H. and POWELL, A. (1997). 'Wales and its Media: Production, Consumption and Regulation', in *Contemporary Wales*, Volume 9, Cardiff, University of Wales Press.

MACKINTOSH, J.P. (1976). 'The Power of the Secretary of State', Edinburgh, *New Edinburgh Review*, No. 31, February 1976.

MADGWICK, P.J. and JAMES, M. (1979). *Studies in Public Policy: Government by Consultation: The Case for Wales*, London, MacMillan.

MADGWICK, P.J. and JAMES, M. (1980). 'Territorial Ministries: the Scottish and Welsh Office's' in Madgwick & Rose (ed) *The Territorial Dimension in UK Politics*, London, MacMillan.

MADGWICK, P.J. and ROSE, R. (1992). The Territorial Dimension in United Kingdom Politics, London, MacMillan.

MADGWICK, P. and WOODHOUSE, D. (1995). *The Law and Politics of the Constitution*, Hemel Hampstead, Harvester Wheatsheaf.

MARSHALL, G. (1989). *Ministerial Responsibility*, Oxford, Oxford University Press.

MAJOR, J. (28/10/94). Interview in the *Western Mail* by David Cornock, p. 7.

MAJOR, J. (1999). *John Major: The Autobiography*, London, Harper Collins.

MARSH, D. (1998). Comparing Policy Networks, Buckingham, Open University Press.

MARSH, D., RICHARDS, D. and SMITH, M. (1998). 'Reassessing The Role of Ministers: Headey Revisited', ESRC award no. L12451023.

MAY, J. (1994). *Reference Wales*, University of Wales Press.

MAWSON, J. (1997). 'English Regionalism: The Developing Policy Agenda', Paper delivered at European Consortium for Political research Standing Group on Regionalism, University of Northumbria at Newcastle, 20–22 February 1997.

MCLENNON, G. (1993). 'The evolution of pluralist theory', in Hill, M's [ed] *The Policy Process: A Reader*, London, Harvester Wheatsheaf, pp. 59–68.

MÉNY, Y. and WRIGHT, V. [Eds] (1985). Centre-Periphery Relations in Western Europe, London, George Allen and Unwin.

MICHAEL, ALUN (1999). 'The Dragon on our doorstep: New politics for a new millennium in Wales', Speech to the School of Politics, University of Wales, Aberystwyth.

MICHAEL, A. (2000). 'The Welsh Assembly: A new start for Wales', Speech to the Business School, University of Glamorgan.

MIDWINTER, A., KEATING, M. and MITCHELL, J. (1991). *Politics and Public Policy in Scotland*, London, MacMillan.

MIDWINTER, A. and MCVICAR, M. (1996). 'The Devolution Proposals for Scotland: An Assessment and Critique', *Public Money and Management*, Vol. 16, No. 4. October–December 1996, pp. 13–19.

MILLER, C. (1990). *Lobbying: Understanding and Influencing the Corridors of Power*, London, MacMillan.

MOORE, C. and BOOTH, S. (1989). *Managing Competition: Meso-Corporatism, Pluralism, and the Negotiated Order in Scotland*, Oxford, Clarendon Press.

MORGAN, K.O. (1980). *Wales Rebirth of a Nation 1880–1980*, Oxford, Oxford University Press.

MORGAN, K.O. (1995). *Modern Wales: Politics, Places and People*, Cardiff, University of Wales Press.

MORGAN, K.O. (1997). *Callaghan: A Life*, Oxford, Oxford University Press.

MORGAN, K. and HENDERSON, D. (1997). 'The Falliable Servant: Evaluating the Welsh Development Agency' in MacDonald, R. and Thomas, H. (ed) *Nationality and Planning in Scotland and Wales*, Cardiff, University of Wales Press.

MORGAN, K. and MUNGHAM, G. (2000). *The Making of the Welsh Assembly, Bridgend, Seren.*

MORGAN, K. and ROBERTS, E. (1993). *The Democratic Deficit: A Guide to Quangoland*, Department of City & Regional Planning, University of Wales College of Cardiff, Papers in Planning Research, No. 144.

MORGAN, R. (2000). Variable Geometry UK, Institute of Welsh Affairs, Cardiff.

NAIRN, T. (1977). *The Break-up of Britain: crisis and neo-nationalism*, London, New Left Books.

NISKANEN, W.A. (1973). Bureaucracy: Servant or Master? Institute of Economic Affairs, London.

National Assembly Advisory Group (1998A). *National Assembly For Wales: Have your say on how it will work*, National Assembly Advisory Group, Cardiff, A Consultation Paper.

National Assembly Advisory Group (1998B). *Recommendations*, Cardiff.

Northern Ireland Office (1997). *Northern Ireland: Expenditure Plans and Priorities: The Government's Expenditure Plans 1997–98 to 1999– 2000* (March 1997), *Department of Finance and Personnel/HM Treasury*, London, HMSO, Cm. 3616.

NORTON, P. (1994). *The British Polity*, Third Edition, London, Longman.

NORTON, P. (1996). *The Conservative Party*, London, Prentice Hall.

OSMOND, J. (1978). *Creative Conflict*, Llandysul, Gomer Press.

OSMOND, J. (1985). *The National Question Again: Welsh Political Identity in the 1980s*, Llandysul, Gomer Press.

OSMOND, J. (1992). *The Democratic Challenge*, Llandysul, Gomer Press.

OSMOND, J. (1995). *Welsh Europeans*, Bridgend, Seren.

PAVELIN, L. (1988). 'The Welsh Office view of the FMI', *Public Finance and Accountancy*, 15 April 1988.

PATCHETT, K. (1996). Power and Politics, *Welsh Agenda*, Winter 1996/ 7, Cardiff, The Institute of Welsh Affairs.

PAXMAN, J. (1991). *Friends in High Places: Who Runs Britain*, London, Penguin.

PELLING, H. (1993). *A Short History of the Labour Party*, Basingstoke, St Martins Press.

PLAYFAIR, E. (1965). 'Who are the Policy-makers?', London, *Public Administration*, 43, Autumn 1965.

PHILLIPS, R. (1996). 'Education Policy Making in Wales: A Research Agenda', *The Welsh Journal of Education*, Vol. 5, No. 2, Cardiff, University of Wales Press, pp. 26–39.

POWELL, W.W. (1990). 'Neither market nor hierarchy: network forms of organisations', *Research in Organisational Behaviour*, Vol. 12, 1990.

Price Waterhouse (1996). *The specification for appointing a Permanent Secretary*, Cardiff, Price Waterhouse.

PYPER, R. (1995). *The British Civil Service*, London, Prentice Hall.

RANDALL, P. J. (1972). 'Wales in the Structure of Central Government', *Public Administration*, Autumn 1972, Vol. 50, pp. 353–372.

RANDALL, P.J. (1975). 'The Origins and Establishment of the Welsh Department of Education', *The Welsh History Review*, Vol. 7, No. 4, 1975.

RALLINGS, C. and THRASHER, M. (1993). *Local Elections in Britain: A Statistical Digest*, Portsmouth, Local Government Chronicle Elections Centre.

'Rebecca', (a magazine published in the early 1980s) October 1981, 'Nicholas Edwards' p. 12.

REDWOOD, J. (1994). *Views from Wales*, London, Conservative Political Centre.

REYNOLDS, D. (1989). The Wasted Years: Education in Wales, 1979–89, *Welsh Journal of Education*, Vol. 1, No. 1., Cardiff, University of Wales Press, pp. 39–46.

REYNOLDS, D. (1994). 'Building Our National Identity: Education Policy and a Welsh Parliament' in Osmond, J's (ed) *A Parliament for Wales*, Llandysul, Gomer.

REYNOLDS, D. (1995a). Creating an Educational System for Wales, *The Welsh Journal of Education*, Vol. 4, No. 2, Cardiff, University of Wales Press, pp. 4–21.

REYNOLDS, D. (1995b). *Towards and Educational Policy for Wales*, Cardiff, Institute of Welsh Affairs.

RHODES, R.A.W. (1986). *The National World of Local Government*, London, Allen & Unwin.

RHODES, R.A.W. (1992). *Beyond Westminster and Whitehall: The sub-central governments of Britain*, London, Routledge.

RHODES, R.A.W. (1996). 'The New Governance: governing without Government', *Political Studies*, Vol. 44, No. 4, pp. 652–657.

RHODES, R.A.W. (1997). *Understanding Governance: Policy Networks, Governance, Reflexivity and Accountability*, Buckingham, Open University Press.

RHODES, R.A.W. (1999). *Transforming British Government: an interpretative guide to the ESRC's White hall Programme*, Paper to PSA Annual Conference, University of Nottingham, 23–25 March 1999.

RHODES, R.A.W. and MARSH, D. (1992). 'New directions in the study of policy networks', *European Journal of Political Research*, Vol. 21. 1992, Netherlands, Kluwer Academic Publishers, pp. 181–205.

RICHARDS, P. (1980) 4th edition. *The Reformed Local Government System*, London, George Allen & Unwin.

ROBERTS, D. (1985). 'The Strange Death of Liberal Wales in John Osmond's (1985) *The National Question Again: Welsh Political Identity in the 1980s*, Llandysul, Gower, pp. 75–99.

ROBERTS, H. (1999). 'Wales in Whitehall', *Agenda*, Spring 1999, Cardiff, Institute for Welsh Affairs.

ROBERTS, W. (1995). 'Fifteen Years at the Welsh Office: Sir Wyn Roberts', *The Welsh Political Archive Lecture 1995*, The National Library of Wales.

ROBERTSON, E.H. (1993). *George: A Biography of Viscount Tonypandy*, London, Marshall Pickering.

ROBINS, L. [Ed] (1987). *Politics and Policy-Making in Britain*, The Politics Association, London, Longman.

ROBINSON, A., SHEPHERD, R., RIDELY, F.F. and JONES, G.W. (1987). Symposium on Ministerial Responsibility (1987) *Public Administration*, Vol. 65 Spring 1987, pp. 61–91.

ROSE, R. (1984). *From Government at the Centre to Nationwide Government*, Centre for the Study of Public Policy, Glasgow, University of Straythclyde.

ROSE, R. (1987). Ministers and Ministries: A Functional Analysis, Oxford, Clarendon Press.

ROWLANDS, E. (1972). 'The Politics of Regional Administration: the Establishment of the Welsh Office', *Public Administration*, Autumn 1972, Vol. 50, pp. 333–353.

Scottish Office (1996). *Serving Scotland's Needs: The Government's Expenditure Plans 1996–97 to 1998–1999* (March 1996), *Departments of the Secretary of State for Scotland and the Forestry Commission*, HMSO, Cm 3214.

Scottish Office (1997). *Serving Scotland's Needs: The Government's Expenditure Plans 1997–98 to 1999–2000* (March 1997), *Departments of the Secretary of State for Scotland and the Forestry Commission*, HMSO, Cm 3614.

SCHMITTER, P.S. (1979). 'Modes of interest intermediation and models of societal change in Western Europe', *Comparative Political Studies*, Vol. 10, No. 1, London, Allen and Unwin, pp. 61–90.

SHAW, E. (1994). *The Labour Party Since 1979: Crisis and Transformation*, London, Routledge.

SMITH, M. (1993). *Pressure, Power and Policy*, London, Harvester/Wheatsheaf.

SMITH, G. [Ed] (1995). Federalism: The Multiethnic Challenge, London, Longman.

SMITH, P. RICHARDS, S. and NEWMAN, J. (1997). 'Remaking the Institution of Government: Studying the Impact of Competition in the Civil Service', paper presented at the annual conference of the *Political Studies Association*, Belfast, April 1997.

STANYER, J. and SMITH, B. (1976). *Administering Britain*, Glasgow, Fontana Orgininal.

STEAD, P. (1985). 'The Labour Party and the Claims of Wales' in John Osmond's (1985) *The National Question Again: Welsh Political Identity in the 1980s*, Llandysul, Gower, pp. 99–118.

STEVENS, A. (1992). *The Government and Politics of France*, London, MacMillan.

STEVENSON, J. (1993). *Third Party Politics since 1945: Liberal, Alliance and Liberal Democrats*, Blackwell, Oxford.

STOKER, G. (1991) 2nd edition. *The Politics of Local Government*, London, MacMillan.

STOKER, G. (1993). 'Local Government Reorganisation as a Garbage Can Process', *Local Government Policy Making*, Vol. 19, No. 4, March 1993, pp. 3–5.

TALBOT, C. (1997). *The Private Government of Public Agencies? – Evaluating the Impact of 'Next Steps'*, University of Glamorgan, Pontypridd.

TALFAN DAVIES, G. (1973). 'The Welsh Office and the Council' in *The Welsh Dilemma*, Morgan, W.J. (Editor), Cardiff, The Merlin Press, Christopher Davies Ltd.

TANSEY, S.D. (1995). *Politics: The Basics*, London, Routledge.

TEWDER-JONES, M. (1997). 'Land-Use Planning in Wales: The Conflict between State Centrality and Territorial Nationalism' in MacDonald, R. and Thomas, H. (ed) *Nationality and Planning in Scotland and Wales*, Cardiff, University of Wales Press, pp. 54–77.

THAIN, C. and WRIGHT, M. (1995). *The Treasury and Whitehall: the Planning and Control of Public Expenditure 1976–1993*, Oxford, Oxford University Press.

THATCHER, M. (1993). *The Downing Street Years*, London, Harper Collins.

THATCHER, M. (1993). *The Path to Power*, London, Harper Collins.

THEAKSTON, K. (1987). *Junior Ministers in British Government*, Basil Blackwell.

THEAKSTON, K. (1992). *The Labour Party And Whitehall*, London, Routledge.

THOMAS, A. (1994). *Language Policy and Nationalism in Wales, Canada and Ireland*, Ph.D Thesis.

THOMAS, A. (1996A). 'The moment of truth: Labour's Welsh Assembly Proposals in practice', *Regional Studies*, Vol. 30:7, Regional Studies Association, pp. 689–693.

THOMAS, A. (1996B). 'Wales and Devolution: A Constitutional Footnote?, *Public Money and Management*, Vol. 16, No. 4, October–December 1996, pp. 21–27.

THOMAS, A. (1996C). 'Region, Culture and Function on the Celtic Periphery: Wales, Cornwall and the EU', *Contemporary Wales*, Volume 10, Cardiff, University of Wales Press.

THOMAS, I.C. (1987). 'Giving Direction to the Welsh Office' in Richard Rose's *Ministers and Ministries: A Functional Analysis*, Oxford, Clarendon Press.

THOMAS, N. (1987). 'The George Thomas Era', Aberystwyth, *Planet*, Vol. 1, pp. 4–8.

THOMAS, N. (1989). 'Welsh Education Funding', *Planet, The Welsh Internationalist*, 74, Aberystwyth, Berw Cyf, p. 120.

SMITH, G., HENDER, D. and KETT, D. (1992). *Local Government for Journalists*, London, LGC Communications.

SNICKER, J. (1998). 'Strategies of Autonomist Agents in Wales', in Elcock, H. and Keating, M. *'Remaking The Union' Devolution and British politics in the 1990s*, London, Frank Cass.

VAN WARDEN, F. (1992). Dimensions and types of policy networks, *European Journal of Political Research*, Vol. 21. 1992, Netherlands, Kluwer Academic Publishers, pp. 29–52.

The Wales Yearbook, 1994 HTV. Compiled and edited by Balsom. D, Aberystwyth, Francis Balsom Associates.

The Wales Yearbook, 1995 HTV. Compiled and edited by Balsom. D, Aberystwyth, Francis Balsom Associates.

The Wales Yearbook, 1996 HTV. Compiled and edited by Balsom. D, Aberystwyth, Francis Balsom Associates.

The Wales Yearbook, 1997 HTV. Compiled and edited by Denis Balsom, Aberystwyth, Francis Balsom Associates.

The Wales Yearbook, 1999 HTV. Compiled and edited by Denis Balsom, Aberystwyth, Francis Balsom Associates.

WALKER, PATRICK (1972). *The Cabinet*, London, Heinemann Educational Books.

WALKER, PETER (1991). *Staying Power: An Autobiography*, London, Bloomsbury.

Welsh Local Government Association (1996). Minutes of evidence to House of Lords Select Committee on Relations Between Central and Local Government, Cardiff, May 1996.

WHITELAW, W. (1989). *The Whitelaw Memories*, London, Headline.

WHITE, G. (1996). 'Public Sector Pay Bargaining: Comparability, Decentralisation and Control', *Public Administration*, Vol. 74. Spring 1996, Oxford, Blackwell Publishers Ltd., pp. 89–111.

Who's Who? 1980. London, Adam & Charles Black.

Who's Who? 1994. London, Adam & Charles Black.

Who's Who? 1995. London, Adam & Charles Black.

Who's Who? 1996. London, Adam & Charles Black.

White, G. (1996). 'Public Sector Pay Bargainging: Comparability, Decentralization and Control', *Public Administration*, Vol. 74 Spring 1996, pp. 89–111.

WILDAVSKY, A. (1979). *Speaking Truth to Power: The Art and Craft of Policy Analysis*, Boston, Little Brown.

WILKS, S. and WRIGHT, M. (1987). *Comparing Government-Industry Relations*, Oxford: Clarendon Press.

WILLIAMS, C.H. (1989). 'New Domains of the Welsh Language: Education, Planning and the Law' in *Contemporary Wales*, Vol. 3, Day, G. and Rees, G. (eds), Cardiff, University of Wales.

WILLIAMS, H. (1998). *Guilty Men*, London, Aurum Press.

WILSON, H. (1979). *Final Term: The Labour Government 1974–1976*, London, Weidenfeld and Nicholson.

WJEC (1993). 'Deep disquiet regarding the Education White Paper', *WJEC Newsletter*, Issue No. 2, Winter 1993.

YARDLEY, D. (1995) 8th edition. *Introduction to Constitutional and Administrative Law*, London, Butterworths.

Yes for Wales (1). *Women of Wales Have Your Say!*, Printed by USDAW.

Yes for Wales (2). *The Welsh Assembly*: What you need to know, Liberal Democrats Wales.

Yes for Wales (3). *The Rose*, Welsh Assembly Referendum, Wales Labour Party.

The Western Mail, Independent, Observer, Times and Telegraph have also been consulted..

Welsh Office

Welsh Grand Committee (1989). *Education and Training for Employment in Wales*, London, HMSO.

Welsh Grand Committee (1990). *Education and Training in Wales*, London, HMSO.

The Welsh Office (1978). The Welsh Office Today (HMSO).

Welsh Office (1987). *The National Curriculum in Wales*, Cardiff, Welsh Office.

Welsh Office (1988). *National Curriculum: A Teacher's Guide*, Cardiff, Welsh Office.

The Welsh Office (1991A). *The Internal management of Local Authorities in Wales: A Consultation Paper*, July 1991, Cardiff, Welsh Office.

Welsh Office (1991B). *Welsh in the National Curriculum*, Welsh Office.

The Welsh Office (1993A). *The Government's Expenditure Plans 1993– 94 to 1995–96* (February 1993): *Departmental Report by the Welsh Office*, HMSO Cm 2215.

The Welsh Office (1993B). *The Government Response to the Welsh Affairs Committee Report on the Work of the Welsh Office* (July 1993) Cm 2276, HMSO.

The Welsh Office (1993). *Local Government in Wales: A Charter for the Future* CM 2155, HMSO.

The Welsh Office (1994). *The Government's Expenditure Plans 1994– 95 to 1996–97* (March 1994): *A Report by the Welsh Office and the Office of Her Majesty's Chief Inspector of Schools in Wales*, HMSO Cm 2515.

The Welsh Office (1995A). *The Government's Expenditure Plans 1995– 96 to 1997–98* (March 1995): *A Report by the Welsh Office and the Office of Her Majesty's Chief Inspector of Schools in Wales*, HMSO Cm 2815.

The Welsh Office (1995B). *Welsh Office Press Release* 28/3/95: 'New Slimmed-Down Senior Management Structure Proposed For Welsh Office', Cardiff, Welsh Office.

The Welsh Office (1995C). *Welsh Office Guidance on Decentralisation* (June 1995), Cardiff, Welsh Office.

The Welsh Office (1996A). *The Government's Expenditure Plans 1995– 96 to 1997–98* (March 1996): *A Report by the Welsh Office and the Office of Her Majesty's Chief Inspector of Schools in Wales*, HMSO Cm 2815.

The Welsh Office (1996B). *Welsh Office Press Release* 29/2/96: 'Welsh Councils Given New Role By William Hague', Cardiff, Welsh Office.

The Welsh Office (1997). *The Government's Expenditure Plans 1997– 98 to 1999–2000* (March 1997): *A Report by the Welsh Office and the Office of Her Majesty's Chief Inspector of Schools in Wales*, HMSO Cm 3615.

The Welsh Office (1999). *The Government's Expenditure Plans 1999– 2000 to 2001–2002* (March 1999): *A Report by the Welsh Office and the Office of Her Majesty's Chief Inspector of Schools in Wales*, HMSO Cm 4216.

The Welsh Office. Trade Union Side (Welsh Office) Mission Statement.

HMSO – Stationery Office – Government publications.

Hansard – Various.

HMSO (1991). *Competing for Quality*: Cm 1730, November 1991, HMSO, London.

HMSO (1993A). *Efficiency Unit: Career Management and Succession Planning Study*, London, HMSO.

HMSO (1993B). *Welsh Affairs Select Committee Report on The Work of the Welsh Office* (17 January 1993) Op. Parl. Sess. 92–93, HCP 259, HMSO, Vol. 393–I.

HMSO (1994A). *Aspects of Britain: Organisation of Political Parties* (1994) 2nd edition, London, HMSO.

HMSO (1994B). *Review of Fast Stream Recruitment*, HMSO, July 1994.

HMSO (1995A). *Standards in Public Life: First Report of the Committee on Standards in Public life*, Lord Nolan, Volume 1: Report Cm 2850–I, London, HMSO.

HMSO (1995B). *The Civil Service: Taking Forward Continuity and Change* (January 1995), London, HMSO, Cm 2748.

HMSO (1995C). *Welsh Affairs Select Committee Report on Wales In Europe* (25 November 1995) Vol. 393–I, London, HMSO.

HMSO. *The Civil Service Year Book*, published annually by HMSO.

The Stationery Office (1997). *Treasury Committee, Second Report, The Barnett Formula*, London, The Stationery Office.

Documentation by the Political Parties in Wales

Conservative Party (1990). *The Dragon Awakes: A Decade of Development, Conservative Central Office for Wales*, McCann-Erickson Payne Golley.

Conservative Party (1992). *The Conservative Manifesto For Wales 1992 The Best Future For Wales*.

Conservative Political Centre (1996). *Strengthening the United Kingdom, The Report of the CPC National Policy Group on the Constitution*, Conservative Political Centre.

Labour Party (1996A). *Domestic and International Policy Committee: Building on Success – the future of the National Policy Forum*, PD3961 DIPC 4/11/96.

Labour Party (1996B). *New Labour New Britain New Vision*.

Liberal Democrats Wales (1996). *A Senedd for Wales: Beyond a Talking Shop, Cardiff*.

Plaid Cymru (1995). *A Democratic Wales In A United Europe*.

Wales Labour Party (1987). *Wales Will Win*.

Wales Labour Party (1992). *It's time to get Wales working again.*

Wales Labour Party (1995A). *'Shaping the Vision: A report on the powers and structure of the Welsh Assembly.'*

Wales Labour Party (1995B). *New Labour – New Wales Report, 58th Annual Conference 1995.*

Wales Labour Party (1996A). *New Labour – New Wales Report, 59th Annual Conference 1996.*

Wales Labour Party (1996B). *New Labour New Life for Wales: What a Labour government means for you.*

Wales Labour Party (1997). *Representing Wales.*

Interviews

Oral or written interviews were held with:

Labour Party

Dr Andrew Bold – former Wales Labour Party Assistant General Secretary (Policy and Information).

Kevin Brennan MP – former member of the Wales Labour Party Policy Standing Committee.

Lord Cledwyn of Penrhos – for Welsh Secretary, Agriculture Secretary.

Ron Davies AM – Interviewed when Shadow Welsh Secretary and later on as an Assembly Member.

Annabel Harle – Wales Labour Party Representative on the National Policy Forum.

Councillor Russell Goodway – (Leader of the City and County Council of Cardiff).

Win Griffith MP – former Shadow Welsh Front Bench Spokesman and Welsh Office Minister.

Alun Michael MP – former Welsh Secretary and First Secretary.

Rhodri Morgan AM – former Shadow Welsh Front Bench Spokesman.

Rt Hon Sir John Morris – (Former Welsh Secretary).

Matthew Taylor – Labour Party Policy Executive.

Gareth Wardell – former MP and Chairman of the Welsh Affairs Select Committee.

Baroness White – former Welsh Office Minister.

Viscount Tonypandy – former Welsh Secretary and Speaker of the House of Commons.

Plaid Cymru

Cynog Davies AM.
Karl Davies – Chief Executive Plaid Cymru.
Janet Davies AM – Former Leader Taff Ely Borough Council.
Jill Evans MEP – formerly Committee of the Regions.
Llio Penfro – Researcher to Plaid Cymru's Parliamentary Party.

Liberal Democrats Wales

Councillor Steve Belzak – former Group Leader, Taff Ely Borough
    Council.
Lord Carlile – former Leader of the Welsh Liberal Democrats.
Nick Buree – former Chair of the Welsh Liberal Democrats Policy
    Committee.
Mike German AM OBE – Leader of the Liberal Democrats.
Judi Lewis – former Liberal Democrats Wales Party Manager.

Conservative Party

Nicholas Bennett (former MP for Pembrokeshire).
Lord Crickhowell.
Ian Grist (former MP for Cardiff Central).
Lord Hunt PC (former Welsh Secretary).
Gwilym Jones (former MP for Cardiff North).
Micheal MacManus – Special Adviser to David Hunt.
Councillor Gareth Neale – Group Leader, Cardiff City Council.
Henry Purcell OBE, former Regional Campaign Executive.
Lord Roberts (former MP for Conwy).
Lord Thomas of Gwydir.
Hwyel Williams – Special Adviser to John Redwood.
Lord Walker of Worcester.
Viscount St Davids.

Former Welsh Office

Robin Abel, Head of Personnel Management Division.

Sir Goronwy Daniel KCB – former Permanent Secretary at the Welsh Office.

Jean Gordon – European Affairs Division.

Mary Evans – Management Planning and Review Division.

Roger Jarman – Local Government Finance, Housing and Social Services.

Alwyn Jones – Environment Division.

Sir Trefor Hughes KCB – former Permanent Secretary at the Welsh Office.

Helen Madge, Welsh Office Trade Union Side.

Hugh Rawlings – Cultural and Recreation Division.

Owen Rees – Agriculture Department.

Mr H.G. Roberts, Director of Information.

Ken Smith – Director Overseas Trade.

D.B. Thomas – Industrial and Training Policy Division 1.

R.A. Wallace – Education Department.

Jane E. Westlake – Social Housing and renovation Division.

Mrs J.E. Westlake, Performance and Resources Unit.

Welsh Office Parliamentary Officer.

Others

Professor John Andrews – Chief Executive – Further and Higher Education Funding Councils for Wales.

Professor David Egan – Head of School of Education, University of Wales Institute, Cardiff.

Paul Griffith – Council of Welsh Districts.

Clayton Haycock, Secretary, WJEC.

Dr Elizabeth Haywood – Former Director, CBI Wales.

Katherine Hughes – Director, Welsh Consumer Council.

Mary James, Policy Executive Officer, Farmers Union of Wales.

David Jenkins, General Secretary, Wales TUC.

Buddug Jones, Agricultural Officer, Countryside Council for Wales.

Meirion Lewis OBE, Executive Director, Institute of Directors.

John Osmond – Director Institute of Welsh Affairs.

Professor Kevin Morgan, Department of City and Regional Planning, Cardiff University.

Roy Thomas – Agency Secretary, WDA.

Iona Wyn Williams – Public Relations Officer – Tai Cymru.

Dewi Williams – Manager for Wales, Agricultural Training Board.
Roger Waters, Director, Country Landowners Association.

Oral contributions

Speeches made at Cardiff Business Club (CBC).

Rt Hon John Redwood 18/3/93.
Sir Bernard Ingham 30/1/95.
Rt Hon William Hague 13/11/95.
Lord Walker 4/3/96.

Speeches made at the Conference on 'The New Unitary Authorities', University Wales College Cardiff 19 January 94.

Ron Davies MP, Shadow Welsh Secretary.
Michael Clarke, Chief Executive of the Local Government
    Management Board.

Speeches made at the Conference on 'The Constitutional Challenge: The Devolution Agenda for the 21st Century', University of Glamorgan, Cardiff, 16 June 1995*

Ron Davies MP, Shadow Welsh Secretary.
Paul Griffiths, Council of Welsh Districts.
Dafydd Wigley MP, President of Plaid Cymru.
Mari James, Campaign for a Welsh Parliament.

* Posts held at that time.

Speeches made at the Wales in Europe Conference, Swansea 1996.
Gareth Wardell MP.

Index

Agricultural policy, *see* Welsh Office and agricultural policy
Anderson, Donald 125
Barnett Formula 29, 179
BBC Wales 151
Bennett, Nicholas 75, 79, 198
Bevan, Aneurin 'Nye' 17, 18
Blair, Tony 219, 220
Bourne, Nick 221
Brecon, Lord 16, 71
Brooke, Henry 16
Bulpitt, James 27–28, 218–219
Butler, Chris 83
Cabinet battles 56–58
Cabinet Committee system and the Welsh Secretaries 58
Cadw 95, 167
Callaghan, James 18, 25, 27, 28, 199
Cardiff Bay Barrage 8, 62, 119, 133
Cardiff Bay Village 225
Carlile, Alex 80, 124
Cathays Park Village 159–176, 184, 200, 225
CBI (Confederation of British Industry) 164, 174
'Civil Servants in Charge' at Welsh Office 104–106, 112–114
Clwyd, Ann 142, 143
Conservative Party and the Welsh Office 125, 138, 216–218
Conservative Party and Welsh administrative devolution 15–16
Conservative Party and Welsh political devolution 157, 216–218
Conservatives, Welsh manifestos 1987 and 1992 5–6, 141, 174
Conservatives and policy creation 136, 141

Conservatives in Wales 136–139, 221
Continuity and Change, White Paper 107
Crickhowell, Lord *see* Nicholas Edwards
Crowther Commission into devolution, also *see* Kilibrandon 26, 28
Curriculum Council for Wales 197, 201, 203, 204
Curriculum Cymreig 178, 188, 191, 195, 197, 201, 206, 207, 209
Cymdeithas yr Iaith Gymraeg 53, 165–166, 187, 194–195, 202
Cymru Fydd 20
Dafis, Cynog 132
Daily Post 151, 152
Daniel, Sir Goronwy 23, 24, 26, 98, 102, 154
Davies, Ron 23, 39, 48, 49, 66, 125, 168, 218, 219, 220–222
Davies, Ron and the setting up of the Welsh Assembly 222–223
Davies, Ron as Shadow Welsh Secretary 142–146
Davies, S.O. 17
Departmental Management Plan (DMP) 93
Educational policy, *see* Welsh Office and educational policy
Educational Policy Community *see* Welsh Educational Policy Community
Educational Policy Making (Welsh) history of 182–183, 188, 192, 202, 211
Edwards, Ness 20
Edwards, Nicholas 11, 30–31, 39, 49, 108, 125, 142–143, 172, 185, 194, 220
Edwards, Nicholas, battle for S4C 53–54, 146
Egan, David 195

Europe, European Union, *see* Welsh Office and/in Europe
Evans, Gwynfor 54
Evans, Jonathan 71
Evans, Sir Hywel 98
Flynn, Paul 220
Garbage Can Model' of policy making 212-213, 214
Goodway, Russell 168
Griffiths, Dylan 4
Griffiths, James 'Jim' 18-20, 23, 39, 55, 64, 154, 222-223, 227
Griffith, Paul 173
Griffiths, Win 219, 220
Grist, Ian 75, 86, 132
Gwydyr House 76, 228
Hague, William 36, 39, 111, 122, 142, 143, 153, 156, 217, 227
Hain, Peter 86
Heath, Edward 26, 27, 49
Henderson's Law, on appointment to Cabinet 50, 232
Henry VIII and the Acts of Union (1536-1542) 14
Heseltine, Michael 32
Hughes, Cledwyn 24, 25, 39, 52, 102, 140, 223
Hughes, Sir Trevor 97, 98
Hunt, David 6, 32, 39, 52, 57, 61, 153, 172, 174, 198, 202
Inkin, Sir Geoffrey 168
Institute for Welsh Affairs 153, 158
Jones, Barry 199
Jones, Gwilym 75, 79
Joseph, Keith 16, 71
Junior Minister, choosing of 72-73
Junior Minister, Welsh speaking 73
Junior Ministers, career paths of 74
Junior Ministers, *see* also Parliamentary Private Secretary
Junior Ministers, Welsh Office history of 69-71, 230-232
Junior Ministers, Welsh Office role 76-80
Kellas, James 1
Kemp, Sir Peter 106
Kilbrandon Commission into devolution 26, 28, 154

King, Anthony, definition of a modern Cabinet Minister 48, 152
Kinnock, Neil 29
Labour Party and policy in Wales 141-142, 145
Labour Party and political devolution 141, 157, 171-172
Labour Party and Welsh administrative devolution 17-21
Labour Party, origins in Wales 139-141
Liberal Democrats (Welsh) and educational policy 199-200
Liberal Democrats (Welsh) and Welsh political devolution 157, 171-172
Liberal Party and Wales 146
Liberal Party and Welsh administrative devolution 15, 20
Lightman, Ivor 112, 153
Lloyd George, Megan 16
Lloyd Jones, Sir Richard 98
Local government 154, 165, 166-167, 173
Lomax, Rachel 97, 98, 221
Major, John 32, 78, 176
Major, John and John Redwood 56, 150-151
Marek, John 220
Maxwell-Fyfe, David 16
McManus, Michael 83
Michael, Alun vii-x, 39, 49, 219, 220, 223-224
Ministerial accountability 61-62
Ministers 'in charge at the Welsh Office' 107-110, 112-114
Morgan, K.O. 139
Morgan, Rhodri 73, 219, 224
Morris, John 29, 39, 49, 223
Murphy, Paul 41, 48
Murphy, Paul 224
National Assembly Advisory Group (NAAG) 223-225
National Audit Office 127, 169
National Curriculum for Wales *see* Curriculum Cymreig
National Curriculum in Wales 9, 110
National Health Service 35, 110, 119, 120, 167, 170-171, 224
Next Steps (agencies) 94-96, 109

Nolan Commission on Standards in Public Life 171
Non Departmental Public Bodies (NDPBs) 168–169
Northern Ireland Office 52, 149, 181
Osmond, John 153, 159
Owen Jones, Jon 75, 219
Parliament, *see* Westminster
Parliamentary Private Secretaries at the Welsh Office 80–82, 87
Parliamentary Private Secretary 69
Permanent Secretary 97, 113–114
Permanent Secretary, post Welsh Office careers 98, 221
Permanent Secretary, duties of 99–102
Permanent Secretary relationship with Welsh Secretary 102–103
Phillips Report on Welsh Office structure 107, 154
Plaid Cymru, foundation of the Welsh Office 19
Plaid Cymru and education policy 199
Plaid Cymru and the Welsh Office 146–147, 157, 171–172
Playfair, Sir Edward, Ministers and Mandarins 103
Policy Community *see* Cathays Park Village
Policy networks 162
Policy theorists Burch 3
Policy theorists Easton 2
Policy theorists Hogwood 3
Policy theorists Jones 13
Policy, definition of 2
Prime Minister, policy centre 178
Prime Ministers, recollection of Welsh Secretaries 51
Prime Ministers and Welsh Secretaries *see* Welsh Secretaries and the Prime Minister
Private Office 112
Public Accounts Committee 111, 117, 126–127, 131, 169
Pugh, Sir Idwal 98
Pwllgor Datblygu Addysg Gyrmraeg (PDAG) 184, 187, 193, 205
Qualifications, Curriculum and Assessment Authority (ACCAC) 211

Questions of Procedure for Ministers (QPM) 151
Redwood, John 5, 6, 10, 11–12, 32–37, 39, 60, 63, 69, 102–103, 111, 122, 130, 153, 155–156
Redwood, John, dealing with Welsh quangos 170–172
Redwood, John, leadership contest 35–36, 217
Redwood, John, Single Mother's speech 150–151
Rhodes, Rod 161, 173, 181, 214
Richards, Rod 80, 83, 205, 221
Roberts, Huw 220
Roberts, Michael 71
Roberts, Wyn (Lord Roberts) 10, 76, 78, 79, 81, 183–184, 189, 190, 193, 197, 200, 203, 207–209, 213
Robertson, George 143
Robinson, Mark 79
Rowlands, Ted 21, 79, 86
Royal Commission on the Constitution *see* Kilibrandon Commission into devolution
S4C, *also see* Edwards, Nicholas, battle for S4C 53, 151, 185
Scholar, Michael 97, 98, 102–103, 221
Scottish Office 52, 143, 148, 149, 161, 181
Scylla and Charybdis 10
Select Committee on Welsh Affairs *see* Welsh Affairs Select Committee
Shadow Welsh Secretary(s) 142, 217
Shadow Welsh Secretary(s) policy role of 144–145
Shelter Cymru 174
Special Adviser 82–84, 87
St David's Day debate (Westminster) 123
Standing Committee and Welsh law making 121–122
Tai Cymru 172
Talfan Davies, Geraint 3
Territorial Policy Community *see* Cathays Park Village
Thatcher, Margaret 6, 27, 69, 154
Thatcher, Margaret, Welsh Secretaries against her in leadership contest 32
Thatcherism and the civil service 94

The legislative process and the Welsh Office 117–121
The New Right 94
Thomas, Dafydd Elis 199
Thomas, George 20, 24, 25, 39, 49, 60, 71, 154, 167
Thomas, Peter 26, 39, 52
Tonypandy, Viscount *see* George Thomas
TUC (Wales) 145, 164, 165, 167, 175
Union (Unionists) 137
Walker, Peter 6, 10, 31–32, 39, 49, 52, 54, 55, 61, 172, 183–184, 194, 202, 227
Walker, Peter, 'Middle Way' for Wales 32
Wardell, Gareth (Chairman of Welsh Affairs Select Committee) 129, 130–132
Welsh Affairs Select Committee 92, 117, 127–132, 169
Welsh Affairs Select Committee, history of 128–130
Welsh Affairs Select Committee and Welsh Office policy 130–132
Welsh Assembly 216, 218–219
Welsh Council 17, 18
Welsh Development Agency 34, 155, 168, 171, 172, 225
Welsh Development Agency, foundation 31
Welsh Economic Council 174–175
Welsh Educational Policy Community 183, 185, 210, 213–215
Welsh Grand Committee 117, 123–125, 198
Welsh Joint Education Committee (WJEC) 184, 188, 191
Welsh language 111, 189, 218
Welsh Language Acts 140, 205, 218
Welsh Language Board 205
Welsh language education 185, 193–195
Welsh Liberal Democrats *see* Liberal Democrats
Welsh Office, cuts in staffing 111
Welsh Office, expansion of policy remit 22–23, 37–38, 219
Welsh Office, internal structure of 89–92
Welsh Office, mini Cabinet 84–86
Welsh Office and agricultural policy 145, 155, 163

Welsh Office and educational policy *see* also Curriculum Cymreig 145, 186, 209
Welsh Office and industry 163
Welsh Office and policy legacy 226–229
Welsh Office and the National Curriculum *see* National Curriculum or Curriculum Cymreig
Welsh Office and the UK media 148–151
Welsh Office and the Welsh media 151–153
Welsh Office and/in Europe 92, 130, 132, 155–156
Welsh Office Ministerial pool 1964–1999 74
Welsh Office quangos 25, 30, 34, 62, 155, 168–174, 225
Welsh Office, bending UK policies for Wales 7–8
Welsh Office, development of 234–240
Welsh Office, foundation of 17–21, 232–234
Welsh Office, policy differences 3–4
Welsh Office, unique Welsh policies 8–9, 12
Welsh Question Time (Westminster) 117, 122–123
Welsh Secretaries, career prospects 52
Welsh Secretaries, Collective Accountability of 59–60, 152
Welsh Secretaries, common factors of 46–48
Welsh Secretaries, personal policy objectives 39
Welsh Secretaries, post holders 230–232
Welsh Secretaries and the Prime Minister 54–56, 137
Welsh Secretary, English based MPs 26–27
Welsh Secretary, establishment of 21–22
Welsh Secretary, policy role 63–65, 157, 174, 227–229
Welsh Secretary, policy skills of 48
Welsh Secretary, selection of 43–46, 137
Welsh Secretary, Shadow, *see* Shadow Welsh Secretary
Welsh Territorial Policy Community *see* Cathays Park Village
Western Mail 151, 152, 170

Westminster and the Welsh Office 116–132

White, Eirene 26, 71

Whitehall Village 161

Whitelaw, William 53–54

Wigley, Dafydd 146

Williams, Hywel 36, 83

Williams, Sir Glanmor 196

'Yes Minister School' *see* Civil Servants in Charge